Conversion in American Philosophy

AMERICAN PHILOSOPHY SERIES
Douglas R. Anderson and Jude Jones, series editors

CONVERSION IN AMERICAN PHILOSOPHY

Exploring the Practice of Transformation

ROGER A. WARD

Fordham University Press
New York • 2004

American Philosophy Series, No. 13
ISSN 1073-2764

Library of Congress Cataloging-in-Publication Data

Ward, Roger A.
  Conversion in American philosophy : exploring the practice of transformation / Roger A. Ward.—1st ed.
    p. cm.—(American philosophy series ; no. 13)
  Includes bibliographical references and index.
  ISBN 0-8232-2313-2—ISBN 0-8232-2314-0 (pbk.)
  1. Philosophy, American—History. I. Title. II. Series.
B851.W37 2004
204.'2'01—dc22   2003024398

A version of Chapter 1 appeared in *Christian Scholars Review*, summer 2000, XXIX:4.

Printed in the United States of America
08 07 06 05 04   5 4 3 2 1
First edition

For Elaine

CONTENTS

ACKNOWLEDGEMENTS

Writing this book was a long and cooperative process. Drs. Carl Vaught and Douglas Anderson nursed my intuitions regarding the notion of transformation into a philosophical problematic. Dr. Andy Carlson read, re-read, and thrice-read the manuscript, providing both incisive criticism and encouragement—a rare combination. Charlie Perkins, my friend and bicycle companion, routinely challenged my thinking and helped me refine my ideas and arguments. I am deeply indebted to these colleagues and friends for their help in this project.

Help of a different sort came from a class of students at Georgetown College who were brave enough to take a course titled "Transformation in Philosophy." These students encouraged me to pursue the ideas central to this text, and many of them are now pursuing their own ideas in various graduate programs and mission fields. Two other students rendered special service: Emily Brandon read and critiqued the earliest version of my chapter on William James and Whitney Purcell aided me in compiling the index and proofreading the text.

I want to thank my colleagues in the philosophy department at Georgetown College, Drs. Norman Wirzba and Bradford Hadaway, as well as Dr. Homer White, a philosophical mathematician beyond compare, for their support and encouragement. My research was also aided by the Pew Foundation in the form of a summer research grant in 1999.

My family has been a constant source of inspiration and support in the production of this book. My mother and father, Jim and Ruth Ward, have always demonstrated the kind of trust in the transformative power of the gospel of Jesus Christ that forms the background of my philosophical understanding. My daughters Rachel and Kara continue to exhibit the remarkable grace necessary for living well together that makes my life of scholarship pleasant and productive. But most of all, this book would not have been possible without my wife Elaine. Her care for me and our family, her extraordinary practical wisdom, and her beauty that shines in so many ways makes my life rich beyond counting and inspires my trust in the goodness of the world. I dedicate this book to her.

PREFACE

American philosophy is best known for the generation of pragmatism, the reconception of philosophy that emphasizes action as the ground and criterion of meaning and truth. Pragmatism has two main opponents: complacence and dogmatism. Lassitude of spirit that simmers into complacence threatens us all with a shrug of the shoulders. Pragmatism challenges complacence with powerful reflection on the depths of intellectual and moral dismay, but it also aims to make a convincing argument about how to live a fully engaged life. Pragmatism attacks dogmatism in order to overcome the false satisfaction of static conclusions held on to for obscure reasons, both personal and communal. Pragmatists work against these opponents by following their desire for things that change the human condition and positively affect its possibilities in terms of inquiry and practice.

Pragmatism seeks a kind of conversion in philosophy by demanding both a radical alteration of philosophical expectations and a renewed expectation of the good available in practice. Pragmatism moves on the conviction that the good of vital practice stands directly opposed to the received tradition of philosophy that privileges abstraction from life and theoretical formulation. Locating the good of philosophy in the emerging possibilities of radical differences in the lives of men and women sets pragmatists apart in the reflective landscape.

This book aims to underscore the ways pragmatism, as it develops in the thought of Charles Sanders Peirce, William James, and John Dewey, reflects the characteristics of religious conversion. This underscoring requires a look into the roots of American philosophy and its relation to religious motivation and meaning. It leads to Jonathan Edwards and his work on conversion in the *Religious Affections* that draws to mind St. Augustine's desire for a healing transformation of his soul and his philosophy. It also leads beyond Edwards to Peirce, James, Dewey, and farther, to contemporary voices in American philosophy. Richard Rorty, Robert Corrington, and Cornel West take up the issues of transformation, religion, and meaning in ways that reflect the origins of pragmatism.

Underscoring connections to conversion in these contemporary voices, however, becomes a platform for pointing to what has been lost and what may yet be recovered for pragmatism and for philosophy. This examination of conversion sets the stage, I think, for a recovery of the spirit of philosophy that responds to the longing of all reflective souls to know more fully the possibilities of human life and change.

Reintroducing a religious term such as *conversion* to philosophy raises several concerns. First is the doubt that such a topic genuinely arises from the consideration of the texts. Is conversion a concern of these American philosophers? I think the answer is clearly yes, and I will demonstrate my reasons for saying so. A second and more powerful concern is whether reintroducing conversion is good for philosophy. Again, I think the answer is yes. Conversion has to do with how a person lives and knows his or her living results from an interaction with a better life, a more profound reality, larger and more vital reasons for living than were available before that interaction. Conversion is a method of establishing a critique of the soul, to borrow an image from Kant. Care of the soul may be the original meaning of the philosopher's task, and recovering this philosophical impulse sends us back to our Platonic origins as well as ahead into the limits that define the lives we may yet live. Philosophy as a way of tending the soul is deeply embedded in our history and practice, and the American pragmatists represent a creative and effective return to this origin and this task. I offer this reflection, then, for those who seek to engage philosophical inquiry for what it may grant in terms of a more fully and meaningfully lived life, and for those who seek a deeper understanding of the American philosophical tradition of pragmatism.

THE PROBLEM OF CONVERSION IN
ST. AUGUSTINE AND JONATHAN EDWARDS

In historical terms, no American thinker is identified by conversion more than Jonathan Edwards. He appropriates the problematic of conversion as the core of his creative theology and critical philosophy. Edwards, like St. Augustine, does not focus on whether he can understand conversion but on how human wills are changed so that they desire God rather than created things. Before we can begin the discovery of conversion in American pragmatism, the historical Augustinian roots of conversion in American thought need to be accounted for. To understand American philosophy, especially with respect to the notion of conversion, we need to understand Edwards. And to understand Edwards's approach to conversion, we need to understand Augustine. The American hope for transformation needs to be connected to the brilliant light of self-reflective evaluation Augustine models in the *Confessions,* reflection that constitutes a new identity and disposition that informs all thoughts, actions, and beliefs. The possibility of such a transformation remains deeply and problematically embedded in our American thinking owing in some part to Edwards's continuation of Augustine's work, which begins with the problem of conversion.

For Augustine, philosophical awareness is a part of his developmental maturation that intertwines with the story of his coming to Christ. Accordingly, Augustine does not argue that philosophy is necessary or sufficient for this transformation (though some may argue otherwise on Augustine's behalf). Rather, philosophy is a precursor and a sign of the power related to the soul's great healing. Philosophical desire is refracted through the healing of Augustine's desire for Christ. Stated negatively, Augustine finds that philosophy lacks healing power. The transition between Manichean dualism and Neoplatonism was significant because of the discovery of an abiding absence in philosophy. Augustine confesses at the end of Book 7 of the *Confessions* that although he was drawn into philosophy for its own sake, "later on . . . I would be able to detect and distinguish how great a difference lies between presumption and contrition, and between those who see where they must travel, but do not see the way, and those who see the way that leads to not only beholding our blessed fatherland but also dwelling therein" (7.26).[1] Even though Augustine glimpses the immaterial God in Book 7, he cannot dwell there.

The narrative movement in the *Confessions* dramatically changes in Book 7. From the "tearing from his side" of his common-law wife at the conclusion of the previous book, Augustine turns to matters intellectual. Principal in this transition is the logical refutation of the Manichean position by Nebridius, although this refutation does little to assuage Augustine's confusion about God's substance or address his wounded soul. It does open the door to the question of the will and the presence of evil in the world. Augustine weaves together the twin problems of the will and God's nature in this book, leading to the realization of a "different infinite" than he was able to imagine before.

What is most striking about this book, though, are the warnings concerning the products of reasoning that proliferate here even as Augustine recounts his significant philosophical discovery of God's spiritual substance. Set free from the limits and errors of dualism, stoked by the books of the Platonists, Augustine proceeds toward this consummatory vision of the reality of God—a vision that breaks the metaphors of container and contained that held him during his Manichean days. The momentary vision of God's nature, unchangeable and encompassing all things, shows the deficiency of the ideas to which he had been committed. The disjunction between a materialistic metaphor and the spiritual substance of his Platonic meditation exposed the significance of his will in relation to philosophical discovery. A reason for his hesitation to commit fully to the Manichees appears that substantiates the logical rejection made by Nebridius, but one that accesses different ground in his soul. His hesitation to commit willingly to the Manichees was a sign of the error contained in that system even before he could articulate it clearly. Philosophical discovery showed him error and also signified a disturbance in his soul that was not simply intellectual. Augustine makes a similar discovery in light of the books of the Platonists. Although they lead him farther than he had been able to go on his own, yet there was nothing of Christ in these books. This awareness points ahead to Book 8, when he is finally able to submit himself willingly to the incarnate one of God.

While philosophy appears in Book 7 as a response to Augustine's sickness and a sign of the depth of his illness and need for healing, healing metaphors surround Book 8 like a gentle vapor. For all the success of having escaped the error of his prior conclusions, Augustine is even more desperate since he no longer has the same fear of error to support his unwillingness to cleave to God. The stories of Victorinus and Ponticainus precede the famous conflict with himself in the garden. But before this ultimate encounter, and in response to these stories, Augustine returns to the problem of the will. Developing the analysis begun in Book 7 of whether the will is the product or cause of evil, he now claims the will is two. In willing we also will a complete will, and to the extent this is not accomplished our complete will is apparent by its absence. His inability to will one thing presses on his wound, and every willing act reflects this absence of the whole will, which is painfully absent. Augustine laments,

> I say that it commands itself to will a thing; it would not give this command unless it willed it, and yet it does not do what it wills. It does not will in its entirety: for this reason it does not give this command in its entirety. For it commands a thing only in so far as it wills it, and in so far as what it commands is not done, to that extent it does not will it. For the will commands that there be a will, and that this be itself, and not something else. But the complete will does not give the command, and therefore what it commands is not in being. For if it were a complete will, it would not command it to be, since the thing would already be in being. Therefore, it is no monstrous thing partly to will a thing and partly to not will it, but it is a sickness in the mind. Therefore there are two wills, since one of them is not complete, and what is lacking in the one is present in the other. (8.21)

The fragmented will is not a story of the moral completion of an intellectual conversion, which would indeed be a monstrous thing. To be converted, but only intellectually—what hope would remain for such a creature? The divided will is the articulated ground of the soul that holds the intellect and the will together in terms of what unsettles them: God's truth. But they are held apart over what satisfies them. Intellectual discovery is essential in exposing the division of the will and preventing premature closure of the will. But this discovery does not afford the rest that the will seeks. Augustine seeks not a replacement for his will, but the transformation of his will through itself into its holistic completion.

Recalling these events and thoughts prevents Augustine from creating a formula for conversion.[2] In the garden in Milan, after hearing the stories of the men who had taken up the way of Christ, Augustine sees himself as a person unable or unwilling to will completely, sick with the division in his will. Is there anything that one could will completely that would be free from the doubt of error yet not a product of vain imagining? The disposition that erupts in his will, "putting on the Christ," resolves the complete/incomplete nature of his willing soul. Entering into the place of the circular walled garden reveals this absence most clearly, and the one thing the Apostle urges, putting on Christ, was the one thing he was clear that he could not do by himself. Urged by the introduction of the possibility, shown his will as it stood in opposition to the words of St. Paul, Augustine came to see his complete will for the first time as a desire to lurk in the shadows of his rejection of willing one thing. To will that one thing, supported by the spiritual reality attained by his Neoplatonic glimpse, brings Augustine to face himself—that there is no opposition to putting on the Christ except his own willing refusal. As he gave up that fight for the last time, he became a new person, in terms not of the substance of his belief but in his disposition toward that belief in Christ as the mediator between God and man. His willful subordination to Christ achieved a character reflecting the infinite good of God in flesh. The sufficiency of this subordination becomes the new object of Augustine's inquiry toward which he can now turn completely, not as a replacement of himself, but as a soul transformed into a will willing. The Christ, the richness of God's infinite healing for the world made flesh, became the principle of his own will.[3]

Still, the part of this conversion that remains a problem is the certainty that Christ is sufficient to make such a willful subordination possible. Overcoming the absence of the will coalesces into a disposition from which inquiry moves to articulate the sufficiency of this transformation. How does this satisfy the will without canceling it? What kind of answer can be given except confession? But the problem of conversion is that it stands on such ground as confession that can always be subject to questions and uncharitable readings. The accomplishment of his Christlike disposition does not respond to these questions as much as it explains Augustine to himself. This disposition is his healing, and is it possible to argue with health?

The problem of conversion Augustine struggles with is the absence of emphasis in the tradition on the change of disposition. If conversion of the heart is so essential to the Christian faith, as it appears to be from his reading of Romans, why has conversion been underplayed? In traditional stories of conversion the focus was on the person being "safely brought into the harbor" of faith, leaving unsaid how the person was transformed from opposing God's truth to acceding God's truth in the only way a will can completely accede.[4] Throughout the text of the *Confessions*, the hints of this possible transformation are laid out clearly for us, even as Augustine himself realizes the hints and suggestions are laid out for his own persuasion. The problem of conversion for Augustine lies not with the intellect but with the will, and Augustine must show how conversion does not reject the tradition but completes it.

EDWARDS AND THE REORIENTATION OF AFFECTIONS

Edwards's spirit of engaging challenging issues of his community is reminiscent of Augustine's detailed account of his personal journey. This character sets Edwards apart from his contemporaries. The formula of conversion in New England Puritanism evolved through the Calvinist appropriation of covenant toward a corporate intellectual assent.[5] Covenant theology established that what could be trusted was not the soul's appropriation of God's grace, since that was impossible to claim without hubris, but that God had covenanted with a part of humanity to be a peculiar people. The affirmation of God's covenant relationship with the community was sufficient affirmation of one's relation to God. According to Conrad Cherry, "[i]n terms of the Puritan morphology of conversion, 'belief upon moral evidence' and under 'a conviction of the judgment and conscience' is equivalent to belief through the saving gift of grace. Therefore, those who cannot profess faith but who prepare themselves through moral endeavor and profess a desire for faith can be counted as believers and admitted to the Supper. For if one is sincere in his moral life and earnestly desires to be in the covenant of grace, even though he cannot in all honesty say he *is* in that covenant, he is 'for the matter of it' a man of faith and a participant in the saving covenant.'"[6]

Edwards found this reliance on covenant affirmation problematic, especially because it bled into other forms of thinking. First, it became the complete expression of a person's responsibility to God. Affirming the covenant replaced the expectation of a personal desire for an experience of God. Second, it bled into the trust that an argument for covenant affirmation, since it was the effective motor of corporate identity and continuance, constituted the goal or telos of preaching and theology. Skillful and vigorous defenses of the rational propriety of the covenant generated more affirmation, so this defense became considered a means of grace. But was God's election influenced by informed consent and intellectually grounded choices made by men and women?

Edwards opposed both ways the covenant theology moved. Edwards opposed the limitation of personal responsibility to covenant affirmation, and he opposed the supposition that a person had the ability to choose God based on coherent grounds presented in rhetorically or philosophically powerful descriptions. Yet Edwards could not deny that souls touched by God's grace would respond to a clear presentation of

the working of God, or that one way the soul properly responds to the
influence of grace is with a desire to know more fully what grace is and
what the soul is that it can be so influenced. In order to address this
problem directly, Edwards undertook a careful inquiry into the nature of
true religious affections.[7] Following the Great Awakening, no longer
defending it or its advocates in the heat of battle, Edwards focused on
discerning the internal dynamism and signs of religious discovery. In the
process he recovered and refined the meaning of conversion for his
Puritan audience.

Recovering conversion from the early Puritan divines further separates Edwards from his contemporaries. His rhetoric is more like the first
generation Puritans than his own. Perry Miller displays the Puritans' self-
castigation over their failure to become the beacon of truth of God's
light in the world.[8] The vision was that New England would be a light
that would draw all humanity to the truth of God's redeeming grace
seen plainly in a well-ordered civil life. But instead of a New World they
found only a *new* England, a repetition of the problems and moral fail-
ures they fled. The failure of conversion marred their civic vision. Was
conversion an impossible task, an inappropriate organizing principle of
this new community? When Edwards takes up the topics of conversion
and spiritual transformation he is engaged in nothing less than scrutiniz-
ing the validity of his own tradition.[9] This project moves Edwards into
sensitive reflective space, and his inquiry probes the absence of coherence and conviction in the corporate Puritan mind. In truth, Edwards
transforms the problem of conversion from the private confessional
ground of Augustine to the corporate covenantal ground the Puritans
relied upon for their theological warrant. Edwards finds a problematic
absence lurking in corporate self-understanding and drives his analysis
directly to this place.

Overcoming the diversion of covenant affirmation is connected to
answering the philosophical principles of Arminianism.[10] But Edwards
does not treat this situation primarily as a theological problem. For one
thing, there was no good biblical evidence to back up Arminian claims
that humanity chooses God based on a natural understanding of good, so
Edwards sees the issue not as a problem for Biblical theology but what
structures theology. Driving this turn toward Arminianism was a philosophical question: What power does the mind have over the most fundamental choices and dispositions? Edwards makes his seminal advance

here. A mental or intellectual conviction in and of itself cannot be a true sign of grace. Even the most persuasive and coherent defense of the covenant is not the same as God's effective power influencing the soul. Yet the mind, as the principal ground of the perception of our souls, is the proper location for discerning the influence of God's grace. If the state of grace of a soul would ever be apparent, and Edwards is confident that God would give us discernible signs to know this, it would be apparent in the conviction of the mind. But again, Edwards's Augustinian spirit appears: it is not the intellect but the will that most essentially reflects God's working. The intellect is the ground for conviction but it is not the end of that conviction. The conviction of truth reveals a sense within the intellect that cannot be attributed to the truths discovered by the "natural" operation of the intellect. Conviction of the truth of the claims of the gospel is in itself a sign of a sense inhabiting and informing the mind. In Sign V of the *Religious Affections,* Edwards writes,

This sense of the spiritual excellency and beauty of divine things, does also tend to directly convince the mind of the truth of the gospel, as there are very many of the most important things declared in the gospel that are hid from the eyes of natural men, the truth of which does in effect consist in this excellency, or does so immediately depend upon it and result from it; that in this excellency's being seen the truth of those things are seen. As soon as ever the eyes are opened to behold the beauty and amiableness that is in divine things, a multitude of the most important doctrines of the gospel, that depend upon it (which all appear strange and dark to natural men) are at once seen to be true. As for instance, hereby appears the truth of what the Word of God declares concerning the exceeding evil of sin; for the same eye that discerns the transcendent beauty of holiness, necessarily therein sees the exceeding odiousness of sin: the same taste which relishes the sweetness of true moral good, taste the bitterness of moral evil. And by this means a man sees his own sinfulness and loathesomeness; for he has now a sense to discern objects of this nature; and so sees the truth of what the Word of God declares concerning the exceeding sinfulness of mankind, which before he did not see. He now sees the dreadful pollution of his heart, and the desperate depravity of his nature, in a new manner; for his soul has now a sense given it to feel the pain of such a disease; and this shows him the truth of what the Scripture reveals concerning the corruption of man's nature, his original sin, and the ruinous condition man is in, and his need of a Saviour, his need of the mighty power of God to renew his heart and change his nature. (301)

Embedded in Edwards's description of this "seeing" is the subtle refutation
of the Arminian ground that the soul is equivalent to its highest intellectual
conviction and affirmation, and that the power of the mind is the same by
which God's truth is appropriated. Throughout the *Religious Affections*
Edwards demonstrates, by appeal to scripture and by common-sense argument, that the will cannot be described in these terms, contradicting many
of his fellow divines. The very people charged to support biblical faith had
been drawn into the error of trusting that whatever prompts a conviction
of the mind is equivalent to the proper conviction of the soul. To make his
separation from this position conclusive, Edwards argues that conversion is
a complete transformation of the nature. This is the most universal human
desire, a desire that struggles against the resistance with the natural state of
mankind, but a desire that remains unsatisfied with any other answer as a
substitute. Second, he argues that the diversion of Arminian thinking, as a
substitute for engaging the absence of one's disposition, could be countered
on the philosophical grounds that it is self-referentially incoherent.
Answering the resistance of philosophy is possible by exposing the error of
this conception of the free choice of the will, the work Edwards takes up in
earnest following his removal from Northampton.[11] In the *Religious
Affections*, however, Edwards makes the positive point that to overcome the
absence of the soul's orientation toward a flawed position entails the
appearance of content to the intellect that becomes the order of a new disposition. The mind perceives this content not as a new thing known, but as
an order of the intellect and the self. The ordering power of this content is
the revelation of an active sense within the mind and intellect that cannot
have its origin in the natural mind.

Just as Augustine is careful to remind himself and his readers of the
limits of philosophical discovery, so Edwards is careful to separate the
sense of the excellence of supernatural truths from the accomplishment
of the mind. What becomes the ultimate sign of gracious affection is not
merely the truth about Jesus proclaimed in the gospel, but the heart
affective results of that discovery. The flexibility of the affections to
reflect this content is the sign of an "other than natural" influence on the
soul. The signs of affection, incorporating the truths of reason and scripture, respond to Edwards's memory of the persuasive structure of philosophy. Following along a path of discovery yields heart affective results
only when the soul is able to recognize that its absence of a sufficient
disposition is answered in Jesus Christ, by both the testimony of the

community and in personal recognition of that sufficiency of ordering the affections. The work of the Holy Spirit is clearly evident in the flexibility of the person's affective character, softened and receptive to a reorientation. But this flexibility of affections is predicated on an original reorientation to the likeness of Christ. The more gracious affections are exercised, the more apparent their brokenness appears, which Edwards connects with the brokenness of evangelical humiliation in Sign VI of the *Religious Affections*. But even the experience of humiliation reveals a gentleness of spirit, open to receiving a shift in orientation that continues the return of the soul to its good, which is God. The opening paragraph of Sign VII describes conversion this way:

> All gracious affections do arise from a spiritual understanding, in which the soul has the excellency and glory of divine things discovered to it, as was shown before. But all spiritual discoveries are transforming; and not only make an alteration of the present exercise, sensation and frame of the soul; but such power and efficacy have they, that they make an alteration in the very nature of the soul; "But we all, with open face, beholding as in a glass, the glory of the Lord, are changed into the same image, from glory to glory, even as by the Spirit of the Lord" (II Cor. 3:18). Such power as this is properly divine power, and is peculiar to the Spirit of the Lord: other power may make a great alteration in men's present frames and feelings; but 'tis the power of a Creator only that can change the nature, or give a new nature. And no discoveries or illuminations, but those that are divine and supernatural, will have this supernatural effect. But this effect all those discoveries have, that are truly divine. The soul is deeply affected by these discoveries and so affected as to be transformed. Thus it is with those affections that the soul is the subject of in its conversion. (340)

For Edwards, conversion is primarily a confessional result of individual souls, but conversion also becomes significant for the institutional career of Puritanism and the church more generally. The corporate absence of the Puritan civic vision did not reveal a need for better ecclesiastical governance; it revealed that this civic failure was a species of resistance to conversion. Edwards dwells at the limits of corporate confession. Even as he accepts the presidency of the College of New Jersey, he admits that he longs to return to the history of the work of redemption in order to establish a completely new method of divinity for his community so that he can finally answer Arminian errors.

Edwards's movement from treating the absence of the individual soul to the projection of the overcoming of the corporate absence of soul is where he is most liable to provoke resistance. Edwards transgresses the confessional space that Augustine opens up in the *Confessions,* in some way not only transforming conversion but also altering the ground of absence to which conversion is connected. After Edwards the need for conversion is always a corporate need, a demand for a content that not only brings souls and God together but that will also become a public platform of regenerative change.

THE PROBLEM OF CONVERSION

The problem of conversion in Augustine and Edwards resolves into the question of whether the impulse of philosophy can be turned toward affective discovery, exploring the dimensions of conviction, habit, and transformation. Negotiating the threats of self-deception and the ground of religious authority opens up the space in which the soul can discover its proper confessional space.

In many ways Edwards is America's Augustine. Edwards's significance for the development of American theology and religious life are well documented. Less so, however, is his significance for the philosophical development in America. Edwards's example of pursuing reflective self-understanding and the connection between this understanding and the meaning of communal transformation indicates that his influence is somehow active in the development of later American philosophy. There is an abiding expectation in American philosophy for a model of corporate conversion that does not exclude the confessional space of the soul, yet one that speaks to the general absence of the communal soul. Through the influence of philosophy resistance has grown to Christian models of conversion to which both Augustine and Edwards were committed. In part this resistance stems from the worry that the Christian model is exclusive, while the experience of God, grace, and transformation must be pluralistic in terms of being openly accessible from any tradition. This resistance also stems from the worry that any divine or non-natural origin of transformation is at base an abdication of human responsibility. Both of these concerns can be addressed but never completely allayed.

Still, the desire for a general response to the absence of conversion persists despite these philosophical worries. For this reason Edwards remains a vital force in American religious life. If Augustine evokes the desire for a personal conversion in making sense of one's spiritual trajectory and thought, Edwards evokes the desire for corporate success and transformation—confession become conversion. The problem of conversion, therefore, remains for philosophy as both a reflective obligation it must answer and a challenge to its authority that it must face. In this book I begin the process of answering this obligation in American philosophy by exploring C. S. Peirce's desire for self-transformation, William James's redaction of Edwards's conversion, and John Dewey's project of corporate transformation. Together these American philosophers construct a kind of triune authority that forms the basis of pragmatism, and it is my goal to examine that platform as thoroughly as possible, unabashedly locating this platform on the grounds of religious conversion.

NOTES

1. St. Augustine, *Confessions* (Image Books, 1960). Subsequent references are shown in the text as book and paragraph.

2. Robert J. O'Connell, S.J., *Images of Conversion in St. Augustine's Confessions* (Fordham University Press, 1996), 269, 278.

3. Ibid., 291.

4. Peter Brown, *Augustine of Hippo* (University of California Press, 1967), 177.

5. Harry S. Stout, *The New England Soul* (Oxford University Press, 1986), 106–108; Joseph Haroutanian, *Piety vs. Moralism* (Archon Books, 1964), 55.

6. Conrad Cherry, *The Theology of Jonathan Edwards: A Reappraisal* (Indiana University Press, 1966), 212.

7. John E. Smith, ed., *Religious Affections: Works of Jonathan Edwards* (Yale University Press, 1959), 2:3.

8. Perry Miller, *Errand into the Wilderness* (Harvard University Press, 1956), 7.

9. Smith, *Religious Affections*, 53ff.

10. Ian Murray, *Jonathan Edwards: A New Biography* (Banner of Truth Trust, 1987), 212. See also Gerald R. McDermott, *Jonathan Edwards Confronts the Gods* (Oxford University Press, 2000), 17–18.

11. Allen Guelzo, *Edwards on the Will* (Wesleyan University Press, 1989), 41. Edwards says, "The will is the mind's inclination." I disagree with Guelzo that Edwards treats the will as a coeval faculty with the intellect. Rather, I would argue that the will is principal in the determination of the substance of the soul, its inclination, which comprises intellect and apprehension. Neither intellect nor apprehension generates inclination, but both correspond to inclination and its changes.

Introduction: Conversion and the Practice of Transformation

American philosophy embodies a kind of criticism in all its parts. Charles S. Peirce, William James, and John Dewey, the founding figures of pragmatism, begin their projects with a deep desire to produce a vital difference in reflection and practice. The difference they seek in philosophy is an opening for a better life, a new world, a guiding principle of action refined by intelligence and human desire. A redirection of communal and spiritual orientation allures their sight, fueled by an optimism that finding a reflective platform connecting the present form of life to a fuller self-consciousness is possible. Their philosophical criticism frames a new kind of discernment of the human soul for the purpose of redirecting and transforming habits and desires. My aim in this introduction is to suggest a way of taking fuller account of the difference pragmatists have made in the broad terms of understanding transformation in human life. This difference, I think, returns some of the vitality of religious ideas and questions to pragmatism. What could have a more profound and permanent effect on our society than a vital difference in our religious self-understanding and expectations?

FROM CRITICISM TO CONSTRUCTION

The constructive character of these classical American philosophers is often hard to discern because of their rigorous focus on criticism. Peirce, James, and Dewey challenge the core beliefs of their society and their intellectual contemporaries, separating them from their fellow citizens and from the tradition of Western philosophy. John Dewey makes a conscious move away from European philosophy by condemning all efforts to construct a positive philosophical program based on foundational methods or claims such as those of Spinoza and Descartes. Dewey argues that philosophy is only the criticism of criticisms. Peirce also insists that the principal failure of philosophy is turning away from exhaustive self-criticism of its method and guiding principles.

Coursing through this critical attitude of American pragmatists, however, is the desire to expand and extend the values of practice and reflection already present in their communities. They are mindful that without a connection to presently lived values their philosophical critique loses its power and meaning. Criticism joined together with a return to lived values is the working faith of American philosophy. This working faith holds that a critical examination of deeply held convictions will yield a fruitful expansion of the living practice of men and women. In this book I aim to make the working faith of the American pragmatists explicit by delving into the philosophical critique they offer, and also by exploring the limits of the transformation of living values that it sponsors. I argue that the success of the constructive project of these American philosophers depends on finding a philosophical platform for describing and enacting a transformation of selves and communities.

TRANSFORMING EXPERIENCE

It would be naive to suggest that thinkers as different as Peirce, James, and Dewey operate from a univocal presumption about the prospects for philosophy and human transformation. They do not share this kind of identity, but I think they had their eyes trained on a similar expectation concerning human life and reflection. Their expectations vary according to their experience and background, but in each of these thinkers there is an agreement of purpose that the redemption of life through transforming practice is possible. It is real. The philosopher's job is to reveal this redemptive capacity and dwell in its power rather than to create it out of whole cloth.

Pragmatism is more about discovering the transformation lurking within our experience and values than about generating a knock-down argument or an aesthetically pleasing story. In this respect, I connect Peirce, James, and Dewey with the figures H. Richard Niebuhr describes in *The Kingdom of God in America* who worked under the powerful vision of turning the kingdom into a principle for constructive action. Convinced that the reality of a new order of life was pressing upon them, they concluded that their responsibility was to find the means to

participate in that economy as best they could. Niebuhr describes their
vision this way: "[T]o put the sovereignty of God in the first place is to
make obedient activity superior to contemplation, however much of
theoria is necessary to action. The principle of vision suggests that the
perfection of the object seen is loved above all else; the principle of the
kingdom indicates that the reality and power of the being commanding
obedience are primarily regarded."[1] The life aimed at is not a product of
human imagination so much as it is a discovery of God's desire for
humanity. Discovering this new life comes through the process of sub-
jecting living values to critical refinement and change, a change culminating in the re-creation of the person in God's image. While the
pragmatists reject the "divine initiative" this vision of the kingdom
entails, they desire a power of transformation of life like this and they
struggle to find ideals that would inspire obedience in action. In light of
these demands, the pragmatists explore goals that dramatically expand
reflective needs in philosophy.

PRAGMATISM'S GOALS FOR THE REFLECTIVE LIFE

Dewey introduces an expansive goal for his pragmatism in "The Need
for a Recovery in Philosophy." "The time has arrived," he says, "for a
pragmatism which shall be empirically idealistic, proclaiming the essential connexion of intelligence with the unachieved future—with possibilities involving a transfiguration." He adds, "Faith in the power of
intelligence to imagine a future which is the projection of the desirable
in the present, and to invent the instrumentalities of its realization is our
salvation. And it is a faith which must be nurtured and made articulate."[2]
James puts it in more personal terms. "The capacity of the strenuous
mood lies so deep down among our natural human possibilities that
even if there were no metaphysical or traditional grounds for believing
in a God, men would postulate one simply as a pretext for living hard,
and getting out of the game of existence its keenest possibilities for
zest."[3] Peirce recurs to New Testament language to illuminate the principle of pragmatism, "consider what effects, that might conceivably have
practical bearings . . . then our conception of these effects is the whole
of our conception of the object." "But [this] is only," he adds in a note,
"an application of the sole logical principle recommended by Jesus: 'Ye
may know them by their fruits,' and it is very intimately allied with the

ideas of the gospel." Producing fruits of practice and inquiry consistent with the character of the universe is the ultimate conception of success, displaying the "process whereby man, with all his miserable littlenesses, becomes gradually more and more imbued with the Spirit of God."[4] If pragmatism is a pedestrian philosophy, then these philosophers have found a walking bridge to the promised land.

I do not think it is an accident that religious symbols and language stand at the root of the connection between commonly lived values and the vision of a new life. The pragmatists capitalized on a common language and hope present in their communities. But they also demonstrate a religious and Christian sensibility that plays a key role in the formation of their ideas. For instance, James caps his "Moral Philosopher and the Moral Life" with a version of St. Paul's use of the Mosaic charge in Romans 10:7–8, "It is not in heaven, neither is it beyond the sea; but the word is very nigh unto thee, in thy mouth and in thy heart, that thou mayest do it."[5] James's profoundly influential *Varieties of Religious Experience* deals explicitly with the way such a word might be translated into a change of identity and practice, and what we might know of the origin of this word in personal religious experience. It is impossible to understand the power of James's conviction about the human need for resolving philosophical questions apart from this religious impetus.[6]

Dewey's naturalism resists the historical encumbrances of revealed religion, yet it retains the character of an evangelical principle.[7] Dewey advocates a form of life that effectively organizes a person's habits and at the same time produces a community that consummates the desire for a satisfying social life. He calls dedication to this community "natural piety," and he underscores the commitment necessary to bring this about in an allusion to the words of Job in *Experience and Nature*: "Fidelity to the nature to which we belong, as parts however weak, demands that we cherish our desires and ideals till we have converted them into intelligence, revised them in terms of the ways and means which nature makes possible. When we have used our thought to its utmost and have thrown into the moving unbalanced balance of things our puny strength, we know that though the universe slay us still we may trust, for our lot is one with whatever is good in existence."[8] Dewey's dedication may stem from a religious experience he had when he was teaching in Oil City, Pennsylvania. In a mystical vision, Dewey saw a glorious merging of ideals and human practice, producing in him a "quiet reconciliation with the world."[9] Hope for a life of realized value like this is more than he finds in religious communities. Dewey does not aim to be nonreligious; he aims to enable his community to be more productive than the religion in his day tended to be.[10]

Unlike James and Dewey, Peirce consistently connects the expansive aspect of his philosophical production to the reality of God and the significance this has for all inquirers. In his late essay "Law of Mind" he remarks that "a genuine evolutionary philosophy, that is, one that makes the principle of growth a primordial element of the universe, is so far from being antagonistic to the idea of a personal creator that it is really inseparable from that idea; while a necessitarian religion is in an altogether false position and is destined to become disintegrated. But a pseudo-evolutionism which enthrones mechanical law above the principle of growth is at once scientifically unsatisfactory, as giving no possible hint of how the universe has come about, and hostile to all hopes of personal relations to God."[11] Peirce's biography is full of the struggle someone with his intellect and demeanor would have with an idea of the divine. In a remarkable letter written in 1898 to the rector of St. Thomas in New York City, Peirce writes,

> This morning after breakfast I felt I must go to church anyway. I wandered about, not knowing where, to find a regular Episcopal church, in which I was confirmed; but I finally came to St. Thomas. I had several times been in it on week days to look at the chancel. I therefore saw nothing new to me. But this time,—I was not thinking of St. Thomas and his doubts, either,—no sooner had I got into the church than I seemed to receive the direct permission of the Master to come. Still, I said to myself, I must not go to communion without further reflection: I must go home & duly prepare myself before I venture. But when the instant came, I found myself carried up to the altar rail, almost without my own volition. I am perfectly sure that it was right. Anyway, I could not help it.[12]

Peirce adds that he is aware that this communion comes with a responsibility to work for the church and that he is prepared to do so, though he leaves the nature of this work vague. An awareness of religious vocation would strike many commentators as an absurd addition to a critical study of Peirce's philosophy, but I think understanding this aspect of the man and his work opens up many interesting and fruitful discussions.[13]

Jonathan Edwards and Conversion

While we see traces and images of the religious hope for transformation in the pragmatists, there is an origin in the American tradition of meeting such questions directly. No person carries this burden more than Jonathan Edwards. Edwards measures philosophical transformation by his biblical understanding of conversion. Historically speaking, Edwards retrieved conversion out of the ashes of his own tradition to accomplish a culture-altering critique of Puritanism, withstanding the harshest of criticisms from those within his own circle. Edwards lifts conversion by an "expropriated" vocabulary from the moralists whereby the true enthusiasm of Shaftesbury becomes the ground for an enthusiasm that only comes from "the knowledge of the loveliness of divine things."[14] Harry Stout finds this a clever way of turning his assailants' arguments against them, and indeed it is clever. But more than cleverness, Edwards reveals a confidence that humankind is made for conversion, and that our fullest potential and truest character is found only in the transformation possible with the Holy Spirit. His facility with philosophy compounds the power of his description of conversion. There is no fear of coming to the end of his tether and realizing he was his own God, as Perry Miller suggests in his beautiful biography.[15]

Edwards is in remarkable continuity with the larger project of pragmatism to make practice intelligent and attain a higher order of clarity in practice through self-criticism. Edwards brings critical self-awareness to the ultimate change of character he discovers at the core of his own tradition. But I think his notion of conversion is broader than eighteenth-century Puritanism or even twenty-first-century Christianity. Conversion is a philosophical platform rich enough to serve as the ground for understanding the development of American pragmatism broadly construed, both in terms of the products it most deeply desires to produce in the person and in the community and in terms of the criticism of ideas and practice necessary to make it a living enterprise.[16]

Expanding Pragmatism through Conversion

So far I have been arguing that the significance of religious metaphors and meanings for Peirce, James, and Dewey is expressed in their method of doing philosophy and the aims for which they engage in philosophy.

Making sense of this meaning, however, depends on overcoming two hurdles embedded in the way American philosophy has long been interpreted. First, the emphasis on naturalism dominant in contemporary discussions of pragmatism blankets the obvious springs of religious motivation and meaning in these thinkers with a smothering rejection. This rejection violates their texts. The pragmatists' critique of supernatural dependence is much more powerful when it is not taken as a simple negation of religious meaning and practice. Strictly segregating religious meaning from pragmatism renders too much of its reflective accomplishment out of touch with its origins. Monolithic naturalism subverts the vitality of the pragmatists, closing off reflection on the kinds of concerns they aimed to render more productive of value in the lives of men and women. I intend to challenge this kind of naturalism by exploring a religious meaning in American pragmatism that is consistent with both its origin and its critique of traditional supernaturalism.

This conviction leads me to the second hurdle that needs to be cleared. I argue from the religious origin and concern of pragmatism that conversion provides a helpful framework for understanding and extending the American philosophical spirit. Conversion entails a holistic change of life that follows a discovery of the truth about ourselves, our community, and God. Conversion also becomes a platform for reorienting practice and reflection. Its power extends in a global critique of the guiding principles of inquiry, and its effect is a pervasive change of the habits and aims of the community and those individuals who find its success as their ultimate obligation and desire. For these reasons, I suggest that conversion forms a general aim of pragmatism's founding figures, who promote a turning from the present world of failing practice to an entirely new kind life and practice for both individuals and communities. Leading philosophy toward conversion inverts the more usual practice of implying a change that needs to be made to religion because of philosophical discovery. While Dewey and James clearly voice the need for a reconstruction of religion, I disagree with writers such as Eugene Fontinell who argue that this reconstruction is the principal aim of pragmatism, requiring the "surrender of much of what we at one time held or may now hold dear."[17] My claim is that no proper reconstruction of religion can be accomplished by an argument that is disconnected from the reconstruction *by* religion of the person and the community if genuine transformation is the desire that holds us.

CONCERNS ABOUT CONVERSION

I am aware that conversion evokes many powerful and troubling images. For many people conversion simply has no value; it is not a live hypothesis, to use James's term. A holistic response to an experience or conviction of the truth about ourselves and God is so remote from current expectations that even suggesting it as a possibility, especially in a philosophical context, appears absurd. For others, the suggestion that conversion is necessary for an ultimately productive intellectual discernment of the self, God, and the world draws active and vociferous resistance because it is perceived as *the* enemy of a self-directed and free reflective life. Despite these worries, conversion remains a powerful image in our common life. A recent poll finds that 41 percent of Americans claim to have been "born again," including both major candidates in the 2000 presidential race.[18] The variety of responses to conversion, and its continuing place in the religious identity of many people, suggests that sorting out its complexity would address live concerns in our common life.

Some concerns about using the language of conversion stem from the belief that religious transformation reflects a static conception of humanity and God. But this is hardly the case. Conversion in the Christian tradition is not as monolithic as its opponents believe and neither is it as reflectively secure as its advocates suggest. The practices and beliefs related to the transformation of human life by a divine influence or a divine principle of concern are as old as Abraham and as convoluted as the controversies among the scholastic philosophers. The presence of this conversation through many centuries of human history reveals the organic need for continuing reflection on the question of a change of human character.

From the point of view of historical theology, the puzzle about conversion is the absence of theological formulation of the doctrine of sotierology. John McIntyre points out that christological controversies and Trinitarian debates structured the development of church practice and theology, but no statement of theological relation of the work of Christ in personal or communal salvation was made. This is interesting from a historical theological point of view because conversion is the crux of worship and church practice. Biblical witness for a conceptual theology of conversion is thin, so when theological development of sotierology did occur it took on the distinct forms based on philosophical conceptions of the person, community, and God of the person writing. McIntyre concludes that trying to bring these diverse formulations together into one kind of development is difficult if not impossible.[19]

Moving in this absence of formal doctrine, however, has opened the way for expansive and creative thinking connected to conversion. The account of intellectual conversion by Catholic theologian, philosopher, and teacher Bernard Lonergan culminates in his work *Insight: A Study of Human Understanding*.[20] Insight is a sudden, unexpected habit affecting discovery that "pivots between the concrete and the abstract."[21] Lonergan takes insight, what I would associate with the discovery of conversion, as the leading principle for an epistemic description of judgment. This epistemic work includes metaphysics, ethics, and transcendence, the tendency of human understanding to "go beyond." Lonergan says his pursuit of insight "has found man involved and engaged in what he happens to be, and it has been confronted with man's incapacity for sustained development and with his need to go beyond the hitherto considered procedures of his endeavor to go beyond."[22] Richard Liddy tracks the development of Lonergan's understanding of intellectual conversion. Following his encounter with Augustine's intellectual grasp of his convictions and in response to the developing scientific worldview, Liddy says Lonergan came to see that "it is the presence or absence of intellectual conversion that is the core issue in the Church's understanding of what is going on in the world and the world's understanding of the meaning and realm of divine revelation."[23]

David Ford takes the question of transformation and salvation in a different creative direction. He asks, "Can this theology of salvation go to the heart of Christian identity?"[24] His answer leads him to engage the Jewish philosopher Emmanuel Levinas and the metaphor of "facing" as a key to reentering the question of salvation. Ford demonstrates both the perplexity of uncovering a single or common word about conversion and salvation in Christian theology and the breadth of inquiry that is possible once this inquiry is embraced. "Flourishings" from his dialogues with the philosophers Levinas, Jungel, and Ricoeur open into the world of Christian identity through singing, facing Jesus Christ, polyphonic living, and feasting. Ford turns to Thomas Trahern for an expression of salvation as felicity, a transformation of God by joy:

> By infusing grateful principles, and inclinations to thanksgiving He hath made the creature capable of more than all worlds, yea, of more than enjoying the Deity in a simple way; though we should suppose it to be

infinite. For to enjoy God is the fountain of infinite treasure, and as the giver of all, is infinite pleasure: but He by his wisdom infusing greatful principles, hath made us upon the very account of self-love to love Him more than ourselves.[25]

Andrew Tallon, in *Head and Heart: Affection, Cognition and Volition as Triune Consciousness,* takes still another tack into the question of transformation. Tallon moves through an analysis of Ricouer's *connaturality.* Tallon summarizes, "as we 'become' through our own agency, by forming habits, thereby constituting our 'second' nature, so we become better able to feel resonance or dissonance, harmony or disharmony, according to the beings we *are,* according to our acquired 'second' nature. . . . In practice, our actions issue proximately from our habits, our modified nature, and only remotely from our first nature, an idea important to Ricouer's general project, namely a theory of the relation of feeling to will and the role of feeling in relation to affective fragility and human fallibility."[26] Tallon's work is significant for the development of a theory of consciousness that makes way for the kind of transformation that percolates through the works of Ricouer, Ford, and Lonergan.

From a completely unsuspecting angle, I also find conversion at issue in the work of the recently deceased philosopher Gillian Rose. Her stunning work *The Broken Middle* puts postmodernity on notice that the privilege of fragmentation will give way to a reflective analysis of value and social reconfiguration. But here I turn to her confessional book *Love's Work: A Reckoning with Life.*[27] In her meditation on what enables some people to live through challenges and experiences that escapes rational explanation, she uncovers the significance of her Jewish heritage and the religious lapses of her dysfunctional family. But what captures me is the organic character of her writing about the deepest issues of life—health, sex, relationships—and that in coming to grips with her own mortality and philosophical reflection she discovers a space in reflection that stands beyond what philosophy can address. Her philosophical consciousness is a prelude to a set of puzzles about what makes it possible to live in light of the ubiquitous threat of death. From this place she can look back at philosophy:

> I find it baffling that philosophers are currently claiming that we have a choice between three alternatives: revealed religion, enlightened rationalism, and postmodern relativism. "Revealed religion" refers to faiths which based their claim to truth on divine intervention and sacred scripture;

"enlightenment rationalism" means the modern authority of unaided human reason, the ability of humanity to achieve unlimited progress and perfection; "postmodern relativism" renounces the modern commitment to reason in view of its negative outcome—the destructive potentiality of science, the persistence of wars and holocausts. It proposes pluralism, localism and reservation as principles, when it has abandoned principles. It is the *unrevealed religion* which troubles us more than any revealed religion: the *unrevealed* religion which has hold of us without any evidences, natural or supernatural, without any credos or dogmas, liturgies or services. It is the very religion that makes us protest, "But I have no religion," the very *Protestantism* against modernity that fuels our inner self-relation. Yet this very protest founded modernity.[28]

Rose's own protests are met with a realization that what holds her is a work of love.

The variety of these responses to human transformation and salvation make a strong case for engaging the question of conversion and transformation with utmost reflective attention and concern. Thinking about conversion reaches across disciplines of psychology, philosophy, and theology, as well as the entire spectrum of religious traditions. Across historical space, even into our own lives, the powerful questions flow: "What is my being, if not an invitation to be transformed?" and "What might be possible for me and my community in light of such transformation?" These questions reformulate the traditional query "What does God require me to be or to do?" My contention throughout this book is that the depth of the American philosophical tradition can be fully seen only in direct relation to these questions.

Plan of Inquiry

This inquiry follows a historical path beginning with Jonathan Edwards. Edwards was aware of his precarious place in the world of ideas and his New England society. He was also acutely aware of the security of the gospel in working toward a completion of redemption and the limits that prevent individuals and communities from participating in that redemptive plan. Edwards's theological creativity in developing the structure of conversion in *Religious Affections* opens this door to participation as widely as possible. His integration of psychological structure and theological content raises pivotal and challenging questions about the soul and the reality of God. These are leading questions, and Edwards is intent on expanding the meaning of God's gracious influence on the soul and demonstrating the forms of life within which this influence can be most clearly known.

Edwards's unique philosophical perspective grows in relation to his theological conviction that an affective transformation of individuals is the healing force of divine grace and revelation. Edwards's role in calling the Puritan tradition to reclaim the ground of conversion emerged from his early preaching career and ultimately resulted in vitriolic opposition to him and his ideas. This opposition convinced Edwards that his generation was in need of a more stable reflective ground in the face of developments in philosophy and theology. Edwards gave his tradition a magisterial corpus and a sound defense of conversion because he realized that resistance to this idea was in fact the same opposition to the truth that necessitates the need for conversion.

Following Edwards, I turn to Charles Sanders Peirce. Peirce left us a full and complex record of his lifelong inquiry into the nature of the self and the universe. Adopting Peirce's semiotic language of the self, I attempt to cash out his conviction that there is a "real and effective force" behind inquiry that pulls us forward into the realization of our continuity in thought with the universe. Rather than a fixed self or a thinking thing, Peirce discovers that the self is stabilized by inquiry aimed at the critical adoption of a guiding principle of thought and practice. This relation of the self and inquiry propels Peirce toward the difficult problems of making sense of brute experience, which does not seem to lead anywhere, and the context of finite time that limits any particular individual's ability to enact a critical transformation. Peirce fails, I think, to make a successful argument about the nature of the transformation of the self. Briefly stated, he fails primarily because he approaches, but resists, the prospect that a particular positive content subtends all human inquiry, rather than facing that issue squarely as the problem. If this is a real failure for Peirce, as I claim it is, it is a very instructive failure.

John Dewey figures large in the American philosophical rejection of religion. He, more than Peirce and James, separates Christian hope for individuals and communities from his pragmatic faith in democracy and humanism. Despite this overt separation from Christian ideals there is too much of the New Testament in Dewey's mature thought to argue that it is a clean break. But this ambiguity in Dewey is not my primary focus. I am more interested in the way Dewey develops the philosophical obligation to deal with human transformation. His description of the community revolves around the critique of public practice necessary to direct it toward a radical transformation of ends and means. Dewey resists disputes about the nature of ends, and the question that is its near relative, the debate over the relative values of theism and naturalism. Rather, he focuses on describing a community oriented toward its own transformation. John Dewey is a spiritual partner of Jonathan Edwards in the task of raising the desire for a new form of life through provocative images and descriptions, even if they both would have rejected each other theologically as extraordinarily misguided and dangerous. Dewey's significance for this study of conversion comes from his goal of prompting transformation without capitulating to any authoritative content for that transformation except experience. Dewey highlights the natural human desire for transformation, and the yearning for a content that make this change possible. Dewey's inability to ground this desire in any kind of tradition and his blunt rejection of the need for a structure of tradition for reflection undermines his project in my view. He, like Peirce, fails to achieve philosophically the transformation that he wants, but this too is an instructive failure.

William James, in distinction from Peirce, works from the emotive and sentimental side of human reflection. He pursues the impulse toward a transformed life through experience, dwelling in the imperative character of transformation. Generally speaking, American philosophy has adopted James's conclusions concerning the sentimental and affective disposition toward transformation, but we have undervalued the problem of the content necessary for the transformation James advocates. James and Peirce disagreed about the importance of resolving the issue of what stands behind the human impulse to seek a holistic change. I explore James's explicit rejection of this content basis for transformation in *The Varieties of Religious Experience* by following his description of religious experience and his systematic dismantling of Jonathan Edwards. James's role in this study of conversion is that of an opponent to the claim that genuine transformation must originate outside or beyond the individual. This claim threatens James personally and philosophically. He engages in a subtle but violent battle with Edwards in order to unseat the prevailing conviction that religious experience always entails an extrapersonal source, like God, as a ground for transformation. James wins, by and large, in the court of philosophical appeal, but I suggest that strong criticism of his argument is warranted. He sets the example for evading conversion by attempting to remove the sting of absence, the phenomena of realizing transformation is *not* possible from our present state. My criticism of James becomes the setting for a thematic treatment of this condition.

Leaving the historical ground of American pragmatism, I explore the absence that emerges in each account of these four philosophers. *Absence* is a term for the general awareness that a holistic reorientation of the self, habits, or the community requires the recognition that the individual or the community is insufficient or in error in its current form. This awareness is expressed in a variety of ways. Absence refers to the existential condition that propels a person to seek transformation such as Augustine felt leading up to his experience in the Milan garden. Absence also refers to the inability to bring a reflective order to satisfactory articulation such as Gillian Rose describes. Philosophy swings between attempting to eliminate all elements of absence in modern thought and embracing absence as the only possible human condition in our postmodern condition. American thinkers try to let the depth of existential absence guide them while striving to bring human consciousness and thought to a functional stability. The irreducible character of absence in reflection is a sign, I think, that transformation and conversion are elemental features of human consciousness. Any spirit of optimism, then, is grounded in the conviction that the blunt experience of absence can become an opening for a movement toward the discovery of a content of reflection that issues in a living stability.

The ability to respond self-critically to the absence of transformation forms the essence of human freedom. Human freedom as creative transformation is the second theme that emerges from an examination of conversion in American philosophy. The possibility of freedom is an accomplishment of spirit discovered in the process of a class of actions related to the self and the community. In this way I understand freedom as a platform for developing an orientation of the self toward some content rather than as a self-oriented ability to select one value rather than another. Thinking about human freedom this way allows for a reappraisal of Jonathan Edwards's claim that transformation from God in conversion demands a completely free human action in response to the revelation of grace. But the principle that establishes this act as a choice of the free will is that the person's affective orientation hangs in the balance.

I conclude this inquiry with a critical approach to recent American philosophy. Three contemporary philosophers who have contributed significantly to the development of pragmatism and American philosophy are held up to the light of conversion. My fundamental question is how conversion enables a critical appropriation and advance from their thoughts. Richard Rorty has obviously influenced the direction of pragmatism and received his share (perhaps a share and a half) of criticism. Rorty associates himself with James, and I find the same tendency to overlook both the content necessary for transformation and the inability or unwillingness to dwell in absence present in his writing. Next I turn to the provocative writings of Cornel West. West picks up Dewey's reforming spirit and recharges it with a jolting shock of charisma. West also falls under the criticism of conversion, but in a different way than Dewey. While Dewey attempted to manufacture the content necessary for transformation, West is clear that his Christian tradition is in play at that point. But West overlooks, I think, aspects of the Christian tradition that are necessary to sustain transformation because it does not appear conducive to his political goals of reconstructing community under an egalitarian warrant.

Robert Corrington, my last example of evading conversion, evokes Peirce's complex interrelation of religious thought, semiotic metaphysics, and psychological insight. Corrington moves between the kind of transformation Peirce perceives he needs and the necessary criticism of Western philosophy's drunken delight in consciousness. Corrington argues against the philosophical privileging of consciousness, and I extend this critique to Corrington himself. The question is not how to get along without consciousness, I suggest, but it is knowing what we are so that we can be transformed and know this transformation.

Making these claims and criticism about the orientation of American philosophy may appear confrontational, and it is. This confrontation appears to the extent that recent American philosophy moves away from lived values and experience and more toward the professional philosophical genre the pragmatists eschewed. I trust that the confrontation of this argument will be seen as an effort to provoke philosophers and reflective individuals to engage the questions of conversion and transformation in a new way. I have not attempted to hide the apologia for Christian content that informs this study of transformation and conversion. This may, and probably should, be taken as a kind of provocation. My own confession is that I have made the discoveries I am exploring here philosophically under the conviction that Jesus, the Christ, is the suitable platform for engaging in this reflection. My defense of this conviction is offered as a dialogical challenge to philosophical programs that reject such content out of hand. My defense of this conviction is also an attempt to test whether a critical evaluation of American pragmatism can be oriented around the core issues of the human soul and communal life. My confession and my philosophical work aim to take fuller account of the difference pragmatists have made, not only in the broader tradition of philosophy, but also more particularly in my own self-understanding. This path of discovery has led to the guiding question for this study, "What could be more profoundly and permanently transforming than a vital difference in our philosophical expectations of religious self-understanding and practice?"

NOTES

1. H. Richard Niebuhr, *The Kingdom of God in America* (Wesleyan University Press, 1988), 20.

2. John Dewey, *John Dewey: The Middle Works,* vol. 10 (Southern Illinois University Press, 1989), 48.

3. William James, "The Moral Philosopher and the Moral Life," *Essays in Pragmatism* (Hafner, 1948), 86.

4. C. S. Peirce, *The Collected Papers of Charles Sanders Peirce* (Harvard University Press, 1931–58), 5:402 and notes.

5. James, "Moral Philosopher," 86.

6. Ellen Kappy Suckiel, *Heaven's Champion* (University of Notre Dame Press, 1996), 114.

7. Richard Bernstein, *John Dewey* (Washington Square Press, 1966).

8. John Dewey, *John Dewey: The Later Works* (Southern Illinois University Press, 1981–90), 1:314.

9. Robert Westbrook, *John Dewey and American Democracy* (Cornell University Press, 1991), 8.

10. Jerome P. Soneson, *Pragmatism and Pluralism: John Dewey's Significance for Theology* (Augsburg Fortress Press, 1992).

11. Peirce, *Collected Papers* 6:157.

12. Letter to Reverend John W. Brown, Rector of St. Thomas's Episcopal Church of New York City. Max Fisch Collection at the Peirce Edition Project, Indiana University and Purdue University at Indianapolis.

13. Michael Raposa, *Peirce's Philosophy of Religion* (Indiana University Press, 1989); Douglas Anderson, *Strands of System: The Philosophy of Charles Peirce* (Purdue University Press, 1995).

14. Harry S. Stout, *The New England Soul* (Oxford University Press, 1986), 205–207.

15. Perry Miller, *Jonathan Edwards* (World Publishing, 1959).

16. John Smith, "Edwards as Philosopher of Religion," *Review of Metaphysics* 30, no. 2 (December 1976): 306–324; Smith, *Jonathan Edwards: Puritan Preacher Philosopher* (University of Notre Dame Press, 1992).

17. Eugene Fontinell, *Toward a Reconstruction of Religion* (Doubleday, 1970), 33.

18. "The State of the Church, 2000" (Barna Research, 2001).

19. John McIntyre, *The Shape of Sotierology* (T & T Clark, 1992).

20. Bernard Lonergan, *Insight: A Study of Human Understanding* (Harper & Row, 1978).

21. Ibid., 4.

22. Ibid., 636.

23. Richard M. Liddy, *Transforming Light: Intellectual Conversion in the Early Lonergan* (Liturgical Press, 1993), 150.

24. David F. Ford, *Self in Salvation: Being Transformed* (Cambridge University Press, 1999), 2.

25. Ibid., 278.

26. Andrew Tallon, *Head and Heart: Affection, Cognition and Volition as Triune Consciousness* (Fordham University Press, 1997), 100–101.

27. Gillian Rose, *Love's Work: A Reckoning with Life* (Schocken Books, 1995).

28. Ibid., 135–136.

Conversion in American Philosophy

1

The Philosophical Structure of Jonathan Edwards's *Religious Affections*

No discourses have been more remarkably blessed than those in which the doctrine of God's absolute sovereignty with regard to the salvation of sinners . . . has been insisted upon.

—Jonathan Edwards, *A Faithful Narrative*

JONATHAN EDWARDS'S CAREER as a pastor, evangelist, and philosopher is unique in American history. His inquiry into *Religious Affections* demonstrates the range and complexity of thought that enabled him to intertwine these disparate roles in relation to the concept of conversion, a concept equally important to his public career and his private devotion. Edwards describes conversion as a change of the inclinations revealed in the discovery of the "sense of the heart."[1] The subject of conversion is the occasion for Edwards's most profound reflection on the way his biblical tradition coheres with his psychological and philosophical observations. No other subject could be as pivotal for Edwards, and no other book in American religious thought has been equal in effect to the *Religious Affections*.

The epigraph to this chapter is taken from *A Faithful Narrative of the Surprising Work of God,* published in 1737, nine years before the *Religious Affections.* In this first attempt to describe the Great Awakening, Edwards established two fundamental points: first, that genuine conversion always indicates God's sovereign activity, and second, that conversion is a proper subject of discourse. Edwards expanded these two points into a thorough inquiry of conversion, which he understood to be the only sufficient way to assess the Great Awakening critically and defend its good against the critiques of prominent clergy, most notably Charles Chauncy.[2]

Yet Edwards did not respond in kind to his attackers. Rather, he saw the controversy over the Awakening as a chance to address the confusion about the possibility and dimensions of religious conversion. In doing so, Edwards supports the results of the revival as the product of conversion that acknowledges God's activity, and he provides a reasoned account of the conditions and consequences of this fundamental change in a person. The argument of *Religious Affections* stands on Edwards's conviction that "all spiritual discoveries are transforming . . . such power and efficacy have they that they make an alteration in the very nature of the soul" (340). This Augustinian character flows through the *Religious Affections* as Edwards examines the transforming effect of grace and reflective discovery. Edwards finds conversion within his tradition, and his conclusions support the role of the Puritan pastors in this process, addressing one of the primary concerns of his critics. But he also expands the meaning of the discovery of divine reality with his understanding of the soul's faculties and what would constitute a "spiritual" effect on those faculties.

Oddly, conversion is not a prominent theme in studies of Edwards's philosophical theology. Indeed, most commentators focus their attention on the novelty of his theological position or its consonance with other traditions.[3] By contrast, I argue here that understanding and describing conversion is Edwards's highest reflective goal, and that in the text of *Religious Affections* he presents a philosophically structured account of religious conversion. Further, I will argue that understanding conversion is essential to taking full account of Edwards's constructive theology and philosophy. I also suggest that the nature of conversion described in the *Religious Affections* gives us a clear way to relate Edwards's later writings, such as *Freedom of the Will* and *Original Sin,* to mention but two, to his earlier career as pastor at Northampton and his involvement with the Great Awakening.

Claiming that conversion is a central philosophical theme opposes some prominent interpretations of Edwards's philosophical theology. Perry Miller, for instance, argues that Edwards discovered the absence of real divinity and turned instead to a naturalism couched in pious language.[4] Sang Lee brilliantly describes Edwards's novel presentation of relational ontology that yields an aesthetic harmonization of the soul and the universe.[5] And John E. Smith explores Edwards's critique of Locke, modernism, and traditional theology, which funds later American developments of a philosophy built on "thick" experience.[6] But what separated Edwards from his contemporaries during the controversy over the Great Awakening is still present in these recent commentators, who are clearly not Edwards's opponents but yet fail to understand Edwards's

focus on conversion. There is a reluctance to embrace the divine transformation of human souls as the culmination of reflective discovery. The
difficulty appears to be centered on accepting the reality of the divine,
articulating the need or desire for a radical transformation of the soul,
and establishing the cognitive or experiential access that enables a reorientation of an individual's actions toward a moral or supernatural good.
For Edwards, however, these difficulties emphasize the importance of
conversion and mark it as the beginning of an inquiry into the kind of
knowing that is necessary to render all knowing as trustworthy.

Edwards's main rhetorical task in *Religious Affections* is preventing the
adulteration of conversion by enthusiasm, the uncontrolled emotional
responses and special "convictions" that attended the Great Awakening.
By describing the limits of conversion, Edwards generates a systematic
account of the convergence of emotive responses and intellectual content in a new "sense" that issues in an effective change of the soul.
Running throughout this description is the theme of discovery: our discovery of God, and God's discovering his reality to us. Edwards uses "discover" in the middle-passive way, the mood of being subject to an
influence where the external or internal origin of the content that
results from this influence is left vague. Edwards extends the traditional
Puritan meaning of conversion to include knowledge, both intellectual
and personal, and faithful living as the signs or aspects of a peculiar continuing discovery, not a single, metaphysically occult event. This discovery is the spirit Edwards finds in experimental religion that opens the
soul to "a new world of knowledge."

ARCHITECTONIC IN *RELIGIOUS AFFECTIONS*

John Smith points out that Edwards is one of America's most systematic
and careful thinkers, comparing him to the logician and scientist C. S.
Peirce. As a systematic thinker, Edwards works out or works toward a
structure of thought. I argue here that the *Religious Affections* is an example of a thoroughly architectonic reflection. The architectonic evident in
the *Affections* is the structure of spiritual and intellectual discovery that
functions as a platform for conversion. This structure forms the outline
of a movement from intellectual discovery beginning within the natural
faculties that yields (with God's grace) a complete reorientation of those
faculties and a conviction of God's active work on the soul, a "salvation

ready to be revealed."[7] Edwards's tone here is one of universal access to the need for and the possibility of experiencing conversion—God's arbitrary choice of applying grace to only a few elect persons does not appear as a limit to conversion in the *Religious Affections*. Rather, Edwards makes the case that in conversion the soul finds a divine object that is "worthy of full acceptance," to borrow missionary Andrew Fuller's term. To say it plainly, highlighting the structure of conversion will conflict with the tendency to categorize Edwards as a typical predestinarian Calvinist. Edwards insists on both the sovereignty of God and the reality of an active human conversion in the *Affections*.

Given the extraordinary dimensions of this topic, there is little wonder that the *Religious Affections* is a puzzling text. Edwards wrote it in three parts, roughly following the pattern of a Puritan sermon of scripture, doctrine, and improvement. The improvement in a Puritan sermon incorporates the scripture and doctrine in a creative expansion of key ideas and makes a practical application of the message for daily living. The scriptural foundation of the *Religious Affections* in Part I is based on I Peter 1:8, "Whom having not seen, ye love: in whom, though now ye see him not, yet believing, ye rejoice with joy unspeakable, and full of glory" (93). Edwards examines the benefits and the necessity of trials in bringing a person's "state of grace"—as converted—to plain view. Opposition clarifies conversion, and genuine spiritual character is revealed only by the deepest kind of spiritual and reflective conflict. This agonistic frame shapes Edwards's reflection throughout the *Religious Affections*.

Part II of the *Affections* is a doctrinal clarification that clears the field of common misconceptions of the process and results of conversion by examining "what are no signs of gracious affections" (127). Edwards presents twelve of these "no certain signs," attacking current formulations of how one might know or be justified in their belief that they enjoy God's grace or have experienced a special revelation. His point in this *via negativa* is to articulate the limits of conversion by describing possible errors of judgment about one's state. Neither "special revelations" nor enthusiastic responses suffice for good evidence of the influence of God's grace.

Part III is Edwards's "improvement" on the subject of knowing one's state, "Shewing what are Distinguishing signs of truly gracious and holy Affections" (191). The last part of the *Religious Affections* has drawn the lion's share of scholarly attention. Edwards presents twelve "marks" of a soul that has come under God's saving influence, a reflective account of a soul persevering and being proven by the "trial" of the affections.

Edwards gives no outline or explanation for the order of presentation of the twelve signs. This leads many readers to suppose that the signs are a list of topics most important to least, or vice versa, or topics that simply came to mind as Edwards thought through the issues.[8] On the contrary, I believe that the signs reflect a discrete arrangement and constitute Edwards's architectonic structure of conversion.

Making the case for Edwards's structure of conversion within the twelve signs of affection depends on establishing three main points. First is that a change in a person's faculties is the proper ground for describing conversion, including its divine origin. I treat this subject in the first section of this chapter. The second point is that Edwards's philosophical and theological description of conversion depends on the arrangement of the twelve signs as an argument that has descriptive and performative dimensions. This point turns on the holistic character of the twelve signs as a single unit of thought. This claim of unity requires an explanation of the internal development of the signs that results in a persuasive argument for conversion, as well as the continuity this argument for conversion has with Edwards's larger ministerial purpose. I present this discussion in the second section.

The third point is that the structure of conversion is central to Edwards's experimental religion. Conversion must not only consist in an ordered process itself, but it must also bring order to our religious experience and practice. This dimension of conversion is discussed later in this chapter.

Amid this positive statement of the effective power of conversion, however, we must not overlook the fact that conversion remained a divisive and problematic feature of Edwards's theology. What remains unresolved about conversion may hopefully come clearer in the process of this examination. It is safe to say, though, that every advance in understanding the complexity of conversion can be properly evaluated only by its potential to provide a continuing ground for reconciliation between the realization of God's demand on humanity and the human efforts to respond sufficiently to that demand, and this clearly cannot be matched by any one thinker. This is the task that Edwards, through the *Affections,* invites us to engage with him.

THE REALM OF FACULTIES AS THE GROUND OF CONVERSION

Edwards begins the discussion of twelve signs of gracious affection with a simple statement of faith, that "it be plain that Christ has given rules to all Christians, to enable 'em to judge of professors of religion," although it is not God's intention to "give us any rules, by which we may certainly know, who of our fellow professors are his, and to make a clear separation between sheep and goats" (193). This is similar to C. S. Peirce's claim that if the creator of the universe "really Be and be benign," then we would be able to reach a settled opinion about this reality within the limits of fallible reason.[9] Peirce suggests that this discovery is possible through the communal practice of scientific inquiry, but Edwards develops his inquiry by delving into religious tradition and scripture. Despite these different approaches, both of these thinkers agree that the ultimate character ingredient in the universe, what they call God, is reflected in a genuine change of human character.[10] Finding the order or principle of human change, therefore, constitutes the ultimate destination of human reflection, and human change in its ultimate form represents the final meaning of the material universe.[11]

Two Kinds of Knowledge

Unlike Peirce, though, Edwards is committed to the pastoral task of describing the signs of such a conversion to enable individuals to know their own state and to enable a right discrimination of true religion from false. Edwards's use of signs, like Peirce's later semiotic theory, argues against an essentialist model of the soul. Gracious affections are the character of the soul changed in virtue of its relation to God, a change that is evident in the alteration of a person's faculties of willing, understanding, and desiring, not just particular conclusions drawn from these faculties.[12] In his 1734 pre-Awakening sermon "A Divine and Supernatural Light," Edwards says "There is a twofold understanding or knowledge of good, that God has made the mind of man capable of." He continues,

> The first, that which is merely speculative or notional: as when a person only speculatively judges that anything is, which by the agreement of mankind is called good or excellent. . . . And the other is that which consists in the sense of the heart: . . . In the former is exercised merely a speculative faculty, or the understanding strictly so called, or as spoken of in distinction from the will or disposition of the soul. In the latter the will, or inclination, or heart, are mainly concerned.[13]

Both speculative knowledge and heart knowledge depend on faculties, but only a change of inclination and will makes "heart" knowledge possible. The discovery of this heart knowledge is the subject of this sermon. Edwards argues that the nature of divine light and its sensible effects are one and the same thing, that the illumination of divine light affects the desires and evokes the "heart," revealing the holistic nature of the person's willing and inclining toward God. Divine light shows what is "excellent," Edwards's term for transcendent reality met within experience. The "heart" appears as the character of the faculties, a soul brought to substantiality by its being made newly "sensible of pleasure and delight in the presence of [divine excellence]."[14]

The emerging awareness of God's excellence reveals the reality the faculties now perceive differently than in their natural state. This perception of excellence shows that the natural faculties have been transcended, and this perceived excellence includes both the objective reality of God and the discovery of a new character, the "heart," within the faculties. Edwards is careful to say that this light does not produce a new faculty in a person, but that the natural faculties are enabled to perceive this excellence in its own functioning, a sign that they have been "awakened" or made newly sensible by the influence of divine light.

Signs of Affection and Four Considerations from "A Divine and Supernatural Light"

"A Divine and Supernatural Light" is especially significant for understanding the twelve signs of the *Religious Affections,* which also treat the possible reorientation of the faculties. Edwards concludes "A Divine and Supernatural Light" with an improvement that exhorts his auditors to "influence" and "move to" divine light by four considerations.

> *First.* "This is the most excellent and divine wisdom, that any creature is capable of," that exceeds "the greatest speculative understanding in divinity, without grace." This knowledge has the most noble object that is, or can be, which is "the divine glory, and excellency of God, and Christ."

Signs

(I)   gracious affections are the result of spiritual operations in the heart,

(II)   the objective ground of the affections is the transcendentally excellent nature of divine things,

(III)   the love of divine things for the beauty and sweetness of their moral excellency is the first beginning, and spring of all holy affections.

Second. This knowledge is peculiarly "sweet and joyful. This light gives a view of those things that are immensely the most exquisitely beautiful, and capable of delighting the eye of the understanding."

Signs

(IV)   arise from the mind's being enlightened to understand or appreciate divine things, becoming a new "sense of the heart,"

(V)   they are attended with the spiritual conviction of the reality of divine things, and

(VI)   with evangelical humiliation, which arises from the spiritual knowledge of one's own failure in relation to the "discovery of the beauty of God's holiness and moral perfection."

Third. This light "effectually influences the inclination, and changes the nature of the soul." This change "assimilates the nature to the divine nature," namely the glory that is beheld in Christ. The effect of this assimilation is a "saving close with Christ."

Signs

(VII) gracious affections are attended with a change of nature to Christ,

(VIII) that this change differs from a false change in that gracious affections "tend to" the spirit and temper of Jesus Christ, and

(IX)   that they yield a softening of the heart and Christian tenderness of spirit.

Fourth. "This light, and this only, has its fruit in an universal holiness of life." This obedience does not arise from a notional or speculative understanding, but from the influence that "reaches the bottom of the heart."

Signs

(X)   saints perceive a beauty of symmetry and proportion inhabiting their affections;

(XI)   they experience a deepening appetite for more complete spiritual attainments including practical service; and

(XII) this Godliness has its full exercise and fruit in a moral Christian practice which is "perfect obedience."[15]

The focus of these considerations is the change in a soul's grasp of a divine object, by knowledge, inclination, and a desire for obedience. The correspondence between the considerations and the twelve signs Edwards develops in the *Religious Affections* is striking. Taking each consideration as a heading or summation, the twelve signs in the *Religious Affections* fall into four groups of three. This alignment between the considerations and the signs suggests that there is a definite structure to the signs, but it also makes it possible to develop the signs and the considerations together as an argument undergirding Edwards's reflection. Let me expand on this alignment by describing the relation I think holds between the considerations and the signs.

The first consideration from "A Divine and Supernatural Light," that the wisdom of God's glory is beyond educated understanding and only possible by grace is developed in the *Religious Affections* by signs I, II, and III: (I) gracious affections are the result of spiritual operations on the heart, (II) the objective ground of the affections is the transcendentally excellent nature of divine things, and (III) the love of divine things for the beauty and sweetness of their moral excellency is the first beginning and spring of all holy affections (197, 240, and 253–254, respectively).

The second consideration, the superlative character of this new knowledge, collects signs IV, V, and VI: gracious affections (IV) arise from the mind's being enlightened to understand or apprehend divine things through a "sense of the heart" (V); they are attended with the spiritual conviction of the reality of divine things, and (VI) with evangelical humiliation, which arises from the spiritual knowledge of one's own failure in relation to the "discovery of the beauty of God's holiness and moral perfection" (266, 291, 311).

The third consideration concerning the effectual change of the inclination to the glory of Christ is developed by signs VII, VIII, and IX: showing that (VII) gracious affections are attended with a change of nature, (VIII) that this change differs from a false change in that gracious affections "tend to" the spirit and temper of Jesus Christ, and (IX) that they yield a softening of the heart and Christian tenderness of spirit (340, 344, 357).

The fourth consideration of "universal" holiness, collects signs X, XI, and XII: (X) saints perceive a beauty of symmetry and proportion inhabiting their affections, (XI) they experience a deepening appetite for more complete spiritual attainments including practical service, and (XII) this Godliness has its full exercise and fruit in a moral Christian practice which is "perfect obedience" (365, 376, 384).

Having suggested a connection between these texts, let me quickly say how they are different. In "A Divine and Supernatural Light" Edwards hopes to encourage conversion by highlighting the realization of the "spiritual knowledge that God is the author of."[16] The four considerations develop the desire or expectation that appeals to the person who does not enjoy this light. Edwards's aim is to promote conversion by speaking about, creating in words, the knowledge that unawakened souls desire but have not yet experienced. His object is different in the *Affections*. Here he examines the same spiritual knowledge as it appears within the living reality of the saints, as the dynamic principle that holds them to God.

Conversion works both ways for Edwards. First, conversion is what he speaks about to draw souls toward the "good" we anticipate in God, and second, he speaks of conversion as an opening into the continuous discovery of the "good" found in the experience of God. In both cases the divine effect of conversion and our realization of it are the same event, whereby God's influence is present in the human experience of a discovery that incorporates the faculties of understanding, willing, and desiring into a spiritual unity. From these two texts it is clear that Edwards treats the faculties as the ground of conversion, both as a feature of existential experience and as the subject for description. In the next section the internal relations of the signs are considered as both the dimensions of a living encounter with the divine and as a way of articulating that encounter.

Signs of Affection as the Content of Conversion

We must still ask this question: Why does Edwards present twelve signs in the *Religious Affections?* As I noted earlier, Edwards says he intends to illuminate "rules" by which "all things whatsoever that the minds of men are the subjects of" come to reflect the order of true religion (89). True religion must be qualified. Religion is true, for Edwards, when it has God for its object and not any self-deceptive replacement. Edwards is not the kind of religious dogmatist Charles Hodge claims he is.[17] Fidelity to orthodoxy is not Edwards's main measure of truth. For Edwards, true religion obtains when "the immediate object of [the soul] is the supreme beauty and excellency of the nature of divine things as they are in themselves" (271).

The twelve signs of affection bring to view the pivotal transitions of a soul in the discovery of its effective change of inclination toward God and the divine character of the object it seeks with its heart. This discovery of the nature of the soul and God shows the inferential character of Edwards's signs, making the set of twelve signs an instance of the argument for conversion from experience. In this way the twelve signs extend outward as examples of the practical and intellectual inferences central to all discoveries of God and self.

The four considerations from "A Divine and Supernatural Light" represent critical transitions on the way to the conclusion of God's reality that Edwards says is made "by one step" (299). Edwards does not presume intuitional or other knowledge of God revealed by non-natural means. The development in the twelve signs traces the discovery of an object within the "things in [a person]" which carries an authority that is divine—a discovery of God in us. Divine authority is not the end in view of this discovery, but the nature of the discovery itself argues for its divine authority. A contrary condition is that "natural" souls, those not having this light, will have no such authority attending their self-discovery. Let me now treat the signs as they appear in the text, paying attention to both their relation to the considerations of "A Divine and Supernatural Light" and the inferential character of the discovery of God and the soul.

First Consideration: Signs I, II, III

Signs I–III reflect the coming to awareness of God's objective character, the "divine glory, and excellency of God, and Christ" of the first consideration from "A Divine and Supernatural Light." Sign I is a spiritual sense that is unique to saints, an awakening awareness that shows that there are operations on the heart that are spiritual, supernatural, and divine (197). In classic Edwardsean style, sign II is what the result of this supernatural operation is not. It is not self-interest. "In the love of the true saint," Edwards says, "God is the lowest foundation; the love of the excellency of his nature is the foundation of all the affections that come afterwards, wherein self-love is concerned as an handmaid" (246). The opposition between self-love and the love of God is the first "objective ground" of gracious affection (240). What is at stake here is best described from the vantage of Edwards's essay on "The Mind."[18] In this essay, Edwards describes the love of excellence that permeates all being as the tendency toward entity. Entity is the unity of manifold being reflected in harmony of arrangement. This harmony is beautiful, and as it draws more and more being into this relationship, entity expands.

Individuals count as entities, for Edwards, since they are able to order their surroundings by beauty and are able to produce or choose harmony in their being. But all entities are relative and dependent on the principle of entity itself. In a work titled "The Mind," Edwards distinguishes between entities (individuals) that partake of this characteristic of being to construct a private and limited harmony, and those that appropriate it as a means of manifesting the universal principle of entity in their relations. The ultimate principle of entity, God, is perceived in universal harmony, and this perception produces those entities in relationship to entity itself. This distinction also separates love from self-love. "Now how improper is it to say," Edwards remarks in the *Affections*, "that one loves himself because what is agreeable to him is agreeable to him, and what is disagreeable to him is disagreeable, which mere entity supposes. So that this thing they call self-love is no affection, but only the entity of the thing, or his being what he is."[19] If the individual is functioning in terms of the natural tendency to entity Edwards does not call this "affection" or love.

An individual develops "affection" by stretching beyond self-interest—and Edwards sees no way this can occur naturally. The only way this stretching beyond is possible is the translation of the principle by which an entity harmonizes being to reflect the principle by which entity itself (God) harmonizes being. In this new state of entity, which is love, the harmony of the individual is the same harmony, but not the same content, as entity itself. The individual expands the being of the entity of God as a new point of expanding the harmony of God's excellence. Love of divine excellence is the sign of a supernatural operation on the heart, not because the natural tendency to entity is eliminated, but because God's harmony of being is appropriated for its "loveliness." The "spiritual sense" of the first sign is this awareness of supernatural excellence within the aesthetic tendency of being, which is shown in opposition to self-love in sign II.

Sign III is the love of God's moral excellence.[20] Moral excellence is the harmony of relations reflective of God's entity in his "exercises as a moral agent, or whereby the heart and will of God are good, right, and infinitely becoming" (255). Objective reorientation of the individual to the entity of God is accomplished when the harmony within the moral character of God is perceived, and Edwards means the character of God revealed in scripture. The transition to love of God's moral excellence is autobiographical of Edwards's own struggle with the "horrible doctrine" of the condemnation of sinners to hell. In his "Personal Narrative," Edwards describes his coming to see that God's eternal judgment of sinners was not simply compatible with the excellence of God's moral character but constitutive of that harmony, at least in terms of human experience.[21] This assent to the moral character of God in the Bible is an ultimate challenge to the natural understanding because it provides the most concrete material for evaluation and judgment and also because it undermines all previous claims to rational harmony. The love of the moral character of God thus disestablishes the intellectual order of the natural faculties, eliminating the integrity of the natural soul, and opening up in an existential way the need for a new order of the faculties.

Before I proceed to the next consideration and the next cluster of signs, let me make two points. First, Edwards calls the love of spiritual things of sign I the "fountain" of all gracious affections (240). This love is indubitable and immediate, that is, it is not a product of inferential reasoning. Neither can it be further articulated by inspecting preceding conditions. Taken in its immediacy simply as love it is without denotable content. There is the love of the spiritual character, like the love for a parent, which inclines the child to seek the particular acts and decisions that manifest that lovable character, but the love precedes this particularity. Edwards's description of this love as prior to particular content has encouraged a portrayal of the gracious affections as an essentially aesthetic disposition, but I do not think this is complete.[22] The immediacy of the saint's love of divine excellence reflects an absence of content that propels the understanding to further discovery. Second, the searching out of this excellence, in response to the immediacy of spiritual love, runs on an abductive hypothesis (to reach ahead to Peirce) of a "new simple idea" (205) that might supply the need for an order to the faculties.

Edwards says that natural understanding excels in following out relations of ideas but not in constructing its own origin or order. So the new simple idea that governs the judgment makes it "entirely of a new sort, and which could be produced by no exalting or varying or compounding of that kind of perceptions or sensations which the mind had before. . . . If grace be an entirely new kind of principle, then the exercises of it are also entirely a new kind of exercise" (205).[23] The focus here is on the nature of the idea governing the understanding, which is revealed by the object the understanding is able to perceive. The object perceivable by the judgment denotes the character of the understanding and also its ordering idea. Edwards establishes the rudiments of pragmatist logic in this connection between our reasoning and the object we can discover with that reason. Recognizing that we have a new or changed understanding requires that a new object has become apparent to our perception.

Second Consideration: Signs IV, V, VI

The second consideration of "A Divine and Supernatural Light" reads, "This knowledge is that which is above all others sweet and beautiful . . . capable of delighting the eye of the understanding." Edwards begins sign IV with a more general point, "gracious affections do arise from the mind's being enlightened, rightly and spiritually to understand or apprehend divine things" (266). "Knowledge," he says, "is the key that first opens the hard heart and enlarges the affections" (266), and the knowledge that is significant "appertains to the salvation by Christ, whereby he now sees how it is, and understands those divine and spiritual doctrines which once were foolishness to him" (268). Here Edwards introduces the sense of the heart: "I say a sense of the heart; for it is not merely speculation that is concerned in this kind of understanding; nor can there be a clear distinction made between the two faculties of understanding and will as acting separately and distinctly, in this matter" (272). Edwards's claim, contra Locke, is that the understanding operates only in strict relation to the order of the inclination, which incorporates the will.[24]

The sense of the heart is the unity of the faculties, where the ordering principle of the understanding and the will coincide. This coincidence is a "sense" because it is not a property of either the will or the understanding. The result of this new principle is not a change in the way the understanding works, but the substantial character it yields to the faculties that was not present before. Edwards does not ascribe to an intuition of the self, or a moral sense that unifies the inclinations, as in Butler's *Analogy of Religion*.[25] The sense of the heart, Edwards says, is "an effect and impression the soul is the subject of, as a *substance* possessed of taste, inclination, and will" (272, my emphasis). The unity of the will and understanding is an inferential conclusion which is possible only in relation to the same kind of harmony perceived in divine "things."

This reciprocal discovery of the substantial character of human and divine reality is the key to Edwards's rational faith. The soul achieves a substantial character as a result of its perception, its sense, of the sort of object that can provide a sufficient order to the understanding and the will, namely "the excellency of Christ's person" (273). The soul becomes a substantial entity as an effect of the understanding and will reflecting the same principle of order perceived in the character of God's moral excellence in Christ. Sign V develops the perception of unity in divine things, which is the basis for the conviction of the reality of the truth of the gospel, "that really Jesus is the Christ, the Son of the living God" (292), a judgment that establishes both the objective nature of God's revealed character and the objective nature of the soul that perceives it. The correspondence between the discovery of the reality of God's character and the reality of personal identity is pivotal in the signs of affection.

Personal identity, for Edwards, is the nexus of will and understanding which becomes substantial as a resisting thing by virtue of a single ordering principle. Edwards's notion of the will is not a power of choosing or refraining from choosing, as he makes clear in *Freedom of the Will*. Rather, the will arises within a person's faculties when the desires are discovered to have a discrete orientation. Likewise, the understanding is a faculty that has an orientation—it has an "object." In a natural condition, a person's will and understanding have different objects and orders. The question is what makes the understanding a proper function of the will, so that the understanding has the same character or focus as the desires. This occurs only if both the will and understanding have the same discrete orientation—toward an object. The "sense of the heart" is the awareness that the understanding is oriented toward an object that requires its full function to engage and that the will is also constrained by the same object as the proper or satisfying object of the soul's desire. The singular focus on this object by both the intellect and the will means that the inclination of the soul has overcome fragmentation. Fragmentation is a feature of our natural condition in which we are unable to perceive what will unify our hearts. In *Freedom of the Will* Edwards says that the soul is determined by its choice of an ultimate object, but no natural object is sufficient to incorporate both the intellect and the will. What Edwards means by "freedom of the will" is making this ultimate decision a conscious one. Really exercising the freedom of the will means choosing the character it will exemplify, and this can happen only when the will is fully engaged in choosing an object that is proper to its power, which is the object discovered in conversion, the excellence of God in Christ. The grace of conversion is the presence of this object in our tradition and revelation. Without this object, the soul is not able to choose the content that unifies the will and intellect, and so its inclinations remain alien to its own cognizance or willful control. This fragmentation is experienced as the being unto death without grace, the universal state of original sin.

The singular focus of the understanding and the will produce the inclinations into a denotable unity, the heart. But unity is not Edwards's privileged category. Instead of the unity of the heart completing his investigation, it becomes the ground for "evangelical humiliation" in sign VI. The character of the soul's inclination is displayed ultimately through resistance and opposition, a recapitulation of the testing Edwards describes at the beginning of the *Religious Affections* and which he repeats at every chance (311).

Evangelical humiliation is a sign of gracious affection because this exercise of the affection is possible only when the order of the soul, as an objective character, is found to be in disjunction with the divine will—not finally separated from God, but at odds in its root order. Cognitively understanding the bad ends of actions and owning the failure to pursue conventionally defined goods is what Edwards calls "legal humiliation." This is insufficient for evangelical humiliation because following out these errors cannot support a holistic judgment of the heart, and these relative differences do not reveal the holistic nature of the separation of the soul from God. Evangelical humiliation is indicative of divine influence because it is the discovery that the affective order of the will and intellect is hideous *as a whole,* which enables a person to "as it were, renounce himself, and annihilate himself" (315).

The discovery of this separation from God is a function of the understanding, since it results from a discerning judgment of the ultimate principle of our natural desires. The knowledge of the heart can be judged as incomplete and lacking in excellence only when compared to God's moral excellence. Judgment is necessary to concretize this lack in human consciousness, but this understanding does not produce a solution or give rest. Rather, this understanding shows the limit of the understanding to describe itself reflexively, since its ultimate principle does not exhibit the excellence to which it is drawn. This judgment also reveals the limit of a change of will without the discovery of divine excellence. Evangelical humiliation is the sign that the natural faculties fail to be the beauty the soul desires, but the absence of this beauty is a conclusion of the judgment, a fact made sensible by "the heart." The perception of this "other" beauty becomes the new object of the understanding; as Edwards summarizes, "Unless this [beauty] be understood, nothing is understood, that is worthy of the exercise of the noble faculty of understanding. This is the beauty of the Godhead, the divinity of Divinity . . . the Fountain of Good" (274), which becomes, "as it were, a new world of knowledge" (275).

Third Consideration: Signs VII, VIII, IX

The "new world of knowledge" is present but also absent in the experience of evangelical humiliation.[26] The felt absence of the sense of the heart, a perception of the "wickedness of sin," results from the sense of the heart seen in relation to God's excellence, although normal models of temporality cannot contain this kind of "resulting." The things of God are wonderfully beautiful, including the sense of the heart, but the understanding comprehends them only from afar, as one outside the gate. The third consideration answers this state of humiliation and fulfills the sense of the heart. Signs VII, VIII, and IX present the individual's conversion, "turning him from sin to God" (341), which is the central dialectic in Edwards's thinking. The immediate limits to this conversion are evangelical humiliation and a turning to "redemption by Jesus Christ, that is the grand subject of the Christian revelation" (346).

In the brief but poignant exposition of conversion in sign VII, Edwards expresses the gracious affection of the human spirit changed to reflect the person of Christ. Just as the centrality of Christ arises in the scripture as the fulfillment of revelation, so the same character arises as the fulfillment of the sense of the heart of the sinner. The Holy Spirit is "united to the faculties of the soul, to dwell there after the manner of a principle of nature, . . . an abiding thing" (342). Sign VIII explores the objective content of this change. Reflecting the passage central to Augustine's conversion Edwards says, "True Christians are, as it were, clothed with the meek, quiet, and loving temper of Christ; for as many as are in Christ, have put on Christ. And in this respect the church is clothed with the Sun, not only being clothed with his imputed righteousness, but also by being adorned with his graces (Rom. 13:14)" (347), which are "forgiveness, love, and mercy" (357). This focus on the objective content of Christ's character is of a piece with Edwards's earlier devotion to discovering the ways of God's working. He says, "We must learn the way of bringing men to rules, and not rules to men, and so strain and stretch the rules of God's Word, to take in ourselves, and some of our neighbors till we make them wholly of none effect" (357).

This alteration that produces the character of Christ as the principle of the heart is an opening into the new world of knowledge of a person's convictions of conscience, described in sign IX. Edwards: "This [conversion] don't tend to stupefy a man's conscience; but makes it more sensible, more easily and thoroughly discerning the sinfulness of that which is sinful" (364). The continuing conviction of sin is a sign that the principle of an individual has altered, even for the saint. Edwards makes a similar point in *Original Sin* when he declares that the Bible is a source of continuing conviction of sin for humanity, and this is a sign that it is a genuine revelation of the character of God—it will not let humanity rest comfortably in separation from its author.[27] The conviction of conscience presented in sign IX is the same principle for an individual. This private awareness of conviction is also the necessary ground for the fourth aspect of gracious affections, the moral life of the saint.

Fourth Consideration: Signs X, XI, XII

The fourth consideration concerns the soul's stretching out in public moral living. This part of Edwards's religious sensibility has been pronounced and, I fear, often disconnected from Edwards's integration of the spiritual sense, the understanding that is ordered by the gracious sense of the heart and the change of nature that produces a new spirit in the person. For Edwards, perfect obedience flows out of the transformed soul only as a reflection of its internal order. It cannot be produced by any natural work or desire. The first sign here, X, indicates "a beauty of symmetry and proportion in the affections" (365). This reference to beauty reflects back to sign I, the spiritual sense of divine harmony. The inclination and taste that reflects divine order likewise perceives the same symmetry in the soul. This self-reflexive awareness of divine order in the soul becomes the ground for genuine "affection" for other people. "The natural body which God hath made," Edwards says, "consists of many members; and all are in a beautiful proportion: so it is in the new man, consisting of various graces and affections" (365). Likewise, a saint's concern for other people is not narrowly spiritual, "[b]ut a true Christian love extends both to their souls and bodies [of others]. And herein is like the love and compassion of Jesus Christ" (369). Being inclined to this harmony involves spiritual as well as physical concern for others as the material in which the harmony of soul and body can be manifested.

Sign XI, "spiritual longing and appetite of soul," is the principal tension that expands the saint's desire for harmony internally in the affections and externally in the world. False affections rest satisfied in themselves but gracious affections do not. "The more he mourns for sin," Edwards says, "the more he longs to mourn: the more his heart is broke, the more he desires it should be broke: the more he thirsts and longs after God and holiness, the more he longs to long, and breathe out his very soul in longings after God" (377). The drive to extend the sense of the heart in practice for Edwards is not principally a duty but a positive response to the possibility of an expanding discovery of the spiritual harmony in all aspects of life. "Spiritual good is satisfying," Edwards says, "as there is enough in it, to satisfy the soul . . . there is room enough here for the soul to extend itself; here is an infinite ocean of it." The graciously affected soul is thirsting "until [it] comes to perfection" (379).

Gracious affections have their "exercise and fruit" in Christian practice according to sign XII, but this practice is ordered by the soul's desire for "perfection." The pursuit of perfection is the longing of the soul to abide in behavior universally conformed to "Christian rules" (383). For Edwards there is no other way spiritual order of the faculties can be fully manifested except by governing action and bringing all habits under the rule of order, to the end that the Christian community is itself one of the "things that are made," which reflects God's divine nature. This sign is also the ultimate test of the spiritual principle in a person and a community, since the spiritual nature of one's inclination is irresistibly manifest in practice. "This fruit of holy practice," Edwards says, "is what grace, every discovery, and every individual thing, which belongs to Christian experience, has a direct tendency to" (399).

Edwards calls sign XII the "chief" sign, and some commentators have taken this as a ground to claim that public moral action is the key to understanding the affections. But Edwards, in sign II, says that "the love of the excellency of [God's] nature is the foundation of all the affections which come afterward" (246), and that in sign III, the love of divine beauty is "the first beginning and spring of all holy affections" (253). And elsewhere Edwards uses the adjective "chief" to mean the temporally present manifestation of a deeper condition, as Saul's sparing of Amalek is the sparing of the "chief" of the Amalekites, a bodily representation of the opposition to God Saul was supposed to wipe out, and this shows Saul's "chief" sin (342). Sign XII is chief in this way. Only by considering practice *universally* is the reality of conversion apparent as the "chief" sign of a person. And this universality includes the complete actions of the individual and the complete actions of the community devoted to "holy practice."[28] The two ways this sign has been developed show the dangers of reading "chief" as equivalent to meaning the ultimate or most determinative sign. One development results in Samuel Hopkins's doctrine of moral perfectionism, the root of the New Divinity movement, and another development is the raising of practice to the ultimate category in personal identity, as in the thought of William James. Both of these approaches deemphasize some aspect of the conversion I have described here. Hopkins rejects the saint's certain knowledge of their condition of grace, which is precisely Edwards's ground for "true virtue," and William James rejects the reality of God's character and the conviction of his "holy" moral beauty as an essential element in discovering the self.

Let me step back a moment to the beginning reflection on the structure of the signs of gracious affection. I remarked that this structure shows up both as a wholeness of content by which Edwards intends to circumscribe religious experience and as a reflective wholeness. I hope the wholeness of the content of the signs is clearer, although I have presented little more than an outline here. The four considerations of "A Divine and Supernatural Light" as they are developed into the signs of gracious affection represent the access to Edwards's continuing reflective discovery of the freedom of the will, the doctrine of original sin, and the nature of true virtue, and its center in conversion. In this way, the signs of gracious affection represent individual self-discovery, but also serve as a platform from which Edwards's thought extends to all aspects of religion.

In this last section I want to offer a brief reflection on Edwards's experimental religion. Taking the *Religious Affections* apart, as I have done here, may present a disjointed image of Edwards's main point. But the text weaves these strands of discovery together in a seamless fabric of transcendent experience and God's excellence. Edwards accomplishes this integration of the four general heads of conversion as well as the twelve particular signs with his "experiential" or "experimental" religion.

EXPERIMENTAL RELIGION

Much of what Edwards found compelling about conversion challenged his religious tradition. His description of conversion directly opposes the Puritan "order of salvation" which is a theological formula adopted as a form for conversion testimonies used for entering church fellowship. Edwards was sensitive to a different structure that is not formulaic. Indeed, Edwards's notion of conversion demands immediate, personal, and "spiritual" experience. This requirement of experience rules out a religion that is merely intellectual, whether witnessed by moral practice or conventional assent. Only an experience that reveals the new supernatural sense of the heart is sufficient, and Edwards is concerned to point to the places in the lives of people where this discovery is evident. In this way Edwards emphasizes the interdependence of experimental religion and conversion. There are three main points to consider here: the form of practice most likely to result in conversion, the reflective opposition that is a necessary counterpart to realizing the spiritual sense, and the nature of discovery that attends experimental religion.

Edwards defines "experimental religion" as the religious practice of worship, prayer, and study of scripture that becomes the most instructive space for discovering the presence or absence of the new spiritual sense. He says,

> not only does the most important and distinguishing part of Christian experience lie in spiritual practice; but such is the nature of that sort of exercise of grace, wherein spiritual practice consists, that nothing is so properly called by the name experimental religion. For that experience which is in these exercises of grace, that are found, and prove effectual, at the very point of trial, or our lusts, are as has been shown already, the proper *experiment* of the truth and power of our godliness; wherein its victorious power and efficacy in producing its proper effects, and reaching its end, is found by experience. This is properly Christian experience, wherein the saints have opportunity to see, by actual *experience* and *trial,* whether they have a heart to do the will of God, and to forsake other things for Christ, or no. As that is called experimental philosophy, which brings opinions and notions to the test of fact; so is that called experimental religion, which brings religious affections and intentions to like test. (452)

Establishing the soul as a fact is Edwards's reflective goal, and the most efficient source of the experience necessary to give this stability to the soul is spiritual practice. Wider experience is certainly a source of spiritual discovery, but the content of religious practice is most significant because it brings the soul into direct contact with the most determinative object, the fact of Christ. Edwards says, "For 'tis only by the discovery of the beauty of the moral perfection of Christ, that the believer is let into the knowledge of the excellency of his person, so as to know anything more than the devils do: and 'tis only by the knowledge of the excellency of Christ's person, than any know his sufficiency as a mediator; for the latter depends upon and arises from the former" (273). Discovering the excellence of Christ's person is the experience that most clearly signifies the spiritual sense of the heart.

Recall the scriptural basis of the *Religious Affections* in I Peter 1:8, from which Edwards shows the necessity of trials for proving faith. He says, "True virtue never appears so lovely, as when it is most oppressed: and the divine excellency or real Christianity, is never exhibited with such advantage, as when under the greatest trials. . . . They tend to cause the amiableness of true religion to appear to the best advantage, . . . but not only so, but they tend to increase its beauty, by establishing and confirming it, and making it more lively and vigorous" (92–93). What kind of a test can bring the excellence of the soul to view? Only the test of conversion arises to this level of facing the objective character of the self and God. For Edwards conversion is the ultimate trial, where the change to the bottom of the heart comes clear and the character of the soul is continually confirmed. Edwards is not alone in searching for the kind of experience and opposition that will identify the character of a person or a community. Dewey locates this kind of identifying opposition in intelligent practice of the community, Royce finds it in loyalty to an ideal religion, James finds it in the will to believe. Edwards contains this opposition that unfolds in conversion within experimental religion.

The twelve signs of conversion in the *Religious Affections* contain a pattern of objective content and opposition central to religious experience. Indeed, the second of each trio of signs contains this objectivity and opposition most concretely. Sign II is the first objective ground of affections, Edwards says, the love of God which is *not* self-love; sign V, the conviction and judgment of the reality of divine things and what is *not* illuminated understanding; sign VIII, the manifest spirit of Christ in a person, which is *not* dissension; and sign XI, moral complacency which is *not* a spirit of discovery. The four movements of the structure of conversion each contain an oppositional and objective core, which directs the process of discovery from the first sign to the last.

Edwards does not attempt to describe this recurring opposition the-matically. I think he does not develop this account because bringing order out of various forms of opposition can be accomplished only in experience, not in any discursive description. Only experience can make the real argument here. Edwards knew that his writing and preaching could not be the instrument of salvation. Preaching is only one occasion among many in which reflective opposition may issue in the discovery of the condition of a soul and the reality of God. The lack of an explicit development of this account of reflective opposition may be Edwards's humble recognition of the genuine mystery of conversion which occurs only in this light; the Spirit blows where it wills and we cannot see from whence it comes, but we can see its effects, namely, that opposition becomes a part of a narrative of transformation and discovery.

It is hard to overstate the importance of discovery in Edwards's exper-imental religion. Time and again he focuses on the discontinuity between what the mind of natural man and supernatural man can per-ceive. But Edwards does not suggest that this discovery is anything else than a personal, revelatory experience over which clergy, parents, social position, or education has little control. Discovery itself is the separating experience as well as the *telos* of experimental religion. Edwards formu-lates it in two ways:

> And besides the things that have been already mentioned, there arises from this sense of spiritual beauty, a true experimental knowledge of religion; which is of itself, as it were a new world of knowledge. . . . And were it not for the very imperfect degree, in which this sense is commonly given at first, or the small degree of this glorious light that first dawns upon the soul; the change made by this spiritual opening of the eyes in conversion, would be much greater, and more remarkable, in every way, than if a man, who had been born blind, and with only the other four senses, should continue for so long a time, and then at once should have the sense of seeing imparted to him, in the midst of the clear light of the sun, discovering a world of visual objects. . . . Yet this spiritual sense is . . . infinitely more noble than that, or any other principle of discerning that a man naturally has, and the object of this sense infinitely greater and more important. (275)

> And besides all this, the truth of all those things, which the scripture says about experimental religion, is hereby known; for they are now experi-enced. And this convinces the soul that one who knew the heart of man, better than we know our own hearts, and perfectly knew the nature of virtue and holiness, was the author of the Scriptures. And the opening to

view, with such clearness, such a world of wonderful and glorious truth in the gospel, that before was unknown, being quite above the view of a natural eye, but now appearing so clear and bright, has a powerful and invincible influence on the soul to persuade of the divinity of the gospel. (303)

Religious experience for Edwards is the discovery of God's holiness that flowers out into an "infinite ocean," a "new world of knowledge," enough to satisfy the soul, that not only withstands scrutiny but that overcomes threats, bringing them to order by the same principle that enlivens the soul. Inquiry is not just a handmaid to theology but is itself the way we discover the reality of an opposing order in "the things that are made," an order that can be experienced and articulated so that it brings our reflective consciousness to stability. Participating in this discovery for Edwards cannot mean turning one's back on intellectual engagement or breaking with the Christian tradition. Rather it entails establishing the limits of self-understanding as it appears in the narrative and reflective accounts of our lives.

The systematic breadth of Edwards's experimental religion seems both attractive and oppressive. Edwards's Calvinism lost its appeal because of its determinism and rational coldness. But Edwards's holistic religious vision still attracts attention from theologians, philosophers, rhetoricians, and historians.

Edwards's fate in our interpretive hands reflects this conflict of desire. On one hand we demand an ideal, all-incorporating structure of experience, as evidenced by the continuing influence of idealism in American philosophy. John Dewey stands in Edwards's wake when he lowers the wall between sacred and secular values in order to fulfill our demands for a holistic account of experience, whether he acknowledges it as ideal or not. On the other hand, Edwards offends our desire for plurality and freedom because of his religious tradition and his absolutist philosophical mien. For Dewey and those naturalists in his line the religious and confessional character of Edwards's systematic breadth is oppressive and philosophically suspicious. Still, we hope for such a philosophy that can provide the reflective stability we need for our pursuit of meaning and community while being open enough to incorporate us all and all of us.

Despite the fact that Edwards never produced a systematic philosophy, there is an elusive wholeness to his thought, like the object that awakens the spiritual sense to the promise of a unity of the heart and the harmony of the soul. Edwards's systematic wholeness appears and vanishes, yet it remains a vague residue in our reading and in the cultural acceptation of his thought and character.

If there is an object that shows Edwards's reflective wholeness, it is his experimental religion based on the kind of conversion described in the *Religious Affections*. Conversion incorporates the aesthetic sense, the integrity of the understanding and the will, the truth of the scriptural witness, and public moral life. These themes taken together give us Edwards's most complete understanding of the whole person.[29] Edwards's conviction that conversion reflects "God's absolute sovereignty" raises the signs of affection as the paradigm of experimental religion. The reflective tension of conversion, articulated within the twelve signs, is arguably the tension "proper" to religion as its most revealing trial in showing the soul's reorientation. The authority of this tension grounds Edwards's hope:

> Whenever a person finds within him, an heart to treat God as God, at the time that he has the trial, and finds his disposition effectual in the experiment, that is the most proper, and most distinguishing experience. And to have at such a time that sense of divine things, that apprehension of the truth, importance and excellency of the things of religion, which then sways and prevails and governs his heart and hands; this is the most excellent spiritual light, and these are the most distinguishing discoveries. (451)

My purpose in this chapter has been to show the significance of the structure of conversion in Edwards's *Religious Affections*. My larger goal, however, has been to call attention to the centrality of conversion in Edwards's larger philosophical and theological enterprise. Edwards's reflective holism is significant for American philosophy and theology today because we are still working from an origin that is peculiarly American, peculiarly Christian, and peculiarly "experimental." The proof of this larger hypothesis of Edwards's significance for American thought requires a continuous reading of our tradition, and the structure of conversion will, I hope, give evidence of its usefulness by the results of further inquiries into Edwards and beyond.

NOTES

1. Jonathan Edwards, *Religious Affections: The Works of Jonathan Edwards,* vol. 2 (Yale University Press, 1959). Parenthetical notes refer to this volume.

2. Iain H. Murray, *Jonathan Edwards: A New Biography* (Banner of Truth Trust, 1987), 207.

3. Two examples are Robert Jensen's *America's Theologian: A Recommendation of Jonathan Edwards* (Oxford University Press, 1988) and Anri Morimoto's *Jonathan Edwards and the Catholic Vision of Salvation* (Pennsylvania State University Press, 1995). Jensen argues that Edwards avoids the traps of modernism in his theological development, and Morimoto argues for a strong connection between Edwards and Roman Catholic sotierology. These are only two examples but are representative of two significant orientations of Edwards scholarship.

4. Perry Miller, *Jonathan Edwards* (World Publishing, 1959).

5. Sang Hyun Lee, *The Philosophical Theology of Jonathan Edwards* (Princeton University Press, 1988).

6. John Smith, *Jonathan Edwards: Puritan, Preacher, Philosopher* (University of Notre Dame Press, 1992).

7. I Peter 1:6.

8. John Smith, in the introduction to the Yale edition of *Religious Affections*, comments only that the signs must not be a recapitulation of the Puritan order of salvation he was opposed to. But Smith does not consider the possibility that Edwards is proposing another structure, one quite different from the tradition. Claude Newlin, *Philosophy and Religion in Colonial America* (Philosophical Library, 1962), states that the first four signs summarize Puritan theology, but does not address the rest. Michael Raposa develops the relation of the twelfth sign to Peirce's pragmaticist position, but gives only a glancing description of the supporting edifice on which this sign is built. "Jonathan Edwards's Twelfth Sign," *International Philosophical Quarterly* 33, no. 2 (1993): 153–162.

9. *Collected Papers of C. S. Peirce* (Harvard University Press, 1934), 6:457: "If God Really be, and be benign, then, in view of the generally conceded truth of religion, were it but proved, would be a good outweighing all others, we should naturally expect that there would be some Argument for his Reality, that should be obvious to all minds, high and low alike."

10. Vincent Colapietro, *Peirce's Approach to the Self* (SUNY Press, 1989), 105. See also Roger A. Ward, "C. S. Peirce and Contemporary Theology: The Return to Conversion," *American Journal of Theology and Philosophy* 16, no. 2 (May 1995): 125–148.

11. See "A Neglected Argument for the Reality of God" and "The Law of Mind," two essays in which Peirce deals with teleological significance of human thought and habit change.

12. Subsequent American thinkers have also expressed a tendency to focus descriptions of value on analyses of change, a tendency I am willing to argue is more or less rooted in this theological conviction of Edwards. I include in this list Dewey, Peirce, Miller, Rorty, and West.

13. "A Divine and Supernatural Light," in *A Jonathan Edwards Reader* (Yale University Press, 1995), 111.

14. Ibid.

15. Ibid., 123–124.

16. Ibid., 106.

17. Charles Hodge uses Edwards against Edwards A. Park; for instance, in "The Theology of the intellect and that of the feelings, II," *Essays and Reviews* (Robert Carter and Brothers, 1857), 571 ff., Hodge states, "Our puritan fathers adhered to the doctrine of original sin as consisting in the imputation of Adam's sin, and in a hereditary depravity; and this continued to be the received doctrine of the churches of New England, until after the time of Edwards. He adopted the view of the Reformers on the subject of original sin and a depraved nature transmitted by descent. But after him this mode of stating the subject was gradually changed, until long since, the prevailing doctrine in New England has been that men are not guilty of Adam's sin, and that depravity is not of the substance of the soul, but is wholly voluntary and consists in a transgression of the law in such circumstances as constitute responsibility and desert of punishment" (575). And further, "We refer our readers to President Edwards's work on Original Sin, and request them to notice with what logical strictness he demonstrates that the denial of the sinfulness of human nature and the assertion of plenary power of men to obey the commands of God, subverts the whole plan of redemption" (593). It is clear that Hodge sees Edwards in fundamental agreement with his own orthodoxy.

18. Jonathan Edwards, "The Mind," *Scientific and Philosophical Writings: The Works of Jonathan Edwards* (Yale University Press, 1980), 6:332–394.

19. Edwards, "The Mind," 337.

20. Conrad Cherry, *The Theology of Jonathan Edwards* (Indiana University Press, 1966). Cherry's emphasis on the incitement to trust and humility from the "posture" of perceiving the excellence of God is certainly correct. What Cherry does not account for as well, though, is the structure of the understanding Edwards depends on to describe this incitement and transformation. 77ff.

21. *The Works of President Edwards* (S. Converse, 1829), 1:60.

22. Sang Hyun Lee, *Philosophical Theology,* 166. Lee's discussion of the ontological task of imagination in Edwards's thought does well to describe the disposition of the mind enabled to decipher the structure of reality. Where I find a lapse in Lee's argument, however, is the relation to objective content necessary for this work of the imagination. For Edwards the mind functions according to its nature only in relation to the objective content of revealed truth, and otherwise it is liable to deception.

23. Smith, *Jonathan Edwards,* 24. Smith discriminates Edwards's difference from Locke on the issue of an order in the mind that is embodied in habit, but is not necessarily "before" the mind "in order for the person to follow the habit." I associate this "order" with the "new simple idea" Edwards connects to "metaphysicians" in the first sign of gracious affections. Edwards enhances

Locke's description of the order of ideas with his claim that the internal structure of "simple ideas" is the ground of substance, or resistance, that makes relations and judgments possible. For Edwards, this becomes the ultimate ground of personal identity and his most marked rejection of Locke. See "The Mind," 386.

24. "The Mind," 386–387. Edwards comments that Locke's description of identity cannot explain the "train of ideas" that constitutes a "person" without the joys and sufferings that affect the tendency of mind. He follows this thought with an outline for a treatise on the mind where he intends to deal with "the influence of prejudice to cloud the mind." The power of prejudice in undermining the ability of understanding is the negative statement of the point made here, that all understanding is reflective of a tendency toward an object, and this object determines the character of the understanding.

25. Bishop Butler, *Analogy of Religion* (Harper and Brothers, 1889). The *Analogy* was first published in 1736. The moral sense Butler describes is one of "propensions, together with moral understanding, as well as including a practical sense of virtue . . . forming an inward constitution," 156.

26. Cherry, *Theology,* 78. Cherry notes the Augustinian and Calvinistic roots of the subsistence of the "old man and new man" together in one person. I am suggesting here that Edwards not only continues this tradition (see sign VII) but that he also incorporates this tension into the dialectic proper to the faculty of understanding.

27. *Original Sin: The Works of Jonathan Edwards* (Yale University Press, 1970), 3:313–314. "This grand distinction between the two Adams, and the other instances of opposition and difference, here insisted on [Rom. 5:12ff] as between the effects of sin and righteousness, the consequences of obedience and disobedience, of the offense and the free gift, judgment and grace, condemnation and justification, they all come to nothing; and this whole discourse of the Apostle's wherein he seems to labor much, as if it were to set forth some very grand and most important distinctions and oppositions in the state of things, as derived from the two great heads of mankind, proves nothing but a multitude of words without meaning, or rather a heap of inconsistencies."

28. But even this notion of "complete" is not without qualification. No sooner does Edwards articulate the "perfect universal obedience" of the saint then he introduces a codicil about the character, which bears failure in particulars but integrity in its wholeness, using King David and Saint Peter as the two prime examples (384).

29. Smith, *Jonathan Edwards,* 44. Smith notes the oddity that so basic a sign as conversion does not appear until the middle of Edwards's signs in the *Religious Affections.* This odd fact has propelled this study to discover the harmony of Edwards's signs.

2

Habit, Habit Change, and Conversion in C. S. Peirce

PLACING A THINKER like C. S. Peirce in context with Jonathan Edwards yields a striking result. Edwards is so closely identified with traditional Christianity that we cannot separate his thought from the community within which it took shape. Although there is no similar identification of Peirce with a community of religious practice, his philosophical researches are widely accepted as full of nutrition for religious speculation.[1] Peirce worked largely on his own. What is striking is the symmetry, maybe even the agreement, between Peirce and Edwards about the central problems of inquiry and the soul.[2]

Peirce is a transitional figure in the American tradition of reflection. Although no enemy of religion, he critiques metaphysically corrupt pietism and dry theological wrangling over the doctrine of predestination. His philosophical consciousness seems to appear out of thin air, marking a dramatic new movement in American thought.[3] His community became the philosophical community in America, and Peirce demonstrates an ability to draw on philosophical resources for answering his deepest questions. But focusing on this philosophical eruption may obscure the religious tenor of the questions that prompted his inquiry. We mistake Peirce, I think, if we fail to consider the impetus of his thought, and such a consideration will suggest that we reconnect Peirce and Edwards by virtue of what they can tell us about conversion.

I begin this chapter by evaluating several avenues of connecting Peirce's philosophical program and religious conversion. Next I turn to an exposition of Peirce's undestanding of habit and habit change. This position of an ultimate habit change incorporates the conclusions of three essays in an argument for a holistic orientation of the thinker fully engaged in self-controlled inquiry. These include the change represented by personality and a belief in a personal creator in "The Law of Mind," the argument for emulating *agapistic* inquiry in "Evolutionary Love," and the belief and logical testing of the reality of God in "A Neglected

Argument for the Reality of God." I conclude with a criticism of Peirce's habit change to a "super-order," as he describes it, and examine several ways to advance Peirce's approach to conversion.

PEIRCE AND CONVERSION

Because Peirce wants to know the fullest measure of reality by knowing the fullest measure of human belief and action possible in self-controlled change, I take up conversion as a theme in Peirce's pragmatism. Let me briefly outline some reasons why conversion appears attractive as a conceptual theme for understanding Peirce and some of the reasons it may appear not so helpful.

Connecting Peirce to conversion makes some sense simply based on the likeness of his thought to Edwards. Edwards and Peirce stand pretty evenly in terms of intellectual power, reinterpreting their traditions and producing epochal shifts in the thinking of their time. They also share a conviction that ultimately determining decisions and self-criticisms entail the integration of the head and heart, intellect and will, thought and faith. The similarity of their "heart" language is a strong linking clue. Edwards finds the affections of the heart connected to transcending the natural functioning of reason and the will. Peirce perceives reasons of the heart illuminating an opposition to self-critical reason. He says, "the heart is more than the head, and is in fact everything in our highest concerns" (CP 4:654)[4] so that the leadings of the heart are properly followed despite not having worked out conceptual problems. This is Peirce's ground for adopting habits based on vague leadings.[5] The opposition of head and heart does not cancel the need for reason so much as it kindles the spirit of fallibilism and humility for the inquirer. Leadings of the heart are significant in Peirce's search for conclusions about the meaning of the self, God, and the object of inquiry. Although trained as a scientist and concerned most immediately with issues of scientific inquiry and logic, Peirce excludes neither divinity nor grace from the realm of reality. He wants to know what is in a person that leads to the conclusion that divine life and grace are real possibilities. For if "God Really be, and be benign," he says in "A Neglected Argument for the Reality of God," "then, in view of the generally conceded truth that religion, were it but proved, would be a good outweighing all others, we should naturally expect that there would be some Argument for His Reality that should be obvious to all minds, high and low alike, that should earnestly strive to find the truth of the matter; and further, that this Argument should present its conclusion, not as a proposition of metaphysical theology, but in a form directly applicable to the conduct of life, and full of nutrition for man's highest growth"[6] (CP 6:457). What God means for human life must be articulated in terms of an inquiry that develops into a self-critical awareness of personality through of a self-conscious exercise of thought, the power of which becomes knowable in the self-controlled action of habit change.

The primary argument for conversion arises from the way Peirce's philosophy leads up to the expectation for an ultimate habit change. Several related lines of thought suggest such a habit change. One aspect of this thought is his suggestion about the integration of the personality in all its parts that is achieved only by perceiving the law of continuity that connects all mind. A second line is Peirce's argument for the evolution of the universe, which he calls *agapism*. This evolution entails a developmental teleology of the person's habits—a continuing character of growth. I think these lines of developmental teleology and the continuity of mind are brought to their final test in the discovery of the reality of God. The continuity between habits of thought and action ensure for Peirce that the object of inquiry is not just to know God as an intellectual exercise, but also to reflect God by participating in the ordering principle of reality. My claim that Peirce's thought leads to an image of conversion draws primarily on this argument for the connectivity between Peirce's conclusions about personality, evolutionary love, and God as components of an ultimate habit change. I think such a claim makes sense of many of Peirce's discussions concerning religion, like this one from an address in 1863:

> [B]efore a man can hear the voice of God or even comprehend an example of religion he must have a notion of what religion is, and that implies he must have had an inward revelation of religion. . . . After the inward revelation comes the objective revelation, and the latter must be the culmination of the former, for bearing as it must a higher message it must itself act suggestively so that its meaning may be perceived. This culminating point will be the phenomenon of perfection in such a form that man can see and know it; that is, it must be perfection in human form. The first condition, therefore, the enunciation of the predicate, was fulfilled at the birth of Christ. (CE 1:110)[7]

Peirce approaches an account of these "phenomena of perfection" in the logic of inquiry that leads not only to belief in God, but to the process of perfecting all one's habits and of the opinions of science through discovering the normative control implicit in thought and the conclusions of this evolving control.

A second reason that conversion coheres with Peirce's thought relates to several broad disjunctions he identifies. There are forms of orientation that represent a deep-seated error, such as greed, or the focus of practical minds and philosophical nominalism. These errors are destructive to the development of self-controlled inquiry. In order to succeed, self-understanding must identify and overcome these attitudes. He characterizes this opposition in the essay "Evolutionary Love":

> The Gospel of Christ says that progress comes from every individual merging his individuality in sympathy with his neighbors. On the other side, the conviction of the nineteenth century is that progress takes place by virtue of every individual's striving for himself with all his might and trampling his neighbor under foot whenever he gets a chance to do so. This may accurately be called the Gospel of Greed. (CP 6:294)

The disjunction between these two gospels represents an orientation in a person's habits that is proceeding toward the discovery of self-control and thought that is not. Avoiding the collapse of reason depends on following signs within thought that identify errors through self-criticism and moves beyond them. This ability to perceive the error of an orientation and adjust the direction of thought in response to it reflects the possibility of a conversion like change.

One last reason conversion is a useful suggestion for understanding Peirce is that it more clearly places his thought in relation to the tradition of productive religious inquiry. Peirce desires to serve the truth he discovers about the universe not for his own aims of success or notoriety, but because the discovery reflects a response to the character and movement of the universe toward deeper community with God. He is deeply connected to the ideals of his community and to demonstrating the ways these ideals translate into august practicality for the conduct of life, even if he often failed to conform his practice.[8] Peirce strives to enter "the process whereby man, with all his miserable littlenesses, becomes gradually more and more imbued with the Spirit of God, in which Nature and History are rife" (CP 5:339n) in order that he becomes a sign of the movement toward an "intimate union of humanity and Deity" (CE 1:110). There is no more apt term for this desired movement then conversion.

Conversion, of course, is not a term Peirce uses in relation to himself or his philosophy. There are several ways that conversion appears to work against Peirce's understanding of metaphysics and inquiry. First, Peirce would reject any notion of epiphenomal change by virtue of an act of will, a dramatic experience, or an "intuitive" revelation. None of these moments constitutes the ground for real change in a person; that is, they cannot be the ground for developing a habit of response. Instead, Peirce suggests that only changes productive of conceptual interpretation have any purchase on the self-control or self-consciousness mentioned earlier. I agree with Peirce in this criticism of conversion, as does Edwards, and attempt to incorporate this demand for an awareness of "general terms" into a more satisfying notion of conversion.

A second challenge is that conversion implies a focus on the will. Peirce was suspicious of the power of volition, as he makes clear in response to James's "Will to Believe," "which pushed this method to such extremes as must tend to give us pause. The doctrine appears to assume that the end of man is action" (CP 5:3). Rather, Peirce holds that we can respond only to what is experienced, and no act of willing can create experience or make a satisfying account of meaning. Another side of this claim is that we cannot fabricate doubt either, so that genuine inquiry cannot begin by virtue of an effort of an individual that is not in continuity either with the limits of inquiry, some phenomenal resistance, or the presence of a tradition. Kelly Parker quotes Peirce's dictum, "Let us not pretend to doubt in philosophy what we do not doubt in our hearts."[9] Again, I think these are valid and useful criticisms. I also think that this criticism places Peirce in clear agreement with Augustine's doctrine of conversion, at least in terms of the need for a resistant notion of God in a tradition and the inability of human will to generate the content necessary to effect a real transformation.

There are several ways that this proposal of conversion provides an advance on Peirce. These will be taken up more fully in the conclusion of this chapter, but let me point ahead just a bit. The primary advance conversion offers in examining Peirce's philosophy is gaining the sense of a holistic power of his system. This holism moves two ways, first as a challenge to claims that Peirce was fundamentally fragmented in his philosophical views of science and religion, as Thomas Goudge claims,[10] and second, it moves toward a criticism of that holism by raising the question whether or not his pragmatism is satisfactory as an argument for understanding an ultimate change of character for persons.

The second advance a consideration of conversion may enable regards focus on inquiry as the principal function of transformation. Can such a discovery be confined to inquiry? The most significant aspect of this question turns on whether Peirce's use of negation as the principal drive of inquiry allows for the image of freedom and creativity that he suggests is necessary for the fullest expression of human thought.

One last advance conversion may allow in relation to Peirce's thought is to more fully engage the connection of inquiry and tradition. While Peirce claims that the church is essential for the understanding of God emerging within the continuity of thought, it is not clear if the church can become anything other than a beginning or reminder of the divine, an *archai* but not a *telos* for action and transformation.

HABIT AND HABIT CHANGE

The opening into the criticism of beliefs, even the most incorporative belief, is habit. "The essence of belief is the establishment of a habit," Peirce says, and "the whole function of thought is to produce habits of action" (CP 5: 398, 400). Access into a critical understanding of inquiry is possible through an understanding of what constrains action and what makes changes in action necessary and possible. A habit is a law governing practice, but a law that can be altered. In this way, habits reflect the power of response through self-control and the discovery of an order both in experience and in habits. Habits are never final or unchangeable, but they are the only indication of the end at which action aims. Bringing the aims of the person to clearest expression entails the critical awareness of habits and the tendency to take habits.

Habits and habit change integrate Peirce's logical categories of First, Second, and Third. As a First, habits are perceived as a quality without determination. As a Second, habits are the resistant features in action; as he says, "each habit of an individual is a law; but these laws are modified so easily by the operation of self-control, that it is one of the most patent of facts that ideals and thought generally have a very great influence on human conduct" (CP 1:351). The tendency to take habits and to change them reflects the condition that a habit is a mediation between one thing and another. This is a habit as a Third (CP 6:32).

The integrative power of habits is manifest in the variety of phenomena Peirce associates with the concept of habit. Through habit feeling is bound into thinking, thought is bound into action, and unconditioned variety is bound into uniformity. Habit and habit change are equally inclusive of all levels of consciousness. The cosmic form of habit taking is expressed in Peirce's "Law of Mind." Communities take habits that bind the many into one (where the "one" is the unified purpose of inquiring after the final object). But the level of habit taking closest to the heart of Peirce's philosophy is that of the person. Like a train station, a person's habits integrate the lines of impression flowing into that consciousness, which then opens out into a multitude of reflections of that moment in action or would-be action. Unlike a train station, there are no finally fixed habits. To carry the metaphor forward we would need to have a dynamic station, one that is capable of moving and changing while still integrating the dynamic lines that meet and disperse there.

Establishing this modal point of habit integration as a character that can become a point of refinement of meaning and criticism brings us to Peirce's notion of habit change. For it is only the change of habits by some other aspect of habit life that makes it a suitable platform for critical inquiry. Peirce seeks a "final logical intepretant" of the effect possible through mental effort. He says,

> It can be proved that the only mental effect that can be so produced and that is not a sign but is of a general application is a habit-change; meaning by a habit-change a modification of a person's tendencies toward action, resulting from previous experiences or from previous exertions of his will or acts, or from a complexus of both kinds of cause. It excludes natural dispositions, as the term "habit" does, when it is accurately used. (CP 5:476)

Exceeding "natural dispositions" is important for Peirce, since what he is after can be discovered only if the fullest power of mental effect as a result of self-control is perceived. A tendency to take habits cannot be a response to any material condition, but can arise only from the consideration of other habits, and particularly, habits taken as signs of some other relation of meaning distinct from what may be present in the person. This desire for an ascending character of habit change is absolutely crucial for Peirce's entire conception of pragmaticism.

In order to focus our discussion on habits and habit changes that illuminate this character of ascendancy we will shortly consider Peirce's descriptions of habit change related to agapism. In order to show this difference, however, it is important to see how habit change works more generally.

HABIT CHANGE

Peirce outlines three possibilities for the instigation of habit change: a striking experience, muscular effort, and imagination. Experience may surprise us with an unexpected fact, like a stone in our shoe, but involuntary experience cannot be the origination of an entirely new habit. Experience can break up habits, but there is no extension of inquiry into "stone in my shoe" that leads beyond the immediate experience. Likewise, muscular effort may produce a habit of response, but "nothing like a concept can be acquired by muscular practice alone" (CP 5:479). Imagination is more vital to habit change. Faced with suggestive experience, and able to differentiate which possible actions are performable, the imagination "traces out alternate lines of conduct" (CP 5:481) that eventually develop into a habit of thinking and action. Fancied irritation yields real habits; "We imagine ourselves in various situations and animated by various motives; and we proceed to trace out alternate lines of conduct. . . . The logical interpretant must, therefore, be in a relatively future sense" (CP 5:481; CP 3:154–166). Peirce recounts a striking example of the effectiveness of imagination on habit formation. During supper one day, a woman spilled some burning liquid on her skirt. His brother Herbert, just a small boy at the time, quickly smothered the fire with a rug. Herbert's quick response astounded the entire family. They asked how he had thought so quickly what to do. He answered, "I had considered on a previous day what I would do in case such an accident should occur." Herbert's action was an example of an imaginary line of conduct giving general shape to future conduct (CP 5:390).

Imagination holds the key to forming new habits, but imagination operates only on the condition of suggestive experience. Herbert had apparently had occasion to imagine someone catching his or her clothes on fire. It might have been a newspaper story or a friend's imaginary tale that presented the occasion for his imagining his action in that situation. But once an experience initiates the active imagination, the limits of physical performance narrow the range of habits that appear possible in that imagination. Herbert's small size allowed him to imagine picking up a rug or a towel to smother a fire, but maybe not a large urn of water. Although neither experience nor muscular performance alone is sufficient for producing a habit change (repeatedly lifting the rug would never have prepared Herbert for his action), Peirce says both are nevertheless necessary elements in that change. What evolves out of such a change is itself another habit, a general concept of action or determination to act in certain ways should a certain situation arise. Pure action is not the interpretant of the concept, since it is not a general rule but only finite to the immediate conditions (CP 5:491).

Even with this open-ended picture of habits, it might appear that Peirce regards habit change as a quasi-mechanical process that does not rely exclusively on conscious control, a "habit of the nerves."[11] We might think habit change is a sophisticated future-oriented reflex to premeditate responses to expected stimuli as a result of experiences that crash into our consciousness. This is not the case. Peirce's notion of habit change is much more human and organic. It is human because deliberation is incorporated into the process of every habit change, which means that by considerations dependent only on the mind, habits are adopted or not. It is organic because the principle of continuing change is present in every habit. No habits are fully unconscious and are therefore always involved in the refinement of self-conscious awareness. The notion of this active determination of habit change is related to Peirce's claim that a habit is the essence of the logical interpretant of any concept.

Concepts that direct choices of behavior are themselves dynamic and resist determinate articulation, just like habits. If we were to rank the concepts that govern our actions at any moment of our lives, we would notice that the most pervasive concepts, the ones that affect the widest range of our behavior, are also provisional and subject to change. But these concepts are the foundation of deliberation about less general habits. These concepts provide concrete direction in the habit-change process via deliberation, but they are of a piece with the same process. The same is true in analyzing a habit's fit in the surroundings. The analysis is contained in the essence of what habits are. There is no external process responsible for taking and laying aside habits other than the tendency to take habits. Peirce calls this the "self-analyzing" of habits. "The deliberately formed, self-analyzing habit—self-analyzing because formed

by the aid of analysis of the exercises that nourished it—is the living definition, the veritable and final logical interpretant" (CP 5:491). Getting
to the "final logical interpretant" of the self, of himself, which appears to
be Peirce's distinct aim in the three essays mentioned earlier, would be
possible only through describing the ultimate beliefs that act as the principles of habit change. Describing the principle behind a person's habit
change, which can finally be seen as a sign of the principle of the universe, makes the person's action the final intepretant to the person's
future thought and to the thought of the community. Concretizing these
principles in a person's practice also becomes a sign of the meaning of
the universe as the logical interpretant of God, since the self is an aspect
of the development. Peirce's dynamic process of habit change removes
any chance of duplicity in self-definition, since the totality of a person's
habits, including the future potential to act in certain ways in particular
situations, completely defines the conceptual framework operating in
that person's thought. There are no other recesses in which a "self" can
hide. This dynamic process also eliminates a hidden God, or at least a
God who resists any logical interpretation. The church is essential or
"penessential" for this reason. A logical interpretant must be in the history of thought. Michael Raposa notes that "Peirce perceived in the
Christian faith the essential ingredients for the development of an ideal
community."[12] Peirce expresses his vision of the church this way in an
1893 essay published in *The Open Court:* "It is the idea of the whole
Church, welding all its members together in one organic, systemic perception of the Glory of the Highest—an idea having a growth from generation to generation and claiming supremacy in the determination of
all conduct, private and public" (CP 6:429).

From this view of habit change, the furthest limits of Peirce's philosophy are in view. The logical interpretant of the person, as a sign, implies
a habit change that is affected by thought working on itself, albeit in
accord with a "suggestive experience." We cannot manufacture a concept of God out of whole cloth, Peirce would say, since this would have
no continuity with any other practice. But neither can a miraculous
occurrence or a forced bending of knee generate a conception of God
that is the logical interpretant of the object God. God, in Peirce's system,
becomes the resistance to false ideas of ultimacy, and also the key to
describing the limits of suggestive experience. The signs we are able to
interpret into habits reveal the full character of our habit-taking tendency.

Making sure that the habits we form are valid, that they do have an object besides our hopeful thinking, is a worry that we will look at in the conclusion of this chapter. Maintaining this validity depends on the retention of the self as separated by negation from that which it is not, so that God will be a possible conclusion only if it is clear that the inquirer is in some real sense not-God. Peirce wants to be sure that any complete habit change, what I am denominating a conversion, is to the real thing and not some simulacra of Holiness.

ULTIMATE HABIT CHANGE AND THE NEGLECTED ARGUMENT FOR THE REALITY OF GOD

What is surprising to Peirceans and non-Peirceans alike in the Neglected Argument is that Peirce brings his thought to a conclusion around one belief, albeit hypothetically, in God. If this belief is that toward which all thought tends, as Peirce says, then this one habit of belief is a striking argument about the collective character of human thought and habit. The force of this generality is why Raposa says it "will prove to be important, in interpreting Peirce's Neglected Argument, to determine the precise role that instinctive beliefs or habits of thought play in that argument, their nature, source, and the extent to which they can be formulated as premises, if at all."[13] Raposa is certainly correct about the need for this precision concerning premises. But for a moment I want to turn this focus around and look backward through the Neglected Argument into the "Law of Mind" and "Evolutionary Love." The Neglected Argument sets the stages of inquiry, but the content on which this argument turns depends on these other arguments. How this collection of arguments arrives at an ultimate conception of a single habit change is a further question, since no intuitive grasp of God is implied. It is important to keep instinctive ideas from welling up into intuitive ones. Peirce's fundamental claim is that the content necessary for the conclusion of God's reality in "a form directly applicable to the conduct of life, and full of nutrition for man's highest growth" (CP 6:457) is available to the inquirer. But without relying on a doctrine of revelation, where does that content come from? Only from inquiry itself becoming substantial as the content for further inquiry. This is why this argument is "odd" in Peirce's own opinion, and why it is significant for an understanding of conversion and what makes such a change possible. Clearly, the God hypothesis attains the place of ultimacy in Peirce's thought or nothing else will.

Peirce conducts a brief rehearsal of the Neglected Argument before he introduces the examination of its "logicality." The logicality of the argument turns on three stages of inquiry that relate to the one conclusion of the reality of God, and these stages are in fact elements of habit change that construct the final logical interpretant of the God hypothesis. So the stages are no preambles to the conclusion that results in an ultimate change; the stages are themselves the fiber of that change being concretized in thought and action. To use a biblical phrase, the stages of inquiry are the temporal structure for "working out" one's conversion.

First Stage of Inquiry: The Hypothesis of God's Reality

> "Enter your skiff of Musement, push off into the lake of thought, and leave the breathe of heaven to swell your sail" . . . From speculations on the homogeneities of each Universe, the Muser will naturally pass to the consideration of homogeneities and connections between two different Universes, or all three. Especially in them all we find one type of occurrence, that of growth, itself consisting in the homogeneities of small parts. This is evident in the growth of motion into displacement, and the growth of force into motion. In growth, too, we find that the three Universes conspire; and a universal feature of it is provision for later stages in earlier ones. This is a specimen of certain lines of reflection which will inevitably suggest the hypothesis of God's Reality. (CP 6: 461, 465)

Musement is Peirce's term for finding an agreeable occupation of the mind that is unproductive in terms of other impulses or practical cares. From undirected observation and its associated experience, the attractiveness of the idea of God abductively emerges in thought as an explanatory hypothesis. This idea of God—not yet a conjecture but a phenomena of some observation from one of the three universes of experience—has an originality in comparison with the other habits of the person. "But a portion of mind almost isolated, a spiritual peninsula, or cul-de-sac, is like a railway terminus. Now mental commissures are habits. Where they abound, originality is not needed and is not found; but where they are in defect spontaneity is set free" (CP 6:301). Peirce seems to suggest that this space of play is available to all inquirers, whether they are willing to let go of other overarching concepts or not.

Whether such freedom is universally available forms into one of the more compelling challenges of Peirce's argument that we will take up later. But at this stage it is clear that the play Peirce is aware of evinces an orientation for an ascending awareness of an ordered character to thought and experience.

Despite the emphasis on play and aesthetic attraction, Peirce uses the term *God* in all its abruptness. Anderson and others associate this use with both the classical arguments for the existence of God and Peirce's scholastic tendencies. Peirce takes care, however, to maintain a critical distance from these arguments by paying strict attention to the emergence of this idea in experience.[14] Peirce is also careful to avoid the case that this argument is theologically driven by emphasizing its dependence on a "vital spark of inspiration" (CP 6:438). What is at stake here is the continuity between thought in its most natural (or unaffected state) and the reality of God. This continuity does not mean that thought produces this idea. Thought is not that reality, and this means at some point the realization of the distinction between the two must emerge clearly. Peirce's connection with the Scholastics and his critical difference turns on this point of establishing a continuity of thought that does not usurp the reality of what it discovers. This is the reason Peirce avoids the language of existence, which he takes as referring to a reaction among like things. Since there is no like to God, there is no ground for existence, but there is for reality: "I define the real as that which holds its characters on such a tenure that it makes not the slightest difference what any man or men may have thought them to be, or ever will have thought them to be, here using thought to include, imagining, opining, and willing (as long as forcible means are not used); but the real thing's characters will remain absolutely untouched" (CP 6:495).

The emphasis in this first stage of inquiry on experience and play excludes the role of the will in developing a content like the hypothesis of the reality of God. In a review of Josiah Royce's *The Religious Aspect of Philosophy*, Peirce comments on Royce's suggestion that the Will can direct its acts to the attainment of universal harmony: "It is absurd to speak of choosing an original and ultimate aim. That is something which, if you haven't it, you have nothing to do but wait till the grace of God confers it on you" (CP 8:52). This act of having an ultimate aim "conferred" implies a dual condition for Peirce, which is completely at odds with what we ordinarily call direct intuitive revelation. In the first place, habits are possible only from a position of need highlighted by a "suggestive experience." Peirce illustrates this point:

> If walking in a garden on a dark night, you were suddenly to hear the voice of your sister crying to you to rescue her from a villain, would you stop to reason out the metaphysical question of whether it is possible for one mind to cause material waves of sound and for another mind to perceive them? If you did, the problem might occupy the remainder of your days. In the same way, if a man undergoes any religious experience and hears the call of his Savior, for him to halt till he has adjusted a philosophical difficulty would seem an analogous sort of thing, whether you call it stupid or whether you call it disgusting. If on the other hand, a man has had no religious experience, then any religion not an affectation is as yet impossible for him; and the only worthy course is to wait quietly until such experience comes. No amount of speculation can take the place of experience. (CP 1:655)

We have already seen the element of experience in Peirce's general account of habit change and his insistence that it alone is not sufficient to attain a concept. Somehow the experience Peirce has in view here comes with some other kind of generality that makes it a suitable ground for an explanatory hypothesis on the scale of the reality of God.

I think this force of experience and generality in the abductive emergence of the idea of God is clearest in Peirce's writings in relation to the Christian church. Although I do not think his argument is anything like a Christian apologetic, I do think that the observations on which Peirce often muses are the instinctive character apparent in religious activity and organization. For instance, Peirce remarks about a meeting in New York,

> When the thirty thousand young people of the society for Christian Endeavor were in New York, there seemed to me to be some mysterious diffusion of sweetness and light. If such a fact is capable of being made out anywhere, it should be in the church. The Christians have always been ready to risk their lives for the sake of having prayers in common, of getting together and praying simultaneously with great energy, and especially for their common body, for "the whole state of Christ's church militant here in earth," as one of the missals has it. This practice they have been keeping up everywhere, weekly, for many centuries. Surely, a personality ought to have developed in that church, in that "bride of Christ," as they call it, or else there is a strange break in the action of mind, and I shall have to acknowledge my views are much mistaken. Would not the societies for

psychical research be more likely to break through the clouds, in seeking evidences of such corporate personality, than in seeking evidences of telepathy, which, upon the same theory, should be a far weaker phenomenon? (CP 6:271)

The phenomena he observes as the "evidence of corporate personality" and the influence of "greater persons" are the kind of connection between universes of thought that would suggest a hypothesis on the order of God.[15] Too much focus on the logical character of abduction as a strictly categorial reality may lead us to exclude observations like this one, but Peirce often refers to the church as a sign of a character within human thought that challenges other explanations. Sympathy with other minds is obviously one of the curious phenomena in the universes of experience on which Peirce muses.

The depth of this musement on the suggestive character of mental sympathy is clear in "The Law of Mind," where Peirce conjectures about three ways this attraction can function. It can affect an entire community, so that anyone in "sympathetic connection" with that community will appreciate the attractiveness of the idea. It can "affect a private person directly, yet so that he is only enabled to apprehend the idea, or to appreciate its attractiveness, by virtue of his sympathy with his neighbors, under the influence of a striking experience or development of thought. The conversion of St. Paul may be taken as an example of what is meant." In other words, sometimes a person has to have a cold slap in the face in order to be abductively awakened to the attractiveness of an idea. Third, and apparently more rare, is the "divination of genius" in which an individual, isolated of other human influences, is struck by the attraction of an idea "before he has comprehended it" simply due to the continuity between his mind and "that of the Most High" (CP 6:307). An example here may be a musical genius, like Mozart, or a religious figure like Abraham who was called out of Haran by Yahweh. Abraham's novel belief in the promised land occurred, according to Genesis 12, even though there was no community present that associated its existence and hope with Yahweh like he did. Abraham was able to hear Yahweh's call, abductively forming the uncomprehended hope of a promised land. The "call" of God is the expression of the obvious continuity of Abraham's mind with God's.

I return to the first two cases. Peirce describes that result in finding an idea attractive, since the third is bound to be obscure since it relies on genius. In these examples, the community is able to manifest the attractive idea without the comprehension of that idea. This precognitive condition, where the possibility is present by virtue of the collection of like minds, is handled here as a striking experience that Peirce attempts to understand with his doctrine of synechism—not the other way around. Peirce describes this same phenomenon working in the context of moral alternatives: "Now, it is not necessary for logicality that a man should himself be capable of the heroism of self-sacrifice. It is sufficient that he should recognize the possibility of it, . . . [b]ut all this requires a conceived identification of one's interests with those of an unlimited community" (CP 2:654). The community spirit, the identification of one's interests with those of the community, invokes the continuity of mind in a way adequate for transmitting the ideas that support agapistic evolution without the cognitive act of some one mind comprehending those ideas. My point here is that the abduction to the idea of God may have much more stable ground in the observation related to communities than on instinct considered as a tendency of an individual's thought in isolation from the community.

As an aside, I wonder where Peirce would place himself in this trifold delineation. I think he would eschew the first, simply by virtue of the fact that he did not feel party spirit. The second, St. Paul's example, may be closer, except that Peirce overlooks the persecution that precedes the striking experience and conversion. I think Peirce is right that even in this persecution Paul had drawn near in something like sympathy with the desire for a revealed Messiah, but the dependence on brute experience to reveal this sympathy does not seem like a way Peirce would identify himself. It is most likely that Peirce would claim the third position of a lonely genius as most indicative of his own experience and most explanatory of the origin of his ideas. What this means for Peirce's larger argument concerning the naturalness of this discovery of God's reality will come more to the fore in the conclusion.

Second Stage: Deductive Explication of the Hypothesis

> The hypothesis of God is a peculiar one, in that it supposes an infinitely incomprehensible object, although every hypothesis, as such, supposes its object to be truly conceived in the hypothesis. This leaves the hypothesis but one way of understanding itself; namely, as vague yet as true so far as it is definite, and as continually tending to define itself more and more,

and without limit. The hypothesis, being thus itself inevitably subject to the law of growth, appears in its vagueness to represent God as so, albeit this is directly contradicted in the hypothesis from its very first phase. But this apparent attribution of growth to God, since it is ineradicable from the hypothesis, cannot, according to the hypothesis, be flatly false. Its implications concerning the Universes will be maintained in the hypothesis, while its implications concerning God will be partly disavowed, and yet held to be less false than their denial would be. Thus the hypothesis will lead to our thinking of features of each Universe as purposed; and this will stand or fall with the hypothesis. (CP 6:466)

The second stage of inquiry is deduction. Inquiry in this stage collects, apart from experience, consequences of the hypothesis. Scientific theism becomes exercised as an edge tool, since there is no dwelling place for habits here, only the anticipation of critical advances by explicating possibilities. The hypothesis of God puts logic to the ultimate test because it is very hard to say what deductively follows from God. "The hypothesis can only be apprehended so very obscurely that in exceptional cases alone can any definite and direct deduction from its ordinary abstract interpretation be made. How, for example, can we ever expect to be able to predict what that behavior would be?" (CP 6:489). Not only is there an incomprehensible object to deal with, there is also the problem of conjoining the consequences of a growing conception of reality with God, since God is thought to already include all in its reality. Despite these problems of drawing deductive consequences, the inquiry moves into this stage with full speed. The most significant logical worry is that deduction is accomplished apart from experience, and so it is liable to become disconnected with the living and breathing power of its object. This is a risk that Peirce argues can be handled only by drawing the prior stage and the following stage, inductive probation, closely around it.

The expansion possible from this second stage of inquiry, then, is most dependent on concepts that are directly connected to the first and third stages. This is where Peirce's argument seeks a content that can become a "platform" for inquiry. The lion's share of the emphasis on Peirce's Neglected Argument focuses on the retroduction of the first stage of this argument, since if a conception of God makes it to the point of inquiry independent of experience it is clear that the argument takes on a much different character. Successfully challenging Peirce's argument for the

God hypothesis depends on draining the first stage of its power, and Peirce is confident that this is not a logical possibility.[16]

Peirce's confidence in the Neglected Argument grows dramatically at the second stage of inquiry, since to doubt it now would involve the critic in a challenge of several arguments that are held together in this one hypothesis. Of course, this also means that if the argument for the reality of God proceeds to the second stage on questionable premises, then the likelihood of error and invalidity multiplies. For this reason, Peirce trains his thought on critical common-sensism in order to either dispel this erroneous conclusion or bolster it with sufficient arguments to silence critics.

With respect to the difficulty of drawing deductive consequences from the God hypothesis, Peirce answers with two characteristics of inquiry. First is the upshot from "The Law of Mind." "[T]o say that mental phenomena are governed by a law does not mean merely that they are describable by a general formula; but that there is a living idea, a conscious continuum of feeling, which pervades them, and to which they are docile" (CP 6:152). Any deductive consequence of the God hypothesis would at least have this character of a living idea that provides for continuity of thought. A second character already mentioned is the character of evolution by creative love. "The philosophy we draw from John's gospel is that this is the way mind develops; and as for the cosmos, only so far as it yet is mind, and has life, is it capable of further evolution. Love, recognizing germs of loveliness in the hateful, gradually warms it to life, and makes it lovely. That is the sort of evolution which every careful student of my essay 'The Law of Mind' must see *synechism* calls for" (CP 6:289). These two principles are symmetrical, in a sense. The presence of a law in mind entails that there is a character that makes such a coordinating law possible. And a coordinating evolutionary process, especially one characterized by love, would require that the increase of love between members would be holistically powerful, reaching to all elements of mind. Continuity is a necessary condition for evolution. These two principles together, then, construct a form of consequence to which the God hypothesis would refer. An early indication of Peirce's attraction to the ideas of growth and continuity taken in relation to God appears in an address from 1863 titled "The Place of Our Age in History."

> If therefore we are Christians it seems we must believe that Christ is now directing the course of history and presiding over the destinies of kings,

and that there is no branch of the public weal which does not come within the bounds of his realm. And civilization is nothing but Christianity on the grand scale. . . . True religion, [this age] will think, consists in more than a mere dogma, in visiting the fatherless and widows and in keeping ourselves unspotted from the world. It will say that Christianity reaches beyond even that, reaches beyond the good conscience, beyond the individual life; must transfuse itself through all human law—through the social organization, the nation, the relationships of the peoples and the races. It will demand that not only where man's determinate action goes on, but even where he is the mere tool of providence and in the realm of inanimate nature Christ's kingdom shall be seen. (CE 1: 108–109, 113)

In this statement, Peirce brings out two themes; that there is a connective law pervading all determinate human action, the basis for his later development of a more explicit continuity in mind; and that there is an irrepressible force of realization in consciously and unconsciously directed action. Taking this early locution as a beginning of Peirce's understanding of God's reality, however, clearly has import for understanding much of his later philosophical work as an effort to bring such a conception to a deductive explication so that it can become an object of inquiry.

The principle of growth Peirce refers to here as "the kingdom of Christ" does not seem to admit of partial acceptance, but rather carries the weight of a universal and universally affective idea. I think Peirce means that any personal relation to God is grounded on the evolutionary universe since the possibility that God can exhibit something like a personality depends on the same evolutionary development. And in just the same way that the whole of the universe is imbued with the motion of agapistic evolution, it only makes sense that a person's whole rank of habits would similarly become imbued with the evolutionary spirit once the association has been broached.

One critical aspect of the "conversion" to the hypothesis of God is worth restating before we draw some further implications of this change in terms of personality. The logical interpretant of any concept is not energetic action, but the habit or general rule that determines how a person will behave in certain situations. So, for instance, the degree to which a person self-critically adopts the teleological harmony of the law of mind (by virtue of adopting the God hypothesis), that person's conduct will replicate that principle in the continuous action of life. Therefore, the openness and association present in the law of mind, that "celestial and living harmony," will be manifest in the person's conduct.

The principle that makes this living harmony so powerful is the unifying nature of this principle. Like the God hypothesis, the law of mind is that most general of principles that incorporates all aspects of experience into a unified whole while maintaining an open-ended view toward future experience. "A general idea, living and conscious now, it is already determinative of acts in the future to an extent to which it is not now conscious" (CP 6:156).

Developmental teleology is Peirce's *sine qua non* of personality, as Colapietro remarks "during any moment of its life, the self is first and foremost a process in which some species of meaning is evolving."[17] It marks the ability to initiate self-control and self-analysis in respect to conduct which is especially significant in choosing an ultimate principle that governs the formation of all other habits. The ability to criticize one's own habits is an imitation, in the good sense of that word, of the law of mind. The individual's representation of the action of the law of mind indicates (and is constitutive of) the presence of developmental teleology. Directly following from the developmental nature of personality is Peirce's claim that personality is an idea that, like all ideas, resists final definition. In concrete terms, the idea of the personality is cashed out in the person's habit, that is, in the general rule of the tendency to take habits that lead to particular actions in certain situations. A notion of personality must affirm the developmental growth of an individual's telos in order to account sufficiently for our experience of the phenomenon of continued growth that persists in personality.

The representation of the law of mind is not only present in the coordination of ideas that constitutes the personality, but it also initiates that coordination as the attractive precognitive idea that draws the mind into the process. Besides meaning that the personality is only completely apprehended when considered in its totality, which includes the entire range of possible actions in all possible situations (CP 6:158), this notion also means that the personality is fundamentally dependent on an initiating moment of precognitive communication. Peirce does not use the term *grace* philosophically, but it would seem appropriate to use it in relation to this precognitive condition of the law of mind that is a kind of origin that makes the development of personality possible. Also, given that the fullest realization of personality depends on a self-controlled habit change of the most general principles governing the soul consistent with the agapistic character of the universe, the elements that Peirce combines in describing the personality seem to draw up to something very much like a conversion of the person.

Peirce says that a difficulty confronts the synechistic philosopher: "In considering personality, that philosophy is forced to accept the doctrine of a personal God; but in considering communication, it cannot but be admit that if there is a personal God, we must have a direct perception of that person and indeed be in personal communication with him. Now if that be the case, the question arises how it is possible that the existence of this being should ever have been doubted by anybody" (CP 6:162). God, then, if our description of developmental teleology has been sufficiently universal, must resemble a person, and so be a "personal God" or "personal creator" as Peirce says. Although our language has been somewhat abstract in the discussion of the law of mind and evolutionary teleology, Peirce's comment here may enable a reconstruction of this account using the metaphor of personal relationship in a way that reflects Martin Buber's language of "I and Thou." The heart of Buber's work, and Peirce's, describes a place of communication between persons that resists objectification on either hand. The activity of communication implies continuity between individuals for the communicative act to obtain, but all communication must reflect an orientation toward semiotic expansion in order for it to cohere into a developing ideal. Developmental teleology, which links God and the human person in this ideal sense for Peirce, is present in its most ideal form in the community. From a practical standpoint, Peirce's argument from personality rests on the presence of a community that expresses developmental teleology.[18] An expectation of this developmental force in a community is, therefore, an aspect of Peirce's argument for the reality of God.

Let me draw out one or two more possible deductive consequences of the hypothesis of the reality of God. From this discussion of the development of the personality, the consequence may be derived that Peirce would expect a conformity of all practice, all of a person's practice and all of a community's practice, with a normative ideal. Such conformity would follow by virtue of Peirce's articulation of growth and continuity. Practice, if growing in connection, would necessarily move into conformity with other practices—be they personal practices or communal practices. And since no part of the mind is discontinuous from the rest, no habit will ever be independent, that is, have a different developmental orientation from any other habit. This evolutionary growth in conformity of action is the only sufficient sign that habits are in fact connected in a law-like way one to another. So, conformity of practice is a deductive consequence of the meaning God.

A third deductive consequence of the reality of God would be to follow out Peirce's confession that this reality claims a passionate "judgment of the Sensible Heart" (CP 6:295). Such a sensible heart would appear, much like Edwards argues, as a sign of the influence of this reality in its affective power. The conclusions concerning the agapistic character of the universe would not be a matter of calculation or indifference. Hence Peirce, like Edwards, expects that if God is real and really benign, passionate sensible hearts would give confessional evidence of this.

The question of the heart, for Peirce, is not a factor that limits the appeal of the reality of God, but is rather an indication of its catholic nature:

> The esthetic ideal, which we *all* love and adore, the altogether admirable, has, as ideal, necessarily a mode of being to be called living. Because our ideas of the infinite are necessarily extremely vague and become contradictory the moment we attempt to make them precise. But still they are not utterly unmeaning, though they can only be interpreted in our religious adoration and the consequent effects upon conduct. This I think is good sound solid strong pragmatism. Now the Ideal is not a finite existent. Moreover, the human mind and the human heart have a filiation to God. That to me is the most comfortable doctrine. (CP 8:262)

The living mode of being is the most complete explication of the God hypothesis, and it follows now to ask what evidences may be possible to suggest that this living obtains for the inquirer. For only this living would constitute the proof of the hypothesis.

Stage Three: Probation of the Hypothesis of God

> I will only add that the third man, considering the complex process of self-control, will see that the hypothesis, irresistible though it be to first intention, yet needs Probation; and that though an infinite being is not tied down to any consistency, yet man, like any other animal, is gifted with power of understanding sufficient for the conduct of life. This brings him, for testing the hypothesis, to taking his stand upon Pragmaticism, which implies faith in common sense and in instinct, though only as they issue from the cupel-furnace of measured criticism. In short, he will say that the N.A. is the First Stage of a scientific inquiry, resulting in a hypothesis of the very highest Plausibility, whose ultimate test must lie in its value in the self-controlled growth of man's conduct of life. (CP 6:480)

The last stage of inquiry brings Peirce's argument for God directly to issue in the conduct of life. Relating Peirce's notion of habit change in light of the God hypothesis makes the most intuitive sense of conversion in this stage. What proves or disproves the God hypothesis is the "commanding influence over the whole conduct of life of its believers" (CP 6:490). Peirce takes this risky position in relation to three types of "men." First is the person who is persuaded by the humble argument for the reality of God and finds an acceptable place in the cosmos in light of this persuasion. The test Peirce proposes is a confirmation of that life, even though that person may not seek it. Second is the "man" who neglects the humble argument for logical reasons. Persuading this person (taking special aim at theologians) seems to be Peirce's focus in presenting the Neglected Argument with its logical back up. The final "man" is most like Peirce himself, skilled in observation and logic—and yet this type also needs the testing or probation of the God hypothesis. This may be Peirce's *apologia pro vita sua* in a logical key. For all these purposes, however, bringing the hypothesis to a test requires transforming an infinite object into finite observations, or finite observations into an infinite character. The issues here are what the conduct of life is that demonstrates this finite-infinite transformation and what kind of inquiry avails here to make this transformation evident. Anderson summarizes this aspect of inquiry in terms of Peirce's pragmaticism. "If one is to test the hypothesis, then, one must move to pragmaticism and the third grade of clearness. That is, one must turn to discovering "just what general habits of conduct a belief in the truth of the concept . . . would develop: that is to say, what habits would ultimately result from a sufficient consideration of such truth."[19] I think Peirce's focus may be more idiosyncratic than persuasive at this stage of his argument. That is, I think he realizes that his discovery of the meaning of himself and his place in the cosmos needs confirmation like the first "man." He has at least articulated the ground he needs confirmed—his logic—so that he is clear about the upshot of this enterprise. If his logic does not issue in the self-controlled development of the conduct of life, if it fails to attain the very generality his realism is based upon, he will collapse into the second "man" he is trying to persuade.

What Peirce means to describe is the living probation of this hypothesis such that the conduct of life is sign of a change in light of the deductive consequences mentioned earlier. These are a complete critical

understanding of habits and habit change and the character of evolutionary love as the principle of that habit change. Every habit must be coordinated with this principle, only now this coordination is the focus of
inductive inquiry. The conduct of life is not limited to normative ethical
practice since there are qualitative as well as quantitative aspects to this
conduct. In response to Royce, Peirce says, "To me, it plainly appears that
such a person, if he have a clear head, will at once reply, right and wrong
are nothing to me except so far as they are connected with certain rules
of living by which I am enabled to satisfy a real impulse which works in
my heart; and this impulse is the love for my neighbor elevated into a
love of an ideal and divine humanity which I identify with the providence that governs the world" (CP 8:47). Ethics is an aspect of this probation only to the extent that it yields this generality of habit
coordinated with God's providence.

What is most clear from the brief description of the probation in the
Neglected Argument is that the results of this change would be the
instantiation of a kind of inquiry, and that this inquiry would have its
ultimate consideration in the God hypothesis. First, this hypothesis
bespeaks a power of generality that comes in the form of "very highest
Plausibility" that reaches an unparalleled height among deliberately
formed hypotheses. This plausibility is a limit of sorts for Peirce's pragmaticism, since the "would be" character of the habits that follow from
this hypothesis would have strength to resist all but the strongest doubts.
Second, the instinct that grounds this hypothesis makes critical evaluation of that belief all the harder since it appears to have its origin not in
any action but only the continuity between his mind and "that of the
Most High." Third, the hypothesis of God is extremely hard to doubt
after it is acquired because it anticipates an order to thought and nature
that stand as limits to the conception of the generality of terms. It is not
clear how such generality or order can ever become an instantiated
doubt that is not "paper doubt." The definition of God as Ens nessescar-
ium entails a "character that is a generalization of order, and that, in the
lack of any word for it, we may call for the nonce, 'Super-order.' Pure
mind must appear as having a character related to the habit-taking
capacity, just as super-order is related to uniformity" (CP 6:490). Pure
mind just is this ordering; hence, habit change, in all its forms, is an
expression of this order that is "sufficient for the conduct of life." This
demand for sufficiency in conduct focuses the claim for authority by

concretizing the order of mind without reducing it to the level of positive verificationism, while at the same time maintaining the ideal nature of the character appearing in conduct. The question of character as a superorder raises a fundamental question about habit change that Peirce is unclear about. What is the origin of the authority evident in habit change? Examining this authority discriminates critical common-sensism from its older form.

> These considerations lead me, quite naturally, to mention another mark of the Critical Common-sensist that separates him from the old school. Namely, he opines that the indubitable beliefs refer to a somewhat primitive mode of life, and that, while they never become dubitable in so far as our mode of life remains that of somewhat primitive man, yet as we develop degrees of self-control unknown to that man, occasions of action arise in relation to which the original beliefs, if stretched to cover them, have no sufficient authority. In other words, we outgrow the applicability of instinct—not altogether, by any manner of means, but in our highest activities. The famous Scotch philosophers lived and died out before this could be duly appreciated. (CP 5:511)

Complete control of the conduct of life entails striking on the authority for change that is absent in terms of instinct. To be bound by instinct would amount to the nominalism that eliminates the possibility of genuine self-control. Peirce leans his logic and metaphysics toward an authority that appears only as a provisional origin of the ordering that yields character. Peirce is correct that it is hard to disprove this origin, and yet its absence does not make sense of the positive individuation that appears in the first "man" who seeks neither confirmation nor provisional ground. What is reserved for Peirce and the third "man" is the realization of the permanent incompleteness of character conjoined with the demand for a proof of the compete control of habits by virtue of a critical apprehension of the authority necessary for self-controlled change. Personality is tested not by its immediate products but by the assurance that its character would, in the long run, come clear as an expression of complete self-control. But there can never be sufficient grounds to make the final determination of the person's character. Conversion, in this way, appears as the ultimate challenge for Peirce's notion of personality.

The dynamic of this provisional but unsatisfactory inductive test of conduct shows up in a comment earlier in the Neglected Argument.

Peirce says, "It is that course of meditation upon the three Universes which gives birth to the hypothesis and ultimately to the belief that they, or at any rate two of the three, have a Creator independent of them" (CP 6:483).

The question is, what "universe" does he mean that does not have a Creator independent of it? Anderson cites Donna Orange: "Even if God is self-creating, God as third has no independent creator." Anderson disagrees, saying that "it is not reason or Thirdness that enjoys an element of freedom from an independent creator but the initial firsts."[20] Both miss the point somewhat because Peirce is not suggesting which universes are complete without consideration of an independent creator, but from which universe can a God *not* be discerned. It is clear that for Peirce this is the universe of Secondness, reaction. This corresponds to the "second man" who neglects the humble argument for God just as the gospel of Greed suggests the same in principle. "Men of action" have no care for what they ultimately produce, and from a platform such as this no meaning concerning a creator is possible. But this denigration of secondness becomes an abyss that keeps pulling Peirce back. Individuation in finite practice can never be general, but firstness lacks power and thirdness rests precariously on provisional symmetries, only ever expecting perfection in the long run. The second, an immediate experience of the self, can never be fully productive of an idea of a personal creator, according to Peirce.

Peirce's emphasis on the third stage of his argument can be more clearly described from this point. The provisional testing of the God hypothesis is not an addendum to make the argument strong; it is the very essence of Peirce's self-understanding. Testing this argument makes human freedom into a test. There is no "want to" or wish for a higher meaning in practice. The Neglected Argument is a challenge thrown down on the road of inquiry. There is not a potential growth into the conclusions of the Neglected Argument. Inquiry either rises to this challenge, integrating induction, deduction, and abduction into this one moment of orientation, or it fails to demonstrate the power necessary for complete self-control. Only in this stage of provisional testing of the God hypothesis can inquiry become a sufficient sign of both the character of the inquirer and the character of the object of inquiry. To establish this habit as a way of life requires a submission to inquiry that is also a submission to the object of inquiry, and the only evidence of this developing control of action is the heartfelt discovery of the object of God. This inquiry, seeking its own overcoming, is the creative obedience of the life of conversion. In "The Law of Mind" Peirce says,

> Were the ends of a person already explicit, there would be no room for development, for growth, for life; and consequently there would be no personality. The mere carrying out of predetermined purposes is mechanical. This remark has an application to the philosophy of religion. It is that genuine evolutionary philosophy, that is, one that makes the principle of growth a primordial element of the universe is so far from being antagonistic to the idea of a personal creator that it is really inseparable from that idea; while a necessitarian religion is in an altogether false position and is destined to become disintegrated. But a pseudo-evolutionism which enthrones mechanical law above the principle of growth is at once scientifically unsatisfactory, as giving no possible hint of how the universe has come about, and hostile to all hopes of personal relations to God. (CP 6:157)

Relation to God is the only way to retain the creative development of habit and habit change that could possibly serve as the ground for confirming the God hypothesis, the character of the person that finally escapes negative individuation. Conversion means this asymmetrical dependence on creative advance that is made at the risk of collapsing into determinism or into secondness where no light is possible.

CRITICISMS AND ADVANCES ON CONVERSION

In the process of this presentation I have made some suggestions about aspects of Peirce's thought that need more attention. One of these points concerns the role of the church in Peirce's thought, especially in the first stage of the Neglected Argument. Another point concerns Peirce's struggle with negative individuation and how this challenges his conclusions about how to determine the character of one's "conduct of life." Before I turn to these two points, however, it is important to raise the critical issue about the use of conversion as a general theme or a general critique, especially since I have not laid down an explicit definition of conversion. I have retained a vagueness concerning conversion so far in this book, a vagueness that I think is essential to uncovering its richest potential meaning, although we can point to some more firmly established elements.

One of the firmer aspects of conversion that comes to light through this analysis is the sense of holism that holds together both the transformation of a thinker and the transforming reality that sponsors that movement. I think Peirce lacks this holism in one sense and finds it in another. The way he lacks holism is in terms of sustained argumentation concerning the principal outcomes of his philosophical musings. I do not think this demonstrates a fragmentation in Peirce's thought, nor do I think that Peirce changed significantly in terms of his more ultimate commitments. Rather, what Peirce lacks is an overarching metaphor from which there is clear access to *all* aspects of his thought. I think this is why studies of Peirce are so fruitful in terms of broader philosophical connections, but why Peirce the man appears more and more elusive even in the course of these studies. "Conversion" may be a possible way to incorporate Peirce's thoughts, and I think a bit of Peirce the man as well, into a more holistic account of his thought. Whether or not conversion is the best platform for a holistic approach to Peirce, I think it is clear that Peirce was profoundly engaged in the issues of God, the soul, and transformation.

The way that Peirce does evince a holism is in terms of his inquiry. The continuity of inquiry becomes Peirce's steed for running through (and sometimes over) reflective problems emerging in a variety of contexts. Kelly Parker has demonstrated this aspect of continuity in Peirce's mathematical and epistemic thought.[21] But this source of holism compromises Peirce's inquiry in several ways. First, it is difficult to make continuity the ground for an argument for an independent creator. Second, Peirce's notion of continuity as identified through resistance undermines any account for positive individuation, despite the fact that Peirce himself seems to have gained a sense of this positive attitude. As he writes to Russell, "Every man sees some task cut out for him. Let him do and feel that he is doing what God made him in order that he should do" (CP 8:138 n.4). The ontological limits of absolute continuity and negative individuation become roadblocks to his inquiry, and much of Peirce's metaphysics is required to move around or past these problems.

My interest in conversion as a platform for appropriating and criticizing Peirce's thought is driven by this observation of his need for an incorporative platform and his clear attempts to find this through the continuity of inquiry. Let me take up two issues then in response to this observation.

The primary issue between Peirce and conversion is his insistence that inquiry is both the sign and product of personal transformation. While his reasons for this are evident, since through inquiry he can collect philosophers, theologians, and scientists in terms of a logical analysis, it also becomes evident that what Peirce could not do was live as a result of that inquiry. Inquiry becomes an end in itself, and in fact, becomes the ground for itself in the Neglected Argument. The proof of his logic stands on the provisional ground of an infinitely developing argument. His reasons for rejecting the pragmatic nominalism of Dewey and James are sound, as we will see next, but what remains absent from Peirce is the sense of a stable platform, a satisfying conclusion, or a spirit of judgment that is really continuous with making discoveries about the universe, the self, and God. This is most evidently a problem in the Neglected Argument, where Peirce's own condition of "influence over the whole conduct of life" comes up looking rather empty when the answer is "but only conduct that always remains future is meaningful." I do not think Peirce was blind to this need, for it occasionally peeks out through his offhanded comments and his struggle with his religious identity, but that makes his philosophical searches all the more surprising inasmuch as these elements do not crash in as the kind of doubts arising in practice his theory of inquiry aims to address.

I have referred to a letter Peirce wrote to the rector of St. Thomas Episcopal Church in New York. Peirce recounts an experience of "receiving permission" to receive communion, although he is aware that he is not intellectually prepared to do so. Nonetheless, he responds and takes communion. My point is not Peirce's inconsistency or a "hidden" conversion. There is not much Peirce hides, and his language of obedience, submission, service, and adoration concerning the church and the object of the church have always appeared to me as signs that he found a resistant, enlivening, and demanding origin in the Christian tradition. Again, these indicate an awareness of his own need for conversion, and without putting things into language like that, I think Peirce strove to realize his own transformation to this reality. What kept him apart from that realization is difficult to say, but I may conjecture that he had more in common with Saint Augustine in terms of the will than he wanted to admit. What I find strikingly absent, therefore, is Peirce's active commitment to the church from which he takes such confidence in the developing character of civilization and such discoveries as the call of the

Savior. I wonder what development of Peirce's thought would be possible if the church he refers to became the place in which his thought could dwell, where his inquiry would find purchase not only in terms of justifying itself but in terms of sustaining the reflective work of bringing creative transformation to bear for the good of all minds, high and low alike. I think this absence is a clue.

Where this clue leads me is to Peirce's difficulty in making sense of the ultimate habit change associated with both the ultimate identity of the character of the individual and the success of his method of inquiry. What is unclear to me is the doubt that sponsors this inquiry—is there a doubt associated with the God hypothesis of equal moment in terms of ultimacy? If there is not, then how does the Neglected Argument develop any differently than Descartes' claim that he discovers an idea of God in his thinking that resolves his problem of the external world. And if there is a doubt behind this inquiry, then it would behoove Peirce to begin with that negation. Regardless of this origin, however, there is another element of absence lurking in Peirce's thought that must be brought to light.

From the broadest consideration of Peirce's claims about the person and God, it is evident that God can only be in the end the ultimate source of negation. To be not God is to be really distinct, and Peirce is unequivocal at this point. There is God, a creator, unlike any other. There are you and me, inquirers, existent and like many others, continuous in thought and action, able to discover this unlike-us God. Agapism as a character looks like a bridge that is crossed through inquiry that yields a kind of mind-meld with God. So, either Peirce becomes a finite-infinite creature—like God, only not able to comprehend his own infinity—or Peirce becomes aware most clearly of his character as not-God. On the first alternative, there is no reason why the identification with God should not be continuous, except that we have a limitation of time (and Peirce never says we do not have the will to be fully self-controlled). But this means that the infinite character is never possibly realized in our thought. It always remains a source of negation for us, if not for the community. And on the second alternative, that we are not-God means that no matter what changes or products of inquiry we achieve or self-critically develop we always remain not-God.

This disjunction reveals an opening for an orientation in Peirce's thought that mediates this split, something like a pragmaticistic model of divine incarnation. What Peirce seeks is a position where the creative function of a personal and provisional inquiry is a full-blooded representation of the power of the church in full awareness of its limit that it is not-God but that it is God's possession. This inquiry, from the platform of the church, can understand God—in fact, grace is God in this finite form—and yet the person by virtue of the community remains distinct from God.

This conjecture of a pragmaticistic incarnation should be viewed in this context as a product of musement, striking upon an attractive idea that needs explication and probation. Taking Peirce as the context for this casting around may make sense of the sign of his thought in terms of what we need to explore to validate his character, which is one of the more open-ended characters in terms of willingness to explore strange worlds of thought. This character is clear when he says "In order that science may be successful, its votaries must hasten to surrender themselves at discretion to experimental inquiry, in advance of knowing what its decisions may be. There must be no reservations" (CP 1:57). To make Peirce's scientific theism critically productive, then, conversion must be examined experimentally and without reservations.

Conversion would mark a dramatic shift in the way Peirce is understood philosophically, and so it is likely that this suggestive proposal will not be well accepted by philosophers familiar and committed to understanding Peirce's thought. But I hope to sustain this argument in order to bring a level of critical analysis to Peirce's thought that it otherwise will not have. In what follows my goal is to realize more clearly the confessional depth of Peirce's recommendation that a person who inquires

> in scientific singleness of heart, will come to be stirred to the depths of his nature by the beauty of the idea and by its august practicality, even to the point of earnestly loving and adoring his strictly hypothetical God, and to that of desiring above all things to shape the whole conduct of life and all the springs of action into conformity with that hypothesis. Now to be deliberately and thoroughly prepared to shape one's conduct into conformity with a proposition is neither more nor less than the state of mind called Believing that proposition, however long the conscious classification of it under that head be postponed. (CP 6:467)

I invoke conversion here to dramatize the transformation of the "springs of action" through self-control realized in the belief in God. Peirce's pragmaticism, Doug Anderson says, "underwrites the possibility of the indirect testing of a vaguely conceived God by way of the habits of persons and the habits of the cosmos. If Peirce were reduced to working only with immediate perception of possible actions, no real God could possibly be understood to emerge in musement or to be testable in induction."[22] This power of testing is connected to Peirce's notion that a "latent tendency toward the belief in God is a fundamental ingredient in the soul" (CP 6:487). The conversion Peirce seeks is a conversion to the criticism of one's ultimate beliefs, and this is a conversion that can and should become catholic in its application and power.

NOTES

1. See Douglas Anderson, *Strands of System: The Philosophy of C. S. Peirce* (Purdue University Press, 1995) for the best extended analysis of Peirce's essay "The Neglected Argument for the Reality of God." Michael Raposa, in *Peirce's Philosophy of Religion* (Indiana University Press, 1989), treats Peirce's religious interests as an incorporating theme of his philosophy.

2. Sang Hyun Lee, *The Philosophical Theology of Jonathan Edwards* (Princeton University Press, 1988), 66. Lee gives an account of Edwards as an objective idealist, and in this sense, a precursor to Peirce. I would extend this connection beyond their shared conceptions of the real nature of Law to include the fragility of disposition by which the reality of the soul as a general term or a habit, is reconstructed through an interaction with an opposing general term or habit. Where they separate is the ontological character of the divine disposition.

3. See Joseph Brent, *Charles Sanders Peirce: A Life* (Indiana University Press, 1998); Kenneth Laine Ketner, *His Glassy Essence* (Vanderbilt University Press, 1998); and Louis Menand, *The Metaphysical Club* (Farrar, Straus & Giroux, 2001).

4. *Collected Papers of Charles Sanders Peirce* (Harvard University Press, 1931–58.) Subsequent references in the text (CP) refer to the volume and paragraph cited.

5. In his 1892 letter to the rector of St. Thomas Episcopal Church in New York, Peirce acknowledges that on a recent visit to the church he was "given permission" to approach and take communion by the "Master." This act of taking communion contravened his problems with the creed that had been the cause of many a "bitter reflection." In this instance, however, Peirce says he was "carried up to the altar rail, almost without my own volition." This, I think, is a case in point of a habit that is adopted on the basis of a vague leading.

6. Anderson, *Strands of System,* 135.

7. *Writings of Charles S. Peirce: A Chronological Edition* (Indiana University Press, 1982). Subsequent references (CE) refer to the volume and page cited.

8. Brent, *Charles Sanders Peirce,* 246.

9. Kelly James Parker, *The Continuity of Peirce's Thought* (Vanderbilt University Press, 1998), 18.

10. Thomas Goudge, *The Thought of C. S. Peirce* (Dover, 1950), 3.

11. Raposa, *Peirce's Philosophy of Religion,* 94.

12. Ibid., 11.

13. Ibid., 24.

14. Anderson, *Strands of System,* 139.

15. Raposa, *Peirce's Philosophy of Religion,* 76–77.

16. Ibid., 104. Peirce distinguishes *logica utens,* a "whole system of opinions and habits of thought that produce bad inferences as well as good ones. Such a system is a precondition of the study of logic and warrants constant and rigorous criticism."

17. Vincent Colapietro, *Peirce's Approach to the Self* (SUNY Press, 1989), 92.

18. Raposa, *Peirce's Philosophy of Religion,* 12.

19. Anderson, *Strands of System,* 173.

20. Ibid., 176.

21. Parker, *Peirce's Philosophy of Continuity.*

22. Anderson, *Strands of System,* 178.

3

Reconstructing Faith: Religious Overcoming in Dewey's Pragmatism

OF THE THREE CLASSICAL AMERICAN PHILOSOPHERS treated in this book, John Dewey is the most expressly antagonistic toward the hold religion has on the expectations surrounding human transformation. The roots of this antagonism are philosophically and psychologically complex. Stephen Rockefeller and others have shown that Dewey's religious attitude permeates much of his professional philosophical work even though he says that his own religious understanding did not constitute a "leading philosophical problem" for him[1] (*Later Works* [LW] 5:149–150). Reading *A Common Faith,* though, challenges this dismissal. If religion is not a leading philosophical problem for Dewey, overcoming religion is. In this way, *A Common Faith* is one of Dewey's most important and revealing philosophical texts.

A Common Faith inadvertently caps Dewey's philosophical career. Rather than put religion in its place, though, *A Common Faith* has done more to put Dewey in his place in relation to religion than vice versa. This raises the question of why Dewey could not overcome religion in the way he intended. Is the religious overcoming that Dewey suggests possible? Does pragmatism stand or fall on the question of overcoming religion? It is clear that Dewey pursues the authority of religious life in order to capture that vitality for his progressivism and to demonstrate that the deepest human values emerge from within experience.[2] Recovering religious power for pragmatism is a confessional task for Dewey, and his passion is evident in his concern "that what is genuinely religious will undergo an emancipation when it is relieved from [the encumbrances of religion]; that, then, for the first time, the religious aspect of experience will be free to develop freely on its own account" (LW 9:4). Dewey longs for the sense of this "free" development of the religious attitude, which is possible only through overcoming "religion" and its false authority. Dewey's confessional challenge is to describe the transformation of common expectations in such a way that men and women are able to abide where there is no middle ground between the religious attitude and religions. This is no bloodless philosophical work, however. Dewey writes to restore and secure religious faith for the men and women who construct the community through reflective action and relationships. This is Dewey's express intention. The only possible ground to criticize *A Common Faith* substantially emerges in terms of this personal transformation—from religion to the religious attitude, but also from no-faith to faith.

My plan in this chapter is to follow the structure of the three essays that comprise *A Common Faith*. In the first section, I examine Dewey's notion of the transformation to the religious attitude in "Religion versus the Religious." Conversion from religion to the religious attitude is the overcoming Dewey thinks is necessary for the democratic community to thrive. Transcending the content of present practice, though, requires an adequate ground for criticism. In the second section, I focus on the content aspects of "Faith and Its Object" that makes this critical advance possible. Dewey wants to stabilize the sources of authority in human practice to enhance the products and consciousness of intelligent control. In the third section, I follow Dewey's ascending polemic against the supernatural in "The Human Abode of the Religious Function." Conversion completes Dewey's thought here in the sense that the religious function is necessary to produce a material effect on practice that manifests intelligent control of the sources of authority in common life. The only material effect that would sufficiently demonstrate this control is the explicit overcoming of supernatural religion. If supernatural dependence is not overcome, Dewey has no ground to claim that the democratic community is secure. I conclude with a critical evaluation of Dewey's attempt to reconstruct faith as the religious overcoming implicit in the growth of the democratic community.

THE RELIGIOUS ATTITUDE

> It is the claim of religions that they effect this generic and enduring change in attitude. I should like to turn the statement around and say that whenever this change takes place there is a definitely religious attitude. (LW 9:13)

On its face, Dewey's interest in the religious attitude constitutes a sort of victory for people who refuse to accede to absolute naturalism. Dewey describes an enduring change of a person's attitude to the spirit or sense of the world beyond what can be accounted by material interaction. He establishes a common ground with ordinary religious expectations that is crucial for all that follows in *A Common Faith*. In this section I will focus on the image of personal conversion as the common ground that Dewey establishes between himself and traditional religions.

Despite Dewey's interest in establishing common ground, the polemic character of *A Common Faith* is evident in the quotation above. Dewey begins his analysis by unsettling the proprietary claim of religion(s) over the religious attitude. Making the distinction between "religion" and "the religious" this way quickly puts Dewey between two camps. On one hand, such a distinction challenges naturalism's rejection of the products or ground of religion. On the other hand, traditional believers are challenged to reexamine the moorings of their faith and to face Socrates' question from the *Euthyphro:* Is the holy what is loved by the gods, or is what is loved by the gods holy? Does religion know the true nature of its practice? Does a love of religion produce the good of religious life, or does the love of the good in religious life produce religion? In both ways Dewey's question leads to the opening of the ground for an understanding of "religious faith" that moves past the easy affirmation of traditional religion and past the easy rejection of naturalism.

Another aspect of Dewey's polemical beginning is less obvious. Dewey must argue that the religious overcoming he proposes is a reformation that arises internally in the self-conscious understanding of religion and equally internally in the communal desire for ideal action. The "religious attitude" must describe a growth intrinsic to religion that in effect cancels that religion. For if "religion" becomes a limit to growth, even a potential limit, at some level emergent value is subordinated to a prior value. In the same way, the "religious attitude" must describe the pressure intrinsic within human action for a fully conscious sense of ideal action. For if there is no opening within action for an unlimited transcendence in terms of the meaning of action, not just its temporal effects, then that too stands as an antecedent limit. The religious attitude gives Dewey a platform to argue against two forms of reification—first, that "God" stands as the ultimate *telos* for all religious value, and second, that the goal of action is the totality of material interactions.

Religion, however, is Dewey's concrete starting point. Dewey uses religion's dependence on supernatural beliefs as a foil in the first sentences of

A Common Faith to move into an evaluation of authority that subtends all practice. From his description of the change to the "religious attitude," we will see that he is contending mostly with the authority of his own Christian background. Dewey's childhood connection to the Congregational church and his mother's Christian influence shows a deep but unquiet relationship. Robert Roth notes Dewey's adolescent involvement with his church in Vermont and Mrs. Dewey's integration of social concerns with her faith, although her son appears to have left these beliefs soon after leaving for Johns Hopkins.[3] What beliefs Dewey held and when they were completely left is an open question,[4] but in his early career Dewey combined his Christian view with the Hegelian conviction that human meaning is completely expressed in its social form. In his 1893 essay "Christianity and Democracy" he writes,

> The significance of democracy as revelation is that it enables us to get truths in a natural, every-day and practical sense which otherwise could be grasped only in a somewhat unnatural or sentimental sense. I assume that democracy is a spiritual fact and not a mere piece of governmental machinery. If there is no God, no law, no truth in the Universe, or if this God is an absentee God, not actually working, then no social organization has any spiritual meaning. If God is, as Christ taught, at the root of life, incarnate in man, then democracy has a spiritual meaning which it behooves us not to pass by. Democracy is freedom. If truth is at the bottom of things, freedom means giving this truth a chance to show itself, a chance to well up from the depths. Democracy, as freedom, means the loosening of bonds, the wearing away of restrictions, the breaking down of barriers, of middle walls, of partitions. (*Early Works* [EW] 4:8)

Despite the passion in these words, Dewey experienced a remarkable change of mind that resulted in his leaving both Hegel and Christianity. This dramatic shift coincides with his move from Michigan to Chicago in 1894.[5] With this change of place, Dewey turns to the natural dimensions of human initiative for transformation. He explores the ways the social expression of human reality breaks beyond what any religion can anticipate or hold and beyond the security any ideal can represent. The church is a finite institution, both in terms of the limit of its membership due to its peculiar intellectual beliefs, and finite in terms of its ability to extend its method of taking new habits and transforming itself. An infinite community, like democracy, avoids these limitations. In *Human Nature and Conduct* Dewey speaks to this vision of democracy:

Democracy as compared with other ways of life is the sole way of living which believes wholeheartedly in the process of experience as end and as means; as that which is capable of generating the science which is the sole dependable authority for the direction of further experience and which releases emotions, needs and desires so as to call into being the things that have not existed in the past. (LW 14:229)

The change in Dewey's thinking between these two conceptions of democracy is significant on several levels. In the first passage, Dewey claims that God's work gives meaning to democracy. The removal of barriers is Christ's immanent work in the world, and so democracy is the evolving reality of that "spiritual" meaning in our practice. Democracy depends on God's authority for its meaning. In the second passage, democracy needs no warrant for its meaning because it is the "sole way of living" in proper relation to the process of experience. This warrant is based on the singularity of the character of democracy. This claim makes an interesting parallel to the charge of exclusivism Dewey lays at the feet of religion later in *A Common Faith*. Further, his reference to science exercising its authority to "call into being things that have not existed" is the counterpoise to John's words concerning Jesus that "not one thing came into being except through him" (John 1:3, *New Jerusalem Bible*). The dialectic between religion and democracy runs into the deepest senses of valuation Dewey can describe. There may be no more meaningful dyad for Dewey than religion and democracy.

Based on these two conceptions of democracy we can see that Dewey's struggle points to the competing authorities of science and God. The confusion in *A Common Faith* is not principally that of the reader. The confusion is a reflection of Dewey's strained effort to achieve a middle ground between these conceptions as he sorts out the ground of his faith into that which makes democracy possible. But this ground only arises in the contest over authoritative power. Moving from God to science as the authority implicit in human action is the question at hand, and the polemic character of *A Common Faith* shows this aspect of Dewey's own overcoming was not yet settled. Further, Dewey's claim that the reformation of religion into the religious attitude is a matter of internal progression, independent of a "special" religious experience or a prompt by a transcendent God, also means that the polemic investing *A Common Faith* is an image of Dewey's divided thinking. The combination of an internal progression related to determining the authority over practice is leading Dewey to the constructive role of conversion in discovering the religious attitude, but there is also an aspect of defensiveness in this development.

Dewey's ability to move through the internal challenge of religion responds to Reinhold Niebuhr's criticism of Dewey's progressivism in the opening pages of *Moral Man and Immoral Society*.[6] For Niebuhr, the ability to choose in anything like "freedom" would be possible only if an individual could act against the society:

> Defiance of a community, which is in control not only of the police power but of the potent force of public approval and disapproval, in the name of the community, which exists only in the moral imagination of the individual and has no means of exerting pressure on him, obviously points to a force of conscience more individual than social. . . . Most individuals lack the intellectual penetration to form independent judgments and therefore accept the moral opinions of their society.[7]

For Niebuhr, then, standing at a critical difference from the prevailing authority of the community is the issue. Individuals, by and large, cannot oppose their own grasp on authority to that of the larger society. Social change depends on an institutional power wielding an authority sufficient to challenge the authority of the community.

In light of this kind of critique, we can appreciate the significance of Dewey's trust in a conversion-like change of perspective concerning authority. Dewey does not dispute the power of social thinking, but he thinks the hope of merging everyday life into an ideal form grips the individual in a way no community can challenge. Dewey's faith is built on the cornerstone "that the reverence shown by a free and self-respecting human being is better than the servile obedience rendered to an arbitrary power by frightened men" (LW 9:7). No person needs instruction to see this "better," and no power of a community or other construct can diminish this "better" of freedom. From this ground of self-respect Dewey dismisses God—not from a metaphysical challenge to the idea of God, or even in opposition to an abductive argument like Peirce constructs—but considering human growth as a universally available good, freedom *from* an unchosen supervening authority and the choice *to* an appearing authority clears up the picture. Since we are able to choose even the authority that we serve, the issue of human progress escapes the bounds Niebuhr describes. All that is needed is for Dewey to say how this choice of authority works.

The question of authority is of central importance for Dewey, for he knows that the spiritual meaning of the democratic community depends on this answer. His task is to describe the critical appropriation of authority that is a product of freedom and that is also sufficient to overcome the Niebuhrean criticism that such a choice is a delusion. A chosen authority would make an internal reform of the individual possible that counteracts the movement of institutions and society despite the apparent imbalance of power. Dewey describes a kind of conversion, then, that is the adjustment of the self into a "unity" in light of an appearing authority that provides a sense of power within his philosophical program.

CONVERSION

I am using conversion here in a limited way. I mean to indicate Dewey's sense that individuals are able to attain a separation from a way of being in the world that is devoid of its highest potential value. This internal transformation must be brought into clear view in order to make the arguments in *A Common Faith* cohere. Without this transformation, Dewey fails to address the mode of becoming in the practical lives of men and women of faith. The religious attitude involves a dramatic transformation of the person, although not necessarily an immediate one.

> [The religious attitude] demands that in imagination we wipe the slate clean and start afresh by asking what would be the idea of the unseen, of the manner of its control over us and the ways in which reverence and obedience would be manifested, if whatever is basically religious in experience had the opportunity to express itself free from all historical encumbrances. (LW 9:6)

This suggestion of "obedience to the unseen" might send shivers down the spines of his naturalist companions, as would the claim that we recognize "its control over us." Dewey is surprisingly close to Edwards's conception of conversion, since both reject the possibility of an interjection of special knowledge or the need for an institutional form of transformation. Dewey is especially close to Edwards in his reference to the religious attitude as a settled transformation of the will that affects an orientation evident in all of a person's habits.

> But there are also changes in ourselves in relation to the world in which we live that are much more inclusive and deep seated. They relate not to

this or that want in relation to this or that condition of our surrounding, but pertain to our being in its entirety. Because of their scope, this modification of ourselves is enduring. . . . There is a composing and harmonizing of the various elements of our being such that, in spite of changes on the special conditions that surround us, these conditions are also arranged, settled, in relation to us. This attitude includes a note of submission. But it is voluntary, not externally imposed; and as voluntary it is something more than a mere Stoical resolution to endure unperturbed throughout the buffetings of fortune. It is more outgoing, more ready and glad, than the latter attitude, and it is more active than the former. And in calling it voluntary, it is not meant that it depends on a particular resolve or volition. It is a change *of* will conceived as the organic plenitude of our being, rather than any special change *in* our will. (LW 9:12–13)

The experience that culminates in this change *of* will to the religious attitude is not Dewey's focus in the text in hand. What is striking is that Dewey leaves out any positive contribution traditional religion has for this change. Whatever *does* bring it about is religious in effect, but what this is remains vague. Dewey's focus is the change of attitude, and dislocating this change from a necessary relationship to a religion works the reversal of origin on which his entire argument turns.

Dewey admits that conversion of the will has been most apparent within particular religious traditions, although he turns this into the critique that this power has been captured and pressed into service as the means of supporting supernatural beliefs. Thus, the power of religious transformation is withheld from the activities from which it genuinely emerges and for which is it most beneficial. There are two claims here. First is that the difference of the religious attitude in the lives of men and women is only coincidentally associated with religions and the supernatural ground of religion. The second claim is that revealing the falseness of beliefs that encumber the power of religious transformation is the reflective task of the philosopher. Persons stuck within "cultural accretions" of religion may not be able to see this lost good, and so the critical attitude of the philosopher is essential to bring these encumbrances to light.

The most direct opposition to the traditional understanding of religious conversion centers on the origin of religious transformation. Dewey offers only one argument here. Imaginative ideals, not the reproduced images or icons of a tradition, are the guide for refining and extending practice. Imaginative ideals are the basis for the expansion of daily experience, and there is no internal limit to the reach of this power of imagining better things or richer experience. There is a difference, however, between the imagination necessary for the religious attitude and imagination concerned with routine activities. In the religious sense imagination stands apart from the day to day activity in order to construct a holistic ideal of the self. Dewey says that the religious attitude results from an interpenetration of imagination in all elements of our being; "The idea of a whole, whether of the whole personal being or of the world, is an imaginative, not a literal idea. The limited world of our observation and reflection becomes the Universe only through imaginative extension. . . . Neither observation, thought, nor practical activity can attain that complete unification of the self which is called a whole" (LW 9:14). The imaginative extension of the whole personal being is an ordering ideal, such that we are "conquered, vanquished in our active nature by an ideal end; it signifies acknowledgment of its rightful claim over our desires and purposes. Such acknowledgment is practical not primarily intellectual. It goes beyond evidence that can be presented to *any* possible observer. . . . [S]uch moral faith is not easy. It was questioned whether the Son of Man in his coming should find faith on the earth at his coming" (LW 9:16).

I have shown the repetition of Dewey's emphasis that the imaginative leap that produces the religious attitude is not a matter of observation or intellectual grasping. This ideal whole emerges only in the imaginative reconstruction of practice that incorporates all aspects of practice but that is never exhausted in practice. "Religious will," Dewey says in his *Psychology*, "is conscious realization that [the ideal and real will] are one because man is a self-determining power. It is the realization that a perfect will is reality. It is the realization of freedom through the realization of the union of finite and the infinite Personality. It is only when we recognize this latter activity of will that we are able really to comprehend the previous forms of activity" (EW 2:362). The power of self-determination is brought into view only through the exercise of a holistic image of life that has a "rightful claim over us." This reflects the tone of Augustine's appeal to God, "command what you will, give what you command," in that Dewey's view of the holism of our being is an active engagement with a compelling authority, not the reflective accomplishment of a belief in an antecedent reality.

Parsing out the meaning of the "rightful claim" that exercises vanquishing power over our practical lives, and yet has its origin in the imaginative extension of our own ends, is the puzzle of Dewey's religious attitude. I do not think Dewey thinks it is wise to dwell on this question too long, as his response to Wieman's and Hartshorne's debate over the question of his theism dragged on. This debate is less important than the fruit that results from the lives of reoriented purpose that are able to endure the turns of fate and the frustrations of failure because of this settled change of will. The common use of "God" to refer to this aspect of human life did not bother Dewey, and his desire to speak in a way that connects to this hope in everyday life further supports his use of the term.[8]

I want to follow through with Dewey's notion that the religious attitude yields a "genuine perspective" of the ends of life that becomes a stable platform for pursuing the work of growing human life in richness. From this platform, Dewey remakes his criticism against traditional religion as promulgating an end of human life that is not with us. In his view, traditional religion calls its adherents to produce what they cannot control, and this is what makes religion an occasion for fear. The end expected from our practice does not, indeed cannot, arise from us. In the remaining sections of *A Common Faith* Dewey takes aim at these fears, first to show that the proper and ultimate end of human life arises organically within that life, and then to show that the anticipated judgment should not occasion the fear of coming up short in terms of a nonhuman criterion, but should occasion widespread dedication and fervor for proving the growth of richness in action for the future judgment of our own community.

STABILIZING THE RELIGIOUS ATTITUDE WITH THE OBJECT OF FAITH

The positive lesson is that religious qualities and values if they are real at all are not bound up with any single item of intellectual assent, not even that of the existence of the God of theism; and that, under existing conditions, the religious function in experience can be emancipated only through surrender of the whole notion of special truths that are religious by their own nature, together with the idea of peculiar avenues of access to such truths. For were we to admit that there is but one method for ascertaining fact and truth—that conveyed by the word "scientific" in its most general and generous sense—no discovery in any branch of knowledge and inquiry could then disturb the faith that is religious. I should describe this faith as the unification of the self through allegiance to inclusive ideal ends, which imagination presents to us and to which the human will responds as worthy of controlling our desires and choices. (LW 9:23)

The first essay of *A Common Faith* carves out the common ground of transformation to the religious attitude. The second essay, "Faith and Its Object," establishes the content that makes such a transformation possible. Dewey's concern for a ground of faith free from disruption is important to note, as is his dependence on imagination to discover ideal ends that sponsor a unification of the self. Working these two concerns together, security from disruptions and the imaginative ground of ideal ends, sets Dewey's notion of religious transformation on a path that leads to a complete rejection of the authority of religion. Here, in a sign of good faith, Dewey advises religion to surrender unconditionally to science.

There are two ways to proceed from this place. Dewey may be advocating a replacement of religion with a devotion to science, disconnected from any prior tradition strictly or loosely termed "religious." This negotiated surrender would in fact become a manifesto of a remarkable trade of "special truths" for general ones that need no evangelistic efforts for their promulgation. A second path takes Dewey in quite a different direction. This is the way of "science" generously understood, that is, so generously that it includes the ideal ends formerly known as "special truths" that are recast in their inclusive and ideal forms as those that have always and will continue to inspire human devotion. What is emancipated by this surrender is the religious person from the task of producing compendia of special truths and ever new methodologies for attaining those truths that have to endure and respond to scientific criticism. Dewey weaves between these two paths, speaking in some instances as a helpful friend and at other times as the most strident critic of religion. His basic commitment to reconstructing faith inspires him to dwell in the reflective space between reconstructing and deconstructing religion. Dwelling in this space means unveiling the authority that is most productive in terms of transforming the experience of the individual.

Dewey's faith is based on the confidence that the ultimate authority for transforming experience arises within the continuum of experience. Simply to be as a human means to be transforming experience, "constantly shaping ourselves to or modifying the environment with which we react," as Michael Eldridge puts it.[9] But the quality or effect of transformation depends on the ends sought, and these reflect the attitudes and dispositions trained into the individual. Concretely influencing the attitudes on which transformation depends seems unlikely. Real reform, even of a person, is nearly impossible even through education.[10] The mystery of personal change and transformation invests all of Dewey's philosophical musings and hopes. For this reason, conversion to the religious attitude becomes even more important as a sign of the character of human intelligence to seek the limits of action by an internal criticism.

Genuine transformation depends on a precarious authority. Unless the content to which we are transformed emerges from the process of transformation itself, the ideal with the practice, there is no intelligent control in transforming and shaping experience. This model of transformation cannot accommodate an ideal already in existence, because if an ideal is somehow already "out there" the transformative moment is a result ordered by some representation, and no transaction of mutual forming can arise in such a representation. It excludes intelligence. Conversion to the religious attitude is all that can at once be religious, in terms of approaching ideal ends, and also transformative, since there is no static image toward which it moves, no set completion that it seeks beyond its own control. Science is the process of moving toward this transformation that does not depend on the authority of an antecedent ideal. But Dewey has yet to show how these scientific beliefs become suitable for a platform for the transformation to a *religious* attitude.

Dewey's way between these two positions—religion that becomes scientific and science that becomes religious—is the true test of the "object" of his faith. On the one hand, he suggests that religious truths and facts of doctrine must be considered symbolically; "they are symbolic of the reality of ends moving us in many forms of experience. The ideal values that are thus symbolized also mark human experience in science and art and the various modes of human association" (LW 9:29). Only in this way can the mode of access to these truths be open to all who obey the structure of inquiry. On the other hand, Dewey's argument also depends on scientific inquiry finding its limit in these "ideal values" common to religious faith. I think this aspect of Dewey's pragmatic inquiry is often overlooked because it requires an inference from scientific inquiry back to religious power. It requires, for instance, the scientific inquirer to seek the ground of the "unity" on which the authority of constructing beliefs stands. This is the needed criticism that religious thinking brings to scientific intelligence that makes it a possible instrument of human transformation. Discovering this potency of ideal ends within the continuum of transforming experience is synonymous with the development of communication.

Communication is Dewey's broadest conception of the human impulse to reconstruct experience. The religious character of emergent communication in *Experience and Nature* inspires Walter Kaufmann to point to Dewey in the introduction to his translation of Martin Buber's *I and Thou,* although he says that Buber is far better in "endowing the social sphere with a religious dimension."[11] Allegiance to ideal ends emerges in communication that enables the whole person to stand in relation to another. The origin of this wholeness in the natural emergence of communication is Dewey's clearest deviation from Hegel, since communication itself becomes the ground of the distinction between the ideal and the material. Rockefeller associates Dewey's immanentism to Feuerbach, but Dewey differs from this inverted idealism in the sense that every experience is an opening for transformation that may have transcendentally effective results on future experience.[12] Some facts have more potentially pervasive effects than others, but none are limited.

> Essence is never existence, and yet it is the essence, the distilled import, of existence; the significant thing about it, its intellectual voucher, the means of inference and extensive transfer, and object of esthetic intuition. In it, feeling and understanding are one; the meaning of a thing is the sense it makes. (LW 1:144)

A fact or a word is not powerful by its existence, but through the inference and transfer of meaning that is possible through it. This distillation of a word to its extensive transfer is found only as its ideal form emerges in action. For instance, language makes description existent but the essence emerges as an ideal in making sense of some range of experience that exceeds the facts of observation. Language transforms experience because it is performative.

> Language is always a form of action and in its instrumental use is always a means of concerted action for an end, while at the same time it finds in itself all the goods of its possible consequences. For there is no mode of action as fulfilling and as rewarding as is concerted consensus of action. It brings with it the sense of sharing and merging in a whole. Forms of language are unrivalled in ability to create this sense, at first with direct participation on the part of an audience; and then, as literary forms develop, through imaginative identification. (LW 1:144–145)

A word opens to view the transformation of action into a possible consensus of action. This ideal of consensus extends beyond the present word through imagination to an ultimate word, an ultimate consensus of action. Religious language is an example of this imaginative consensus that seeks an ultimately incorporative word. Although religious language is not a compendium of "special truths" for Dewey, he recognizes its performative power for constructing communities. What is true of language in general is true of religious language in particular: "it becomes a word by gaining meaning; and it gains meaning when its use establishes a genuine community of action" (LW 1:145).

The community of action religious language constructs, however, is not bent on realizing a concrete union of divine and human existents. It is bent on realizing the union of actual and ideal practice as a method of extending the consensus of transformative action. The religious nature of language is a reflection of its authority to develop ultimately comprehensive ideals in action. Here Dewey moves directly against Hegel. While accepting the conclusion that the ultimately real is the social realization of human life, Dewey holds that the development of this real is contingent on the emerging authority of a method of producing an imaginative whole in human action. This movement in action has the method of discovering authority for consensus as its content. "For a perceived mode of becoming," Dewey says, "is always ready to be translated into a method of production and direction" (LW 1:183).

The power of religious language follows from the awareness that it is continuous with a method of establishing the authority of ideal ends. This is the sense of Dewey's suggestion about religious beliefs and terms in "Faith and Its Object."

> What would be lost if it were also admitted that they have authoritative claim upon conduct just because they are ideal? The assumption that these objects of religion exist already in some realm of Being seems to add nothing to their force, while it weakens their claim over us as ideals, in so far as it bases that claim upon matters that are intellectually dubious. The question narrows itself to this: Are the ideals that move us genuinely ideal or are they ideal only in contrast with our present estate? (LW 9:29)

Dewey's deepest question in "Faith and Its Object" is how it is possible to test the genuineness of religious ideals. How is it possible, to say it a little differently, to bring religious ideals to the fiery crucible of practical evaluation of their effectiveness for transforming experience? Avoiding this test is precisely what traditional religion does that raises Dewey's concern.

> What I have been objecting to, I repeat, is not the idea that ideals are linked with existence and that they themselves exist, through human embodiment, as forces, but the idea that their authority and value depend upon some prior complete embodiment . . . where all facts and truths are already discovered and possessed, and all beauty is eternally displayed in actualized form. (LW 9:33)

Dewey is confident that his criticism of religion is helpful to its cause. Although "religion" has not yet secured its method of discovering the authority for its development, it continues to function based on the power of its language to construct communities of action performatively. This vitality and power can be improved by scientific criticism. Religion's openness to scientific critique and development is another sense of Dewey's "object of faith." The object of faith is to use all means to produce the integration of motive values and scientific confidence in practice. Religion's refusal to adopt the scientific method of establishing values puts it out of step with its desire to influence the practical lives of men and women. Conversion to the religious attitude discovers this lapse of method most effectively, as we will see in the next section.

What remains open and questionable concerning Dewey's object of faith, I think, is the origin of the impulse for the "whole" will. The discovery of the wholeness of will is different from the movement of authority in the development of practice. The sense of the whole person turns up from time to time in Dewey's thought as a casual reminder of something important but missing, and something that creates a host of problems. For instance, consider this statement from *Human Nature and Conduct:* "Each impulse is a demand for an object which will enable it to function. Denied an object in reality it tends to create one in fancy, as pathology shows" (*Middle Works* [MW] 14:98). Remembering the warnings of Jonathan Edwards concerning the genuineness of religious affections, it is fair to ask what the impulse for a whole will is, and how Dewey's story of communication escapes this hint of pathological fancy. If there is any strictly religious ground in Dewey, I think it concerns this sense of the wholeness of will and the genuineness of the impulse toward that wholeness. This is the third sense of the object of faith that I find in this chapter. From this third sense, it is possible to make a fair explanation of Dewey's notion of God.

Dewey's religious faith in the wholeness of the person emerges in continuity with communication and the development of consciousness. Consciousness, Dewey says, "is an idea, is that phase of a system of meanings which at a given time is undergoing re-direction, transitive transformation" (LW 1:233). How one attains consciousness is bound up with this redirection and transitive transformation of experience. Wholeness must emerge with or because of a transformation that is holistic in its effect. For this to occur there cannot be an existent "other" from which we draw imagistic content, or an existent soul seeking to be clothed in action, or a metaphysical communion with God to which we are drawn to return, although this may be the closest metaphorically to what captures Dewey's imagination.

So far in this account we have respected Dewey's reluctance to generalize the will to power. There is only the inherent pressure of every activity of transformation to find an adequate manifestation. Dewey's argument for the wholeness of will is not based on an ascending development of transforming power. Rather, the wholeness of will is based on a search for an opportunity to use a power already existing. It mirrors Leibniz's proof for God: that this Being, if possible, must exist. So Dewey claims that human transformational consciousness, if possible, must become materialized in the wholeness of a personal will. The object of faith is this possibility of materialization.

Of course, Dewey's object of faith has a lot in common with a Christian object, namely the incarnation of God in Jesus Christ. But Dewey does not treat the similarities or differences between his incarnational model of intelligence and the incarnation of Christ, even in a wisdom sense that might avoid the problems of the historical Jesus. The absence of a consideration of Jesus Christ in "Faith and Its Object" follows, I think, because any mention of Christ might spark up Dewey's fear that he is in the neighborhood of transforming an essence into an existent. He could invoke "God" but not Christ, because the latter is fraught with an existential power that would compromise any scientific inquiry into that term. Faith is anticipatory action, and to be fully anticipatory it cannot give over its content to a prior term, even by allusion. This puts Dewey in an odd place. It is as if the revelation of Christ was essential for Dewey's religious understanding as a first term in realizing the limit of an ideal humanity, but then this term had to be forgotten in order to make this ideal limit forceful again in practice. Dewey has to become his own Christ in order to exercise anything like religious faith; he must be novel, purely reflective of the merging of ideal ends and actuality, and an unshakable incarnation of intelligence. Christ might not be mentioned in the text but this idea is still forceful even in its absence. The force of the Christological union is behind Dewey's compulsion to honor the union of ideal and actual: "It is this active relation between ideal and actual to which I would give the name 'God'" (LW 9:34).

> Whether one gives the name "God" to this union, operative in thought and action, is a matter for individual decision. But the function of such a working union of the ideal and actual seems to me to be identical with the force that has in fact been attached to the conception of God in all the religions that have a spiritual content; and a clear idea of that function seems to me urgently needed at the present time. (LW 9:35)

This notion of God, qualified even as it is, almost overwhelms Dewey. He must assert his intelligent power in determining his essence, for this is the true test of freedom. "God" stands for the imaginative coherence of the uncoerced union of the ideal and actual in our practice. Faith is the unlimited perspective of our responsibility for the creation of practice in accord with this ideal end, and, in a way, the creation of ourselves *as* the content to which experience and nature lead. Dedication to this faith is perceived in instances of scientific inquiry that are subordinated to the service of human freedom.[13] Science, as a method, is complicit in achieving the end of controlled reflection, but science is subordinated to the power of an unlimited inquiry that alone expresses authority in the transformation of life. Dewey's faith is secure to the extent that whatever science discovers it cannot outrun the platform of transformation. It remains for the last essay of *A Common Faith* for Dewey to say what this free creation of ourselves is *for.*

IDEAL ACTION AND THE HUMAN ABODE OF THE RELIGIOUS FUNCTION

> The third stage would realize that in fact the values prized in those religions that have ideal elements are idealizations of things characteristic of natural association, which have then been projected into a supernatural realm for safe-keeping and sanction. Note the role of such terms as Father, Son, Bride, Fellowship and Communion in the vocabulary of Christianity, and note also the tendency, even if a somewhat inchoate one,

of terms that express the more intimate phases of association to displace those of legal, political origin: King, Judge, and Lord of Hosts. . . . Unless there is a movement into what I have called the third stage, fundamental dualism and a division in life continue. The idea of a double and parallel manifestation of the divine, in which the latter has superior status and authority, brings about a condition of unstable equilibrium. (LW 9:48–49)

In this last essay of *A Common Faith,* Dewey suggests that the movement from religion to the antisupernaturalism of the religious attitude is a relatively simple, uncomplicated linear progression.[14] Leaving religion is what happens when intelligence rules expectations. But Dewey knows the progression is not linear and neither is it simple. The impulse for realizing the religious function of the community emerges only as a reaction to a diremption in the experience of the individual. The realization of the religious function of experience involves conflict. In Dewey's inimitable way of saying it, "the social center of gravity of religion" has shifted from an incorporative living explanation to the defense of beliefs in light of scientific discovery (LW 9:41). "[A] kind of polite deference to the notion [of the supernatural] remains along with a concrete transfer of interest. The general mind is thus left in a confused and divided state. The movement that has been going on for the last few centuries will continue to breed doubleness of mind until religious meanings and values are definitely integrated into normal social relations" (LW 9:44). This "movement" that breeds doubleness of mind is the basis for Dewey's three stages of growth, from the assumption that man is evil and must be overcome by an external power, to the stage where natural values are elided with religious values and kept safe in supernatural vaults, to this third stage where value is seen for what it is—naturally available, fully productive of "religious" value, and needing no supernatural validation or protection.

The transition to the third stage is Dewey's ground for apologetic. This transition is what human intelligence seeks, where doubleness of mind is replaced with secure and meaningful practice. Attaining this stage, though, occurs only when corporate human action fully realizes its freedom by choosing its own authority—converting human association into a democratic community. Dewey focuses on the effect of overcoming religion as the means of perceiving progress toward the democratic community. From this perspective, his advocacy of this overcoming is an expression of care: "Criticism of the commitment of religion to the supernatural is positive in import. All modes of human association are 'affected with a public interest,' and full realization of this interest is equivalent to a sense of a significance that is religious in its function" (LW 9:53).

A nearly irresistible sense of religious progression emerges in *A Common Faith* as Dewey moves from a beginning in naïve supernatural faith, through an articulation of the intelligent object of faith, in this last chapter, that makes it possible to reconnect with practice in "The Human Abode of the Religious Function." The proper domain of the religious function is the human community, but exercising this function depends on the transformation of individuals to the religious attitude and the stabilization of the object of faith. Dewey self-critically challenges this form of progression, though. The first line of this chapter reads, "In discussing the intellectual content of religion before considering religion in its social connections, I did not follow the usual temporal order. Upon the whole, collective modes of practice either come first or are more important" (LW 9:40). He is careful to make this qualification because his organic reflection on religion inverts the trajectory of *Experience and Nature* where social connections do precede intellectual content. *A Common Faith* constitutes a challenge to his understanding of the natural emergence of ideal action. Dewey is pressed to recover the priority of social relations as the ground of human transformation, although now this becomes a spiritual rather than a temporal priority. He argues that achieving the religious function of the democratic community results from the progressive impulse to overcome the "gospel of salvation" in which individuals are held by supernatural expectations. Achieving ideal action, at least in *A Common Faith,* depends on establishing religious overcoming as the common ground between the individual and the community. I think this is where Dewey makes his most explicit argument that the good of the community must overwhelm individual interest. Individuals must undergo a conversion *to* the community, and this requires the abandonment of supernatural religion.

In the previous section we noted that the religious function of seeking a transformation to a "whole" self makes the community possible, holding diverse acts of intelligence into a workable union as a gathered and gathering focus. Dewey seeks to describe the space between the gathered focus of the good of human association that intervenes in and directs behavior, and the gathering focus of human behavior emerging within all aspects of intelligent human behavior. The space between these two foci is where redirection of the community can occur. Dewey interjects the challenge of religious overcoming into this space as the principle of reorienting the direction of the community.

Implicit in this effort toward redirection is the realization that the authority that presently "holds" the community is different from the authority that "holds" individuals within the community. If there is no difference between these then there is no ground for an internal dialect that issues in progress. Dewey suggests that the prospect of a supernaturally funded reprieve from the limits of the finite power of individual life is still attractive, despite the problems it raises. Such a hope still holds many individuals. But the development in the community follows a hope that is focused on the adoption of the authority of science. This is the root of the change in the "social center of gravity of religion." Aligning the prospects of individuals and the community is the primary exhortative work of this essay. Dewey is not responsible for generating this conflict or this content. He can, however, point out the disjunction and how it may be resolved. To accomplish this, he must persuasively describe anew the individual in terms of an aspect of the community's progress toward good, and second, he must describe the community's good as a collation of the gains made by the intelligent practice of individuals. Religious overcoming makes sense of the individual as a rejection of the "hold" of supernatural authority in deference to the community. This third essay is necessary to build the common ground between individual and community for this transition to occur. Overcoming the desire for individual salvation, then, is not a function of the power of the individual's will; it is the test of the reality of the community.

> The outcome will not be a gospel of salvation but it will be in line with that pursued, for example, in matters of disease and health. The method if used would not only accomplish something toward social health but it would accomplish a greater thing; it would forward the development of social intelligence so that it could act with greater hardihood and on a larger scale.

Transport into the realm of human life where intelligence has meaning beyond overcoming "this or that" individual concern means, in essence, a complete reversal of the hope for a "gospel of salvation." Such a reversal is a sign that the authority of the community has attained its proper place.

It is not clear whether Dewey thinks such a reversal of hope must be *advocated*—do this!—or merely *described,* as a condition that follows a preceding condition. If Dewey takes the role of advocacy, which I think he does, then *A Common Faith* is more like a sermon on the "calling to which we have been called" than a philosophical treatise that presents "what is." Dewey vacillates between these poles, and because he is unclear about his purpose this text occasionally escapes his control.[15]

Between the role of preacher and philosopher, however, Dewey manages to articulate the fact that the conversion of authority is the great good, the natural good, of human life. Only such a conversion of the whole context of practice can counteract the "social reign of accident" in which the supernatural is trusted to accomplish *our* aims. Religion, as the communal reflection of this trust, is the primary target in getting around this limiting dependence on the supernatural. But the trust that religion still incites in people that depends on little or no evidence, that constrains individuals to refine their practice in accord with an ideal community, that is carried from generation to generation through the passionate commitment of men and women—this trust must be collected together by Dewey into the conversion of authority for the community. Dewey's appeal is that individuals must be religious about overcoming religion.

> Were men and women actuated throughout the length and breadth of human relations with the faith and ardor that have at times marked historic religions the consequences would be incalculable. To achieve this faith and élan is no easy task. But religions have attempted something similar, directed moreover toward a less promising object—the supernatural. It does not become those who hold that faith may move mountains to deny in advance the possibility of its manifestation on the basis of verifiable realities. There already exists, though in a rudimentary form, the capacity to relate social conditions and events to their causes, and the ability will grow with exercise. There is the technical skill with which to initiate a campaign for social health and sanity analogous to that made in behalf of physical public health. Human beings have impulses toward affection, compassion and justice, equality and freedom. It remains to weld all these things together. (LW 9:54–55)

What Dewey finds necessary for this description of the religious function of experience is an ultimate disjunction. The content he establishes for the "religious attitude" is a negative content: it must be all things appearing in human practice, but it *cannot* be religion. The authority Dewey desires for establishing the power of intelligence can be discovered only in this opposition to the supernatural. Dewey is not an aggressive atheist, but he is an aggressive naturalist (read "antisupernaturalist"). Whether this is opposition or positive criticism, Dewey's emphasis comes down to the authority that moves individuals to act in light of ideal ends and the community gathered around these ends. The success of his description of the religious function stands on the claim that the authority of supernatural responsibility cannot move individuals in the same productive ways as the *absence* of that supernatural responsibility. I wonder, however, at his grounds for saying this. What sort of community is he trying to evoke, for clearly he is trying to evoke one. What would a human community completely absent of supernatural expectations mean? ("Ask Zarathustra," a friend recommends. Another time, another place.) We have no way of anticipating this community, and even if we could, how would it not be completely discontinuous with the whole history of human social existence?

I do not think Dewey wants to fashion a new community. I think he wants to evoke a "formerly supernaturally religious" community out of the present one. Like a prophet or a reformer he is calling his community to leave the false god of "God" and serve only the true and living "God" of the democratic community.

> I cannot understand how any realization of the democratic ideal as a vital and moral spiritual ideal in human affairs is possible without surrender of the conception of the basic division to which supernatural Christianity is committed. Whether or no we are, save in some metaphorical sense, all brothers, we are at least all in the same boat traversing the same turbulent ocean. The potential religious significance of this fact is infinite.

But this democratic realization will always remain derivative on the supernatural community since he cannot deny that the urge for the religious attitude comes bound up with it. Dewey confirms that the democratic community will always carry its opposite, supernatural religion, with it. Other insistent naturalisms, like the "death of God" theology, also work the opposite of what they intend, even as militant theisms are most productive of their counters in atheism.[16] Using religion's language to counter its strength, and attempting to emancipate its good from its traditional authority, involves Dewey in a set of problems that exceeds his control. He desires the power supernaturalism extends over the lives of its adherents. He is jealous of that power, and he would be wiser in its use, better able to aim the motive force of the religious attitude toward truly productive ends. Prometheus would be so bold.

Although Dewey claims that he is describing what has always been the "common faith" of mankind, the conclusion of this third essay comes across as a performative exercise. Dewey is attempting to speak this community into existence. John Smith finds a similar point in Dewey's use of the term *nature*. Dewey claims that nature is "all there is," and thus it does not entail a principle of difference. But if there is no difference, Smith says, *nature* is a gratuitous term. Smith's point can be extended to say that Dewey's naturalism is not just an effort to discover a complete description of "what is"; it is a platform for making a criticism.[17] Dewey's naturalism is unclothed in *A Common Faith* as a fundamental critique of supernaturalism. This text is a recapitulation of Dewey's long struggle to explain his dramatic transition from the authority of the supernatural to the authority of democracy. This opposition orients his pragmatism. His willingness to confront this opposition, internal to his thinking, funds his role as America's leading naturalist, and his leadership stands on his ability to cut across boundaries otherwise respected. Dewey throws himself into the balance as the living image of the personal conversion he attempts to encourage in this concluding essay of *A Common Faith:* "Ours is the responsibility of conserving, transmitting, rectifying and expanding the heritage of values we have received. . . . Here are all the elements for a religious faith that shall not be confined to sect, class, or race. Such faith has always been implicitly the common faith of mankind. It remains to make it explicit and militant" (LW 9:58).

The "salvation" of Dewey's pragmatism depends on the success of speaking the democratic community into existence. The religious progression that structures this "common faith" needs a push. Dewey whispers confident words in the ears of his auditors; "finish the good work that was begun in you." If his speech does produce a community it would not have a supernatural origin but a basis in the method of science. The religious attitude emerging from this community, propelling it toward the discovery of deeper and richer associations, affecting the shift of individual wills toward this content as an image of wholeness, would confirm that Dewey's faith in the common faith of mankind is not vanity.

RELIGIOUS OVERCOMING

The common faith Dewey gives us is only possible by individuals over-coming religion. The natural origin of this conversion of the whole person from religion to the scientific choice of authority validates his hope for the evolving democratic community. Without such a conversion, Dewey's project fails descriptively and programmatically. Dewey needs the transition of religion to the religious attitude as a screen to complete his project.

Dewey's confession in *A Common Faith* is an example of a monumental overcoming of tradition by personal discovery, similar to what we have seen in Augustine and Edwards. In each of these cases the individual becomes the moment of significance for the community's transformation. This expectation exposes a peculiar limit to Dewey's pragmatism. How does the individual become held by the community in such a way that transformation is possible between them—the individual transforming the community and the community transforming the individual? Dewey's model suggests that the goal of transformation is establishing the continuity between individual and community, but in practice transformation seems to emerge in the disjunction between these. The individual is necessary to have substantial criticism of the community, and the community exposes the narrowness and the (ir)relevance of the individual. This marks a significant difference between Niebuhr and Dewey. For Niebuhr the question of social progress is twofold, overcoming the sinful rejection of responsibility and countering the force of the communal authority with an equally powerful authority. This is the reason Niebuhr sees the vital role of religion in social progress while Dewey sees the need for the church to lay aside its present method and take up the interests of society.[18]

Niebuhr's insight is a powerful check on Dewey's optimism. While Dewey's conversion to the religious attitude sheds light on the immanent aspects of transformation in both the individual and the community, he cannot fully explain the permanence of the destabilizing forces that produce the disjunction between supernaturalism and trust in the authority of science. Claiming these are both the products of nature is nominalistic, and such nominalism subverts inquiry, just as Peirce says it does. There is more going on in the interaction between religion and the religious than Dewey suggests. The impulse of the person to find religious ground is more than a desire for a formal character of a settled will. There is an urge to discover an appropriate content for the will. Dewey claims that this content is negative—the content of the will most apparent in *A Common Faith* is opposition to the authority of supernatural control. But to be genuinely communal this rejection has to arise within an actual communal shift. This is the most serious challenge to Dewey's description of faith. If the rejection of "the supernatural" for "the religious attitude" is made on the basis of some appearing good, some content, I do not think the "unity of ideal ends" in an imaginatively projected community can sustain the material transition in the community. I agree that the challenge to supernaturalism's hold on communal expectations is an organic occurrence, but I think there is some other content sought in this experience. Dewey's description fails to account for the origin of instability in individual and communal authority. The force within inquiry that resists idealistic claims of comprehensiveness is the realization of an absence of transformation rather than a discrete pursuit of growth. Supernaturalism represents this recognition of the absence of transformation for Dewey, for he often claims that in supernaturalism ideal ends are final and unmoving. Overcoming the absence of transformation is the core of Dewey's faith, and this is where his faith is genuinely a common faith. Dewey's remaining Protestantism is evident in the sense that no community or institution captures the enlivening demand for transformation emerging in individuals. He strives to collect this impulse into his argument for democracy, and in so doing he transforms it from an *absence* to a positive quality, *growth*. But if the growth of the democratic community becomes the *telos* of transformation that is fully realizable in experience, what further transformation would be necessary? Dewey produces an absolute and unquestionable verity that rivals any supernatural belief.[19] But at the risk of repeating the error he criticizes, Dewey seeks to capture the vital engine of religious passion from religion for the democratic community. To accomplish this purpose he must overcome religion, personally and philosophically, and reconstruct the faith of his community.

The confidence in Dewey's analysis that enables him to locate a content that reorients the faith of the community is intoxicating. The evaluation of the practical ends of religion and religious faith are compellingly simple—if there is not a "good" end to religion, what is the good of religion? And the human community is all that can be anticipated as the ground for this good or any good. There are no metaphysical prizes that translate into reasonable ends for everyday living. This is the positive contribution Dewey makes. And locating the necessity of conversion of the individual to this appearing end extends that contribution. There can be no mistaking the commitment necessary for transforming our present experience into a better, richer, more humane experience. It does not happen by accident and it does not happen as a by-product of an orientation toward an abstract realm of rarified existence.

On the other hand, Dewey's religious vision produces precisely what he strives to avoid. In order to co-opt his democratic vision, the breadth of tradition must also be abandoned or, if not abandoned, reclaimed as purely symbolic in just the points that in *our* past have been the most productive of progression toward humanity. Dewey makes his religious faith into a radical disjunction between the philosopher and the common believer that cannot be overcome by qualification. Dewey excises his tradition, and all tradition, from the conception of the religious attitude and the conception of a democratic community. Faith, in Dewey's sense, is not the trust that the truth embedded in our tradition is sufficient for the next challenge. Faith is a kind of power that cannot be justified by observation nor restrained by tradition. Faith means excising one's self from the fabric of continuity of habits for the sake of what is beyond. Dewey seeks ground for a religious work that extends not from a passionate fidelity but from a passion for unfettered power. In this way, the democratic faith Dewey expounds becomes the twin of the abusive religious power he rejects. For Dewey's religious faith to be redeemed, it must be brought back into the tradition from which it emerges. This would truly amount to the religious overcoming Dewey seeks in order to secure the continuation of human progress in the social values that construct a better community.

NOTES

1. Stephen Rockefeller, *John Dewey's Religious Humanism* (Columbia University Press, 1992); Robert J. Roth, *American Religious Philosophy* (Harcourt, Brace and World, 1967).

2. Daniel Rice, *Reinhold Niebuhr and John Dewey: An American Odyssey* (SUNY Press, 1993), 44. Horace Friess gives an account of a talk Dewey gave in 1930 that demonstrates both Dewey's reflection on religion as a mode of

experience and not just an approach to a "common faith." Friess recounts Dewey's interest in the "hymnology, the prayers, the meditations" that move toward pertinencies of specific circumstances rather than the 'eternal verities' of religious dogma. Dewey says, "I would rather like to throw my emphasis tonight on that side of the importance of religion as a channel in which that kind of expression can flourish."

3. Robert Roth, *American Religious Philosophy*, 89.

4. See Bruce Kucklick's *Churchmen and Philosophers: From Jonathan Edwards to John Dewey* (Yale University Press, 1985) for an argument that Dewey never completely leaves the Calvinistic belief in the sovereignty of God or good.

5. Roth, *American Religious Philosophy*, 94.

6. Rice, *Reinhold Niebuhr and John Dewey*, 18–19.

7. Reinhold Niebuhr, *Moral Man and Immoral Society* (Scribners, 1960), 36.

8. Robert Westbrook, *John Dewey and American Democracy* (Cornell University Press, 1991), 426–427.

9. Michael Eldridge, *Transforming Experience: John Dewey's Cultural Instrumentalism* (Vanderbilt University Press, 1997), 23.

10. Eldridge, *Transforming Experience*, 50.

11. Martin Buber, *I and Thou* (Scribners, 1970), 30.

12. Larry A. Hickman, ed., *Reading Dewey: Interpretations for a Postmodern Generation* (Indiana University Press, 1998), 137.

13. James Campbell, *Understanding John Dewey* (Open Court, 1995), 103.

14. See, for instance, Robert Benne's *Quality with Soul* (Eerdmans, 2001) for an example of this description of Dewey from religious faith to a progressively liberal and idealized faith.

15. Richard Bernstein, *John Dewey* (Washington Square Press, 1966), 196.

16. Michael Buckley, *At the Origins of Modern Atheism* (Yale University Press, 1987), 36.

17. John Smith, *Reason and God* (Yale University Press, 1961), 114.

18. Niebuhr, *Moral Man and Immoral Society*, 62: "Religion is always a citadel of hope built on the edge of despair. But the same absolutism which drives them to despair, rejuvenates their hope. In the imagination of the truly religious man the God, who condemns history, will yet redeem history." Dewey states, "The surrender of claims to an exclusive and authoritative position is a *sine qua non* for doing away with the dilemma in which churches now find themselves in respect to their sphere of social action" (LW 9:55).

19. John Milbank, *Theology and Social Theory: Beyond Secular Reason* (Blackwell, 1991).

4

Transforming Obligation
in William James

RELIGIOUS LANGUAGE and ideas course through William James's essays like a rough breeze. James finds vital strength in religion, and almost all of his philosophical reflections incorporate religious themes. He self-consciously affirms his devotion when he says, "Religion is the great interest of my life."[1] A part of his interest is in the unfinished and unanticipated character of religious impulse and meaning. The exigencies of the spirit blow where they might, and they often propel James into saying things that he, or his later followers, might sometimes wish he had left unsaid. But his openness to the influence of spiritual forces, and his demand that the philosophical life pay attention to this influence, separates James from most other philosophers. His philosophical writings often border on affective manipulation as he tries to change, not only what his readers think, but also what they feel. I am sure he writes this way because he feels he has been manipulated in the same manner by the reality of the universe. In the spirit of truth, James knows no better occupation than discovering what sponsors such movement in his character and what the results might be if this prime mover is followed without fear.

Despite James's religious character and my own focus on the meaning of conversion in this book, I turn to James reluctantly. His influence has overwhelmed American Christianity and philosophy. It is hard to stand at a critical distance from James without risking offense to many of our more fondly held beliefs. The ultimate privacy of religious experience, the failure of organized religion to meet the deeper needs of religious people, the pragmatic justification for the freedom of the will, and the need for a radically empirical approach to the problems of reflection are a few of these beliefs for which James is largely responsible. As Stanley Hauerwas observes, "The challenge facing Christians today is that James's world has so thoroughly become 'our' world that we can imagine nothing else."[2] I agree with Hauerwas's observation and would extend it to American philosophy's dependence on naturalism. Many philosophers, and most American philosophers, cannot imagine a philosophy of religion that varies substantially from James. I think this is a problem, because anything that limits imagination often leads to a reduction of genuine inquiry.

James did not intend to become a stumbling block to philosophical or religious inquiry, as Ellen Kappy Suckiel convincingly shows.[3] He wanted to open up the world, not close it down. That his work has become a kind of restraining limit to reflection is largely our fault. We want to believe as James believed. We want to hide in his penumbra without facing the difficult issues ourselves. Nevertheless, I think James must bear his share of the responsibility for the present poor condition of our religious and philosophical reflection on personal transformation. James leads us down a fair path, but I fear he walks away from—and consequently leads us away from—the kinds of discoveries that can better ground our reflection and action.

James writes as an observer of religious value, claiming the distance of an objective observer. With the presentation of these observations, he produces a powerful argument that reforms the way we think about religious obligation and personal transformation. James's reforming intention is evident in *Varieties of Religious Experience* (VRE), particularly in his treatment of conversion. When his survey of religious experience reaches this central Christian tenet—that God's active spirit changes the form and character of human lives—James departs from his purely observational stance and sharply critiques the belief that religious change is dependent on content or ideas apart from the self. His critique is interesting for several reasons, as we shall see. In general terms, it reveals a shift in James's approach—from seeking to *discover* the grounds of religious experience and transformation to seeking to *determine* the ground of personal transformation. Simply put, James wants to mold religious experience in his own way. Sorting out James's resistance to the traditional understanding of conversion will not only clarify part of the ambiguity in his treatment of religion, but it will also enable us to articulate more clearly the dialectic internal to classical American philosophy over ultimate personal change and the extrahuman grounds of such a transformation as conversion.

The plan of the present study is to describe the connection between the obligation James finds in the reflective life and the resultant personal transformation that provides access to the meaning of that obligation.

The relation between obligation and transformation leads James to claim that the development of personal character is a proper aim of philosophical inquiry. I will develop this line of thought by following James's treatment of conversion in *Varieties*. As I show, James uses his analysis of character and personal transformation to separate himself clearly from the traditional doctrine of religious conversion, and particularly from Jonathan Edwards. I conclude with an analysis and critique of James's position against conversion and ask what this means for his work in transforming the obligation to the religious life.

THE OBLIGATION TO TRANSFORMATION

In his early essays, William James shows little interest in pedestrian topics such as the epistemological and metaphysical status of general concepts. Rather, he seeks to understand why men philosophize by exploring the motive behind their reflection. He wants to weigh in on the question of whether or not the universe is a moral game. If it is not, James observes, there is little need for the regretful hand wringing that occupies much of our living and thinking. But if the universe *is* a moral game, then it *does* matter what we do, and why we do it. It was in beginning to sort out the question of the moral universe that James realized there must be a restive condition common to reflective persons. He calls this condition *obligation*. Without some sense of obligation, a prerational form of an "ought," there would be no vital connection between acting and thinking. There would be no demand to be reflective at all.

In the essay "The Moral Philosopher and the Moral Life" James argues that an obligation emerges within the reconciling function of thought. Our primary objective is not to change the world or our selves but to achieve intellectual rest with our selves and the world. The path toward this elusive intellectual peace requires sensitivity to motive forces in action and a willingness to articulate the character of obligation that informs our reflection.

Accounting for this motive force in the reflective life leads James to two speculative conclusions. The first is that "goodness, badness, and obligation must be *realized* somewhere in order to really exist; and the first step in ethical philosophy is to see that no merely inorganic 'nature of things' can realize them" (*Will to Believe* [WTB] 150). A second conclusion is "*that the essence of good is simply to satisfy demand. The demand* may be for anything under the sun" (WTB 153). James's first suggestion here, that no obligation can be real unless it is fully realized in some form, leads to a hypothetical connection between God and morality. Without a supreme obligator, there is no temporal possibility for understanding the drive for strenuous moral living. Interest and excitement in living the good life with vigor must have a tangible ground—this way of life must fulfill a discrete obligation. Idealism will not suffice to explain the vigor of concrete moral action.

James's second speculative conclusion, whatever the good is it must at some point satisfy a demand, gives us the range of his moral thought. On one pole stands the moral philosopher, who is good to the extent that a demand is satisfied. At the opposite pole is whatever originates the obligation, and this origin is good in terms of demanding action continuous with the abilities and affections of reflective persons. The obligation comprises the middle ground of good in humans and the good of the universe. "The philosopher, therefore," James says, "who seeks to know which ideal ought to have supreme weight and which one ought to be subordinated, must trace the *ought* itself to the *de facto* constitution of some existing consciousness, behind which, as one of the data of the universe, he as a purely ethical philosopher is unable to go. This consciousness must make the one ideal right by feeling it to be right, the other wrong by feeling it to be wrong" (WTB 147). James extends the ontological character of this "feeling" a step further when he adds, *"we see not only that without a claim actually made by some concrete person there can be no obligation, but that there is some obligation wherever there is a claim."* Obligation, in other words, is simply a feature of the claim. There is no ground for separation or dialectic. Statements like these seem to suggest that James holds to a kind of moral intuitionism, but his emphasis on "some claim" and "some concrete person" muddies the waters on this point. It is not clear how he could arrive by intuition at the feet of "some concrete person." The problem here is akin to the discontinuity that Charlene Haddock Siegfried indicates in the larger flow of the "Moral Philosopher," where James "takes back this ethics developed in light of our finite temporality" by saying that ethics must wait on metaphysical and theological beliefs to be final.[4]

James lays stress on the character of obligation itself at this point. It has the feel of something objective and external, something *organically authoritative* over the moral philosopher. A moral philosopher is a person who has become aware of this obligation and is thus awakened to the changes in action that follow. Ignoring this obligation reduces one's ability to live as a human being, but living in its observance implies the difficult task of self-judgment.

Self-judgment, however, is not a sufficient response for the moral philosopher. James says, "Obligations can thus exist inside a single thinker's consciousness; and perfect peace can abide with him only so far as he lives according to some casuistic scale which keeps his more imperative goods on top" (WTB 159). Perfect peace may sound a bit fantastic, but I think this is one example of James's tendency to use scriptural phrases to bolster his point. And though, in this example, perfect peace is an extreme point, an elusive and impossible task, such is the focus for persons who try to make their way by piecemeal judgments toward a moral existence. James is leading his reader toward the unsatisfactory limit of the casuistic response. Simply judging between obligations is not enough. Rather, James pushes the reader to recognize moral obligation as a force pressing us beyond the ability to judge between imperative goods, and toward a metaphysical realization of character.

Only this pressure toward a dramatic realization of character explains what James means by an awareness of obligation. That a moral principle is "not made up in advance" means that it has some other ground, something else giving it stability. And James is fascinated with the kind of action undertaken where the immediate good is not apparent. The ability to endure hardship for the sake of a more imperative good is the sign of a moral life. The division *in human character* between persons who respond to this kind of obligation with strenuous action and those who affect an easygoing mood is most distinctive in James:

> The deepest difference, practically, in the moral life of man is the difference between the easy-going and the strenuous mood. When in the easygoing mood the shrinking from present ill is our ruling consideration. The strenuous mood, on the contrary, makes us quite indifferent to present ill, if only the greater ideal be attained. The capacity for the strenuous mood probably lies slumbering in every man, but it has more difficulty in some than in others in waking up. It needs the wilder passions to arouse it, the big fears, loves, and indignations; or else the deeply penetrating appeal of some one of the higher fidelities, like justice, truth, or freedom. . . . When, however, we believe that a God is there, and that he is one of the claimants, the infinite perspective opens out. The scale of the symphony is incalculably prolonged. The more imperative ideals now

begin to speak with an altogether new objectivity and significance, and to utter the penetrating, shattering, tragically challenging note of appeal. . . . The capacity for the strenuous mood lies so deep down among our natural human possibilities that even if there were no metaphysical or traditional grounds for believing in a God, men would postulate one simply as a pretext for living hard, and getting out of the game of existence its keenest possibilities of zest. (WTB 160)

James's rhetorical power here is admirable, especially as he moves seamlessly from human moods to the infinite moral claimant, God. The strenuous mood is the character of a person who responds to the challenging note of moral obligation—whatever the cost, however dark the outlook, the person is aroused to enter the fray. The capacity for living in the "strenuous mood," James argues, lies deep among our natural human capacities. It lies buried within us, but active, seeking manifestation and opening into universal meaning. The reflective life is a part of the impulse to engage the "wilder passions" so as to awaken this character in us. Given our human capacity and the objectivity of compelling ideals, it seems strange to think that anyone would willingly stand on the side of the easygoing life, ignorant and unresponsive to the obligation that yields the keenest possibilities of zest in existence. Strength seems to bubble up from James's description of the moral life, and the positive character of the philosopher rises above the superficial problems and contradictions that haunt intellectual accounts of this life. God does not overcome contradictions, and besides, we can exercise our deepest moral capacity within the ambiguities of the reflective life.[5]

Despite this positive word about the reach of our natural capacities, raising this kind of obligation as the goal of reflection puts James at odds with both philosophy and religion. Responding to a felt obligation means moving philosophy beyond its traditional role as an abstract discipline, and many philosophers will resist making such a move. James, however, points to a guiding sentiment that lies beneath the practice of philosophy, its particular topics, and the facts of experience upon which it must work. If not awakened to the reality of moral obligation, the philosopher stands compromised, an unwise lover of wisdom. The strenuous mood is a direct challenge to philosophy.

James raises a two-headed specter for religion. First, the God religion serves may be a self-created god of easy satisfaction, and not a "God-for-strenuous-living." Second, even if there is no God, people may have good reason to invent one for the sake of living well. Religious traditions may be well rehearsed and useful, and terribly mistaken.

James's critique of philosophical and religious practice remains veiled in the "Moral Philosopher" as he struggles to grasp the buried character of moral reflection and draw it out of the habits and clichés caked around it. He shakes obligation loose from the glozing of idealism and the false face of rationalism. To see this obligation means a spirit of unrest, action without full grasp of consequence, will without belief. Religion is of interest precisely because it sponsors practices that translate an obligation that does not rely on explicit formulation. Philosophy, especially idealism, resists this demand for particular action unsupported by theoretical wires. Philosophy is morally recalcitrant in its dreamy satisfaction with theory divorced from the actual facts of life, comfortable with smooth intellectual formulations that avoid the coarse texture of intellectual unrest in light of an obliging reality. While religion always moves toward praxis, philosophy does not. James sounds a clarion call for philosophers to face this failure of philosophy, and this is the reason he writes philosophical essays rather than sermons. James is an evangelical philosopher for philosophy. He will reproach religion for other errors later.

Let me return for a moment to the ontology lurking in James's account of obligation. This ontology finds its fullest form in later essays where James expands the ground of moral action to a more universal application. In "Pragmatism and Religion," he writes, "The only *real* reason I can think of why anything should ever come is that *someone wishes it to be here*. It is *demanded*,—demanded, it may be, to give relief to no matter how small a fraction of the world's mass."[6] The ontological character of demand is peculiar. The "what is" depends on "what relieves," and further, "what is" can be realized only in the action of persons who are awakened to the reality of "what relieves" that produces the charge to live the strenuous life. Moral life is a transformation of the easygoing life. I think James's point in "Pragmatism and Religion" is that nothing beyond this transformation explains the creative power in the universe, and that obligation is all that is needed to realize fully this creative power. Moral living is equivalent to dwelling in the ontological fabric of the universe.

Few philosophers have utilized the persuasive philosophical essay better than William James. His intuitive sensibility of the philosophical and spiritual condition of his auditors guides him in how far he and they can travel together. This distance is often astounding, as when "Moral

Philosopher and the Moral Life" begins with the claim that there is no ethical philosophy made up in advance. That essay concludes this way:

> "See, I have set before thee this day life and good and death and evil; therefore choose life that thou and thy seed may live"—when this challenge comes to us, it is simply our total character and personal genius that are on trial; and if we invoke any so-called philosophy, our choice and use of that also are but revelations of our personal aptitude or incapacity for moral life. From this unsparing practical ordeal no professor's lectures and no array of books can save us. The solving word, for the learned and the unlearned man alike, lies in the last resort in the dumb willingness and unwillingnesses of their interior characters, and nowhere else. It is not in heaven, neither is it beyond the sea; but the word is very nigh unto thee, in thy mouth and in thy heart, that thou mayest do it. (WTB 162)

These words build on Paul's exhortation in Romans 10:5–8, but James inserts his own meaning in the frame of Moses' and Paul's exhortation. In place of the Law, which Moses warns is not beyond the sea but in the mouth and the heart, James inserts the willingnesses and unwillingnesses of the interior character. And James stops his quotation of St. Paul short of verses 9 and 10, where the apostle supplies his understanding of the content in question here: "That is the word of faith which we preach; because if you confess with your lips that Jesus is Lord and believe in your heart that God raised him from the dead, you will be saved. For man believes with his heart and is so justified, and he confesses with his lips and so is saved." This is the word of faith that Paul claims is "nigh unto thee," on our lips and in our hearts. The demand for a transformation of character, a change in our willingness to cleave to the moral life, is equivalent to the persistence and power of the Law for Moses and the confession of Jesus for Paul. James is not subtle in his use of this text. Ultimate meaning, he exhorts his readers, is available in the way one chooses to live. The transformation of one's character is all that can be called to witness for the appropriation of ultimate meaning, and the ability to choose is all the ground one needs to make such an appropriation.

CHARACTER AND PHILOSOPHY

Philosophy does not comprise neutral ground for James. Philosophy is instead an expression of a person's character and temperament. Rather than establish sufficient distance to enable a person to evaluate analytic claims critically, philosophy is a task that reveals and solidifies one's character. What is at stake in philosophical reflection is the apocalypse, the unveiling, of the philosopher. Confession, especially by philosophers, is a difficult task. Pragmatism's general insistence on confessional philosophy is one reason I think logical positivism found a fertile field among American intellectuals in the middle of the last century. Rather than endure the discomfort of confessional reflection required by thinkers like James, philosophers found it easier to ask what it is like to be a bat.

James, however, meets the soulful questions of confessional discourse with an ease that is not just elegant, but also inspiring. His demand that philosophers enter confessional waters requires James to offer his own character as the potential result of such difficult work. "By their fruits," he says repeatedly, "shall you know them." I think the realization of the importance of his own life to his philosophical project leads James to shift from the exuberance of discovery in his earlier essays to more of a defensive character in some of his later writings. James drifts from an attitude of provoking a desire for a better self to defending the claim that a better self is the *source* of the obligation to the moral life. This is a crucial shift since it alters the ground from which he will argue that his or any person's character is sufficient.

The demand for a sufficiency of character appears throughout James's work. This sufficiency requires openness to satisfying as many demands as possible. A temperament of openness places the person in the mainstream of the moral current of the universe. It is only against this current that we can discover our willingness or unwillingness to live the strenuous life. Yet, in James's later essays, the search for salvation through action leads to the claim that the person acting is the salvation, not only of himself or herself, but of the world. James writes in "Pragmatism and Religion,"

> Every such ideal realized will be one moment in the world's salvation. But these particular ideals are not bare abstract possibilities. They are grounded, they are live possibilities, for we are their live champions and pledges, and if the complementary conditions come and add themselves, our ideals will become actual things. What now are the complimentary conditions? They are first such a mixture of things as will in the fullness of time give us the chance, a gap that we can spring into, and, finally, *our act*.[7]

All that can be required of us, James asserts, is what is possible in action. If an ideal cannot be discovered within the active capacity and freedom of the person, then it is not a true potential or ideal. The impossibility of realization is one reason James rejects the imitation of Christ as a proper content for religious practice. If complete Christ-likeness is impossible for mortal sinners, then it cannot serve as the kind of ideal to which we are truly drawn to act.

Clearly, James thinks the reflective life leads to this place where action secures those ideals that are the salvation of the world. He is also aware that there is a temperament behind this activity that requires dedication to ideal action. Such a temperament is realized only through an interaction with the prospective meaning of this life. It cannot be generated by intellectual castle-building or wishful thinking. The philosopher either responds to this reality or remains insensible to it. What kind of transformation is it that makes engagement in the kind of action James here suggests possible, where strenuous living reaches beyond the immediate occasion and *becomes* the good of the universe? Where does this conviction originate, and what warrants it? How does this ideal form of human action take shape in a person's character and philosophy?

The origin of James's dependence on human transformation, it would seem, lies more in existential than metaphysical confidence, though I do not think these can ever be completely separated. To raise questions about the function of transformation in James's philosophy, as I am doing here, means asking where this task begins for him. We must ask what inspires his willingness not only to engage the demand for transformation, but also to approach transformation as an acceptable content for reflection. What does the transformation he describes seek to overcome?

John McDermott calls attention to an event in James's youth that sheds light on his interest in a transformation of character. In what we now know is an autobiographical account of a "vastation," an experience of emptiness, James writes,

> [T]here fell upon me without any warning, just as if it had come out of the darkness, a horrible fear of my own existence. Simultaneously there arose in my mind the image of an epileptic patient who I had seen in the asylum. A black-haired youth with greenish skin, entirely idiotic, who used to sit all day on one of the benches, or rather shelves against the wall, with his knees drawn up against his chin, and his coarse gray undershirt, which was his only garment drawn over them inclosing his entire figure. He sat there like a sort of sculptured Egyptian cat or Peruvian mummy, moving nothing but his black eyes and looking absolutely non-human. This image and my fear entered into a species of combination with each

other. *That shape am I,* I felt, potentially. Nothing that I possess can defend me against that fate, if the hour for it should strike me as it struck for him . . . It gradually faded, but for months I was unable to go out into the dark alone. . . . I have always thought that this experience of melancholia of mine had a religious bearing. . . . I mean that the fear was so invasive and powerful that if I had not clung to scripture-texts like "The eternal God is my refuge," etc., "Come unto me, all ye that labor and are heavy-laden," etc., "I am the resurrection and the life," etc., I think I should have grown really insane.[8]

This episode is followed by a journal entry in 1870 that McDermott claims is especially important for James's life and thought. James writes,

I think that yesterday was a crisis in my life. I finished the first part of Renouvier's second "Essais" and see no reason why his definition of Free Will—"the sustaining of a thought *because I choose to* when I might have other thoughts"—need not be the definition of an illusion. At any rate, I will assume for the present—until next year—that it is no illusion. My first act of free will shall be to believe in free will. . . . I will go a step further with my will, not only act with it, but believe as well; believe in my individual reality and creative power. My belief, to be sure, can't be optimistic—but I will posit life (the real, the good) in the self-governing resistance of the ego to the world.[9]

These episodes are, as McDermott notes, instructive for understanding James's development as a thinker. The intellectual problem of the freedom of will is secondary to the moral question of choice, and confirming this priority is approached as a task of faith. James's interest in religion emerges, I think, in the connection of his struggle with depression and the scriptural phrases and ideas that helped him arrive at the platform of willful self-direction he discovers.

What I find most interesting about these accounts is James's awareness of his own crisis of transformation. First, he is aware that he is susceptible to a negative transformation, into a form like the asylum patient. Without a positive content or focus, James feared becoming like that—withdrawn, unable to communicate, unable to act, unable to *appear* human. In the journal entry, however, James moves completely beyond the framework of despair, deliberately latching on to the prospective significance of his own free action. The possibility and potential of this act overwhelms, for the time, his intellectual doubts about the freedom of the will. In respect to the first occasion above, this prospective attitude is possible in light of a God who claims, "I am the resurrection and the life." James's description of religious experience as focusing on dependence obviously connects here. Moreover, his philosophical modus operandi of combining religious warrant and prospective intellectual ground has a clear antecedent in his own experience of transformation.

I think the energy that drives James to write *Varieties of Religious Experience* emerges from this personal ground of his own character development. Religion plays a part in James's encounter both with his despair about his "shape," and the reality of his freedom to mold that "shape." The role religious hope sometimes played in his life, and the role it ought to play in the general hope of human transformation and strenuous living, is at stake in *Varieties*. For this reason, I find *Varieties* much less a species of observation than a prolonged persuasive essay. Or, as Ralph Barton Perry puts is, *Varieties* is James's *justification* of religion. Perry connects this justification with James's recollection of his "father's cry" that religion is real, and that "the thing is to 'voice' it so that others shall hear."[10] *Varieties* may, in fact, be James's best sermon.

Given this relation between his own transformation and his religious thought, I find it fascinating that James's philosophy of transformation does not rely on the language or tradition of a community. His careful avoidance of borrowed language means that philosophy has to speak a double word. Philosophy is pressed into service as the language and context for the transformation to the strenuous life, yet it also continues to work in its accepted role as a tool for critical evaluation. Sometimes the priority of raising the banner of strenuous character overwhelms the task of philosophical critique. But James must defend the ambiguity of the role of philosophical argument in order to secure his larger project. Defending this position, I think, propels James to claim that philosophy cannot produce any final evaluative judgment, either of a person's character or of the particular meaning of an idea. His resistance to finality spreads over both the sufficiency to interpret the many "demands" people live under and the "clash of temperaments" that describes philosophical debate. Philosophers neither can nor should seek resolution in a final, single, or ultimately determinative meaning.

James's defense of his peculiar philosophical manner and his emphasis on transformation set the stage for his dramatic encounter with religious experience and Christianity. Any philosophy that has finality as its origin or *telos* receives explicit repudiation. Any religious system that locates the content for transformation in a hard and fast way, either in historic truth-claims or explicit moral demands, assaults James's "individual reality and creative power." His resistance is honest. His transformation arises within himself and by his own will; any suggestion that it happened otherwise would compromise *his* ground and *his* character. But extending this position beyond himself philosophically means that no particular con-clusion to life, to transformation, or to moral obligation can stand in the universe.

Fleshing out this philosophy of freedom and moral openness demands a kind of rebirth for James. Born into the world where finality and per-manence are most often the hallmarks of the good, James enters a new world that is largely unacknowledged by the religion and philosophy of his culture. In his world, finality is equivalent to death. But his rebirth is apparent only in his confidence that he can find a way through the many pitfalls of finality and despair in the reflective life, traversing a path that can be navigated only by careful articulation and persuasion. Religious experience represents a part of human life with a high concentration of pitfalls, so James is compelled to confirm his transformation by plowing through the varieties of religious experience.

Despite his reservations about final claims and orthodox Christian beliefs, James is attracted to the character of primitive Christianity. The willingness of early Christians to act on truths that demand absolute and reckless commitment without the possibility of intellectual certainty attracts him. He wants to share in a ground that gives him hope his action is not in vain. Only in a state of action-sans-certainty can human life be fully open to creative power and all its possibilities. James's many arguments for the value of religious meaning are based on the expecta-tion that more creative power for action is available within such a world than in a world that rejects religious meaning. Suckiel points to the fol-lowing passage from *Varieties* that bears out this ethical point: "If radically followed, [the precept love your enemies] would involve such a breach with our instinctive springs of action as a whole . . . that a critical point would be practically passed, and we should be born into another king-dom of being."[11] This expectation for creative action *via* the religious worldview is so central to James's philosophical position that it amazes me that a philosopher such as Richard Rorty can miss the import of James's religious arguments so badly.[12] On the other hand, despite the positive value for creative action we find in James's account of religious experience, his own critique of conversion in *Varieties of Religious Experience* undermines the ground of personal transformation that he tries so hard to secure philosophically.

CONVERSION IN *VARIETIES OF RELIGIOUS EXPERIENCE*

James's charged religious moralism and his desire for an interaction with a compelling, life-transforming obligation would seem to be compatible with religious conversion. James's use of the biblical imagery in "setting before you this day" the alternatives of life and death supports this view. But in chapters 9 and 10 of *Varieties of Religious Experience,* James argues that conversion is *not* the ground for the creative transformation that he seeks.[13] Rather, he argues that religious conversion, as an instantaneous event revealing a new center of the person in a dramatic and unanticipated way, is incoherent, unnecessary, and dangerous. It is incoherent because no "distinguishing mark" separates converted persons from the unconverted. It is unnecessary because natural transformation produces the same results. And it is dangerous because diabolical ideas may, in fact, be imported into such instantaneous transformations. The religious view does not, nay *cannot,* either depend on or benefit from a conversion event.

This argument represents a significant shift in James's account of religious experience. His warm appreciation of religious experience for its unique value in responding to "objective ends that call for energy, even though that energy brings personal loss and pain" (VRE 45) changes dramatically. Instead of arguing for the power and possible significance of an event like a conversion experience, he focuses on what is potentially wrong with it. I think something about conversion worries James, perhaps because it undermines his own account of the transformation necessary for the religiously powered moral life. He aims to set aside this eminently practical aspect of religious experience and reduce its hold on reflective minds by capitalizing on the conversion anxiety in his readers.

James's treatment of conversion moves in three ways. First, he reduces conversion to a defensive position. In the first paragraph of chapter 9 he states that, in general, conversion signifies the process whereby "a self hitherto divided, and consciously wrong, inferior and unhappy becomes unified and consciously right, superior and happy . . . whether or not we believe a direct divine operation is needed to bring such a moral change about" (VRE 189). Later in the chapter he recognizes "man's liability to sudden and complete conversion" as one of our more "curious peculiarities," and then asks, "What, now, must we ourselves think of this question? Is instantaneous conversion a miracle in which God is present as he is present in no change of the heart less strikingly abrupt?" (VRE 230). The posture here is more instructive than the words. From the outset James involves his readers in evaluating conversion from some ground beyond the description of its occurrence or the ground it claims for itself. James introduces a division between conversion and the divine, and his examination turns on exploiting this separation.

Second, James critically examines several experiential characteristics of conversion based on the presumption that these effects are all that can be said about conversion. He draws his data from personal experience and the accounts of such representative thinkers as St. Paul, Martin Luther, and Jonathan Edwards. Edwards appears as the authority most closely identified with the suspicious doctrine of conversion. James's attachment to Edwards is significant because they have very different conceptions of conversion. There is something of a battle of wills or a clash of temperaments going on in these chapters, and it is to James's credit that he selects a strong opponent. Recall that Edwards says no genuine conversion is possible without God's immediate presence, and that if God were present to a person it would affect a complete reorientation of the person's affections, of all their ideas and all their desires. The rhetorical value of a critical appropriation of Edwards into James's psychological account of religious experience would be dramatic. In the heat of battle, however, I think James either seriously mistakes or intentionally misrepresents Edwards's understanding of conversion. He does so in part, I think, in order to avoid confronting some of the deeper issues that are at stake here. We will take up this examination in a moment.

The third movement within James's argument builds from the opposition that grows between him and Edwards. James argues that the good desired in conversion can be explained better as a natural than a supernatural transformation, and that the expectation of a sudden or momentary change of character undermines the prospects for creative transformation. James plies the positive side of this argument as well, suggesting that redeeming the "fruits of evangelicism" (VRE 239) requires a different kind of distinction between people than the bifurcation of "converted" and "unconverted." Such an abrupt distinction is too pedestrian to work as a satisfactory account of religious transformation that accesses the higher and lower limits of a person (VRE 230). Such criticism of sudden or momentary conversion that separates souls into two distinct categories carries for many later American religious thinkers, including the superbly articulate account in H. Richard Niebuhr's *Christ and Culture*.[14]

Part of my aim here is to show the seriousness with which James addresses conversion. He alone among American philosophers gives the topic careful consideration. But I also want to demonstrate the effectiveness of the argument James makes against conversion. James is in such complete control of his text that his rejection of conversion is not an unintended by-product of his larger religious view or a rhetorical overstatement. Conversion pushes James's philosophy beyond its limit. Uncovering the basis for his resistance to conversion will enable us to see a different side to his account of obligation and personal transformation.

CONVERSION ON THE DEFENSIVE

James's suspicions about conversion are warranted. It would be absurd to accept uncritically an event where "religious aims form the habitual center of [a person's] energy" (VRE 196). Adding the conception of *divine* influence to such an event raises further questions that must be answered. James's focus on conversion is good; his suspicions are justified. But the facts are that the curious notion of conversion is a central tenet of Christian doctrine. It is not a peculiarly American or evangelical invention. Christianity is built on the foundation that interaction with divine power remarkably changes a person into a "new creature."[15] Conversion is not a tangent of theology but the very heart of the Christian tradition, as Karen Armstrong points out in her work on Islam.[16] Conversion is Christian territory. James knows this. My unhappiness with James is not that he examines conversion critically, but that he does not examine it critically enough. His program limits inquiry into conversion, and thus limits inquiry into the obligation that stands behind religious experience.

James creates the rhetorical space for his argument against conversion by asking his auditors at one point to wait for his assessment of the divine aspect of conversion until he has made some "psychological remarks" (VRE 230). Holding the divine aspect of conversion in abeyance allows James to lay out another frame for the change of disposition toward religious life. This frame of expansion includes "the Subject's range of life," and "a new sphere of power" (VRE 48).

This psychological inquiry hides a critical strategy, though; it is part of a tactic of holding tough questions in abeyance that begins early in the book. James is not simply offering an objective description of religious experience and conversion, that is, using personal narratives on the one hand and psychological terms on the other. He is bringing religion and conversion to a critical philosophical test. "If the *fruits for life* of the state of conversion are good," he says bluntly, "we ought to idealize and venerate it, even though it be a piece of natural psychology; if not, *we ought to make short work with it, no matter what supernatural being may have infused it*" (VRE 237, my emphasis). James introduces the prospect that conversion may not yield good results for human life, effectively shifting the ground under conversion. Its position seems precarious. By suggesting that we "make short work of it," I take him to mean that if conversion is not in some way demonstrably *good for us*, we ought reject it and eliminate it from our conception of *good* religious experience. The burden of proof is therefore placed on the side of those who claim that conversion is good; they must show that it is good for life, and also that it does not warrant suspicion. James has sealed off the argument that conversion is good *because* of its divine origin, having narrowed the description of "religion" and "good" to effects obviously apparent in the active life of the subject. Thus, he demands from conversion an answer he knows it cannot give.

Examining religious experience in this way represents a remarkable shift away from James's willingness to embrace the infinite perspective of moral obligation that comes with an awareness that "God is there" in "The Moral Philosopher." It reveals an inconsistency in James's thinking that needs sorting out. Why does James find himself in such opposition here? The reason for this opposition is more evident when we consider his interaction with Jonathan Edwards.

EDWARDS'S *AFFECTIONS* IN *VARIETIES OF RELIGIOUS EXPERIENCE*

Jonathan Edwards's *Religious Affections* and William James's *Varieties of Religious Experience* are the two most significant books in American religious thought. Edwards and James both seek the reality behind religious experience, but they reach conflicting conclusions. Edwards discovers the rules or patterns in experience that enable individuals to judge whether their affections have been graciously (divinely) changed, since if God desires such a change in us God will also enable us to know it. Human transformation is completed by divine influence and known by discovering this divine influence in our affections, our "lively actings of the will or inclination" (*Religious Affections* [RA 98]). James arrives at a quite different conclusion. What is most good for human life is good whether there is a divine influence behind it or not. James argues that if religion is good for life, then all of its aspects should be accounted good, including claims of divine influence. Conversion is a problem, however, because it testifies to a direct divine influence on the individual's life, and this dependence on the divine moves the achievement of the religious life out of the range of human power or philosophical understanding. This dependence on divine power, taken as a negative limit, is the aspect of conversion that James finds most unfruitful for life.

Although James and Edwards are clearly at odds, James refers to the *Religious Affections* several times, primarily as he concludes his own remarks on conversion. I think James plays on Edwards's authority by casting his own psychological formulation over Edwards, subtly leading the reader toward the claim that there are more important tasks than establishing the divine ground of transformation. If an explicit philosophical incompatibility between James's description of religious experience and orthodox Christian belief arises, it will appear in regard to conversion.[17] But James wants to avoid a showdown between himself and orthodox theologians like Edwards, if this is possible. To avoid this fight James must persuade his readers that they can be Christian and religious—even more religious—without conversion.

James uses Edwards in the introductory lecture of *Varieties* to support his basic premise that effects in life are the only suitable grounds for assessing the value of religious character. He attributes this passage to the *Religious Affections,* though he does not give the reference for any of his uses of this book. In forming a judgment of *ourselves,* Edwards says (according to James), we should use the same evidence that God uses: "The degree in which our experience is productive of practice shows the degree in which our experience is spiritual and divine" (VRE 20). James sets this up by attributing to Edwards the idea that "the roots of a man's virtue are inaccessible to us. No appearances whatever are infallible proofs of grace" (VRE 20). Edwards would, in fact, agree with this, because any final judgment is God's business alone. But that is not the force of the point James is trying to make. James implies that searching after "the roots of religious virtue" is a problem because these roots cannot be known, and they actually do not make a difference when our focus is on the quality of our practice; at best, they are a distraction. James lobs this problem in Edwards's direction. For Edwards, though, determining the roots of one's affections is both challenging and necessary, since without this inquiry we will not know whether the truth of our condition is based on God or self-deception.

James again cites Edwards in the discussion of the form of conversion as a matter of social suggestion. In a footnote (VRE 200), he records a passage where Edwards notes that the pattern of conversion is clearly influenced by suggestions from the social practice of religion. James takes this as confirmation that the form of conversion has more to do with following cultural expectations than finding divine roots. But Edwards's point in the text is very different. In fact, this passage is from Part II of the *Affections,* where Edwards is giving an account of what *are not* signs of truly gracious affections. Following steps or conventions gives us no ground for considering our hearts to be genuinely affected by God, since even Satan can reproduce steps in our experience. What Satan cannot do is reproduce the content of the gospel in such a way as to change souls. This is the unequivocal sign of God's grace. Again, then, James draws on Edwards's authority, but their points do not lie together.

In both of these instances, it would take a reader familiar with the *Religious Affections* to see the depth of philosophical separation between Edwards and James. This separation becomes much more apparent in the culminating instances of James's use of the *Religious Affections* and his use of David Brainerd. *The Life of David Brainerd,* a narrative of the life and service of the missionary to the Delaware Indians, has a history of its own. David Brainerd was a friend and admirer of Edwards. After his dismissal from Yale, Brainerd stayed with Edwards before he began his mission work. Brainerd returned to Edwards's home after his missionary tour, deathly ill, recounting his journey and delivering over his journal. Edwards's daughter Jerusha nursed Brainerd as he died, then followed him in death a few months later. Their graves are side by side in recognition of their deep spiritual communion.

Edwards edited Brainerd's journal, added an introduction, and gave it the title *The Life of David Brainerd.* The popularity and influence of this book exceeded all of Edwards's other writings both domestically and abroad. *The Life of David Brainerd* is regularly cited as the inspiration for the modern missionary movement, with Brainerd's example becoming the acme of personal piety and self-sacrifice for the cause of Christ. Joseph Conforti quotes John Wesley, who edited and distributed his own version of this book, as saying: "Let every preacher read carefully over *The Life of David Brainerd*. . . . Let us be followers of him, as he was of Christ, in absolute self-devotion, in total deadness to the world, and in fervent love to God and man."[18] Brainerd was not only Edwards's ideal saint, but he was also canonized as the model of vital piety and Christian service for most of the nineteenth century.

James quotes from David Brainerd's narrative at the end of chapter 9 before moving into his critical analysis of conversion. In the passage quoted, Brainerd describes his resistance to the persuasion of Christ, his inability to affect the change he desired by his own will, and his ultimate yielding to God: "I was attempting to pray; but found no heart to engage in that or any other duty. . . . I thought God had quite left me. . . . Then as I was walking in a thick grove, unspeakable glory seemed to open to the apprehension of my soul. I do not mean any external brightness, nor any imagination of a body of light, but it was a new inward apprehension or view that I had of God" (VRE 213). James uses Brainerd's narrative to describe the condition of emotional exhaustion that often attends conversion. In such cases the "exhaustion of the lower and the entrance of the higher emotion" is simultaneous, James says (VRE 214), and this reveals the subconscious ripening of the one affection and the exhaustion of the other. The pneumatic language of this exchange of emotional states is the subtext for James's chapter on conversion, and for this reason James does not reflect on Brainerd's claim of a "new inward apprehension of God"; he only notes that Brainerd moved from exhaustion to a glorified peace. This emphasis on Brainerd's emotional state, while discounting the content connected with the emotional state, parallels James's direct response to Edwards.

James's emphasis on Brainerd and the emotional state of exhaustion are certainly strategic in this argument about conversion. The psychological description of Brainerd's conversion as the result of exhaustion and being overwhelmed in weakness by a "higher activity" is a direct challenge to Edwards. James's suggestion is that Brainerd's state of exhaustion and loss of control are determinative for the likes of Edwards and other advocates of conversion. Conversion and critical philosophical reflection must therefore be incompatible. Brainerd, as Edwards's most noted disciple and exemplar, makes the path of conversion appear hyperbolic. The close association between Brainerd and Edwards, which would have been very clear to James's auditors in Scotland and at home, sets up James's explicit conflict with Edwards.

James closely aligns Edwards with this depiction of conversion as dubious and dangerous. Reliance on social suggestion, the common feature of psychological exhaustion, the strong desire for safety and the instantaneous effect of this change—all these ideas circulate around Edwards. James praises the religious power of the conversion experience, and he calls Brainerd an original saint, since there is no doubting his presence and power in the story of American Christianity. James then glosses the Puritan thinker Henry Alleine and Edwards together, writing, "More-over the sense of renovation, safety, cleanness, rightness, can be so marvelous and jubilant as well to warrant one's belief in a radically new substantial nature" (VRE 228). Notice that into this sentence James slips the warrant that a "new substantial nature" is a conclusion drawn from the quality of the marvelous sense of safety and jubilation, not from the content of intellectual, scriptural, or philosophical descriptions. He quotes from Edwards's *Religious Affections* to support this connection between a "new substantial nature" and certain gathered effects. James quotes at length from the *Religious Affections:*

> Those gracious influences which are the effects of the Spirit of God are altogether supernatural—are quite different from anything that unregenerate men experience. They are what no improvement, or composition of natural qualifications or principles will ever produce; because they not only differ from what is natural, and from everything that natural men experience in degree and circumstances, but also in kind and are of a nature far more excellent. From hence it follows, that in gracious affections there are also new perceptions and sensations entirely different in their nature and kind from anything experienced by the same saints before they were sanctified. (VRE 228–229)

The new perceptions mentioned here seem to correspond to the ideas that appear on the ragged edge of consciousness, as James describes it. These appearing ideas become the ground for claiming divine significance due to the overwhelming pressure the subject feels in relation to them. In this way, the "supernatural" is an addition to these perceptions. James continues quoting from the *Affections* concerning the bifurcation of a person's experience into one of two states: life without grace, and life with it.

> As those who are saved are successively in two extremely different states of justification and blessedness—and as God, in the salvation of men, deals with them as rational and intelligent creatures, it appears agreeable to this wisdom that those who are saved should be made sensible of their Being, in those two different states. (VRE 229)

Edwards's statements seem to cohere very nicely with James's theory. Based on the experience of a dramatic shift in perceptions and sensations a person is able to claim the presence of divine influence. And this divine influence is extended to mean a complete sundering of the old man from the new—the sinful man from the grace-filled man. These additions to the experience of transformation are in view when James says,

> What, now, must we ourselves think of this question? Is an instantaneous conversion a miracle in which God is present as he is present in no change of heart less strikingly abrupt? Are there two classes of human beings, even among the apparently regenerate, of which the one class really partakes of Christ's nature while the other merely seems to do so? Or, on the contrary, may the whole phenomenon of regeneration, even in these startling instantaneous examples, possibly be a strictly natural process, divine in fruits, of course, but in the one case more and in another less so, and neither more nor less divine in its mere causation and mechanism than any other process, high or low of man's interior life? (VRE 230)

James retraces the lines of Edwards's inference. From the claim of divine nature, we can regress to the experience of dramatic change without losing any descriptive power. Edwards's suggestion that two discrete states of the person would clearly appear is treated more condescendingly. Are there really two classes, James asks, two utterly separate parts of humankind with no continuity between their moral existences? What fruits could support such a claim? Are the differences in the active lives of such people so stark that a difference in *divine status* can be claimed? If the goal of religious life is good fruit, the good fruit is all that matters, not an obscure and problematic division between converted and nonconverted. No such distinction is possible, James says, and the issues of divine ground, instantaneous change, and a unique and comprehensive alteration of character are unnecessary additions to the natural process of change and growth.

This claim rests on James's conviction that responding religiously to moral obligation does not include such a once-and-for-all change, or the knowledge of such a once-for-all change. James puts it this way:

> Were it true that a suddenly converted man as such is, as Edwards says, of an entirely different kind form a natural man, partaking as he does directly of Christ's substance, there surely ought to be some exquisite class-mark, some distinctive radiance attaching even to the lowest specimen of this genus, to which no one of us could remain insensible, and which so far as it went, would prove him more excellent than ever the most highly gifted among mere natural men. But notoriously there is no such radiance. Converted men as a class are indistinguishable from natural men; some natural men even excel some converted men in their fruits; and no one ignorant of doctrinal theology could guess by mere everyday inspection of the "accidents" of the two groups of persons before him, that their substance differed as much as divine differs from human substance. (VRE 238)

One wonders what kind of class mark James would accept even if Edwards could describe it. My guess is that there would never be a "distinctive radiance" of which no one could be insensible, so this criticism is disingenuous. Everyone will fail to meet a standard that no one, by definition, can meet, but very little is gained by pointing this out. I think James's remark here hides a deeper purpose. At every critical juncture James reinforces the centrality of fruits in forming our religious self-conception, but he has cleverly transformed the expectation of these fruits into philosophical terms of stability and freedom instead of the "fruits in keeping with repentance" that grounds this biblical phrase. These are the fruits by which Jesus claims we can discriminate false teachers from true, not those that attest to our freedom or our action.

James's remark about a radiance that cannot be found is a further critique of Edwards's claim that believers are asymmetrically dependent on divine content in their understanding of conversion. Since we can identify fruits, and since we can manifest them or not by our willingness to make them our "center of energy," James argues that we are not dependent on a tradition, scripture, or divinely revealed content in order to have the good of religious experience. This conflicts somewhat with James's earlier depiction of religion as awareness of our dependence. What James is doing here—especially in light of what he has to say on conversion—is redefining religious dependence. "For when all is said and done," James says, "we are in the end absolutely dependent on the universe; and into sacrifices and surrenders of some sort, deliberately looked at and accepted, we are drawn and pressed as into our only permanent positions of repose" (VRE 51). This dependence is not without deliberation, even in this high prose, and therefore obligation in moral and religious life falls more on the side of "choose this day" than "See, I set before you life and death."

I think James has to "make short work" of conversion in this way because the very notion of conversion exposes a problem in his understanding of obligation. He recognizes the abrupt character of moral and religious ideas and their emotional influence. Yet, he also wants to make room for Emersonian religion, the religion of the healthy-minded. If Brainerd is Edwards's ideal saint, Emerson is James's, despite the fact that James is clearly a sick soul himself. After all, he did require a year to recover his emotional equilibrium before he could write *Varieties of Religious Experience,* Josiah Royce graciously taking his place in Edinburgh during his absence. James wants to secure the healthy-minded passage through life even if he is not constitutionally able to live it. He longs for that stability that would anchor each moment of volition; "whereas the merely moralistic spurning takes an effort of volition the Christian spurning is the result of an excitement of a higher kind of emotion, in the presence of which no exertion of volition is required" (VRE 46). James seems to move between affirming and rejecting this kind of life. The stability of a converted character attracts him; the finality of a converted character repels him. He is clear that "[religion] ought to mean nothing short of this new reach of freedom for us. With the struggle over, the keynote of the universe sounding in our ears, and everlasting possession spread before our eyes" (VRE 48). "So with the conversion experience," he concludes, "that it should for even a short time show a human being what the high-water mark of his spiritual capacity is, this is what constitutes its importance which backsliding cannot diminish, although persistence might increase it" (VRE 257). James wants the place of the converted, but without the content of a tradition to limit or define him or his choice.

Oddly, Edwards agrees with James. It is true that there can be no single emotional center for the many religious or converted souls. Such a center would set up opposition between the one and the many, and also between the person and himself or herself. Nor does Edwards seek a limiting content in conversion, but rather an access to a "new world of knowledge." This is why, in opposition to James, Edwards rejects "new perceptions and sensations" as the proper ground of conversion. Rather, he claims that a different discovery is made. Let me return to the passage from the *Affections* James quoted earlier. Where James cites Edwards pointing to "new perceptions and sensations," Edwards's unabridged text reads, "through the saving influences of the Spirit of God, there is a new inward *perception* or *sensation* of their minds, entirely different in its nature and kind from any thing that ever their minds were the subjects of before they were sanctified." Edwards's focus is the content that appears in the mind, the person's perception of himself or herself. To continue, Edwards says that what appears in the mind is "what some metaphysicians call a new *simple idea*" (RA 205). These words do not appear in the text James apparently used for *Varieties,* which is an emended and abridged version produced as a volume of the *Evangelical Family Library.*[19] The "new center" of the person cannot be a combination of any naturally occurring ideas, but can only distinguish the mind as being aware of a completely new content—which is discovered *in* the mind, *in* its products, *in* the person's affections.

Edwards prefers to call this a discovery of a new foundation in the soul. This foundation is not a philosophical accomplishment or a product of the mind, but the creation in the heart and mind of the individual of a new kind of reflective order. The new ideas we have are not miraculous or divine, but the new idea we have of ourselves is. James found the right passage but did not have the right text. Still, from a more thorough reading of the text he did have, James could have found this statement:

> What a spiritual conviction is, we may ascertain from what has been said already of spiritual knowledge. Conviction arises from the illumination of the understanding. . . . Hence it follows that a spiritual conviction of the truth of the gospel is such a conviction as arises from a spiritual view or conception of the Gospel. And this is also evident from the Scriptures, which often represent a saving belief of the reality and divinity of the things exhibited in the Gospel, as springing from the enlightening of the mind by the Holy Spirit, so as to give us a right conception of those things. (EFL 169)

In this passage and many others, Edwards connects the illumination of the mind with the discovery of the truth of the Gospel concerning Jesus Christ. As I have said in other places, the dual character of the self and the content of the Gospel are closely related for Edwards. The discovery of the "simple idea" in the Gospel parallels the discovery of the new foundation in the soul. But this kind of asymmetrical dependence on the Gospel for religious discovery is antithetical to James's account of conversion and his account of religious experience.

James won the battle for conversion, at least in the court of common appeal. But I think he lost more in this battle than he gained. His understanding of obligation undergoes changes in several ways in order to negotiate the waters of conversion, and these changes reveal some of the philosophical weaknesses of his account of moral living and religious experience. These weaknesses, though, point us in the direction of some further transformations necessary for understanding obligation.

Transforming Obligation

James reminds me of the sort of person who likes to preach but cannot stand to listen to a sermon by someone else. He brings his readers to the point of realizing their choice about which world they will occupy. All of his essays are persuasive; he wants to move the reader to his position. This is what makes him an excellent philosopher—his arguments are never useless icons, they are working thoughts. They aim to have an effect.

The effect James has on me when I read this text is that I am aware of his transference of religious expectation from the world to the individual. Whatever is religious in the universe is for the well-being of individuals, for James himself as a matter of fact. When I read *Varieties*, I am most struck by the idea of "what the universe does, or should do, for me." I think this is the reason James's treatment of conversion rubs me the wrong way. It is all about the subject. If our deepest religious experiences are idiosyncratic, if they do not put us into commerce with a community, the critics of religion are right to condemn them, as Patrick Dooley notes.[20] If the height of religious experience only confirms my success in prescinding the meaning of the universe into the transformation of my emotion, then what have I gained? What connection is there between my success and the moral state of the universe? Whether conversion is moral or metaphysical, stretching out from my own personal experience to the reality of human experience beyond me is essential. James faced this problem in the "Moral Philosopher" when he claimed that every moral impulse requires a kind of universal applicability. He was once prepared to bring this universal sense of obligation to the fore. But the universality of obligation breaks down under pressure from conversion. There must be transformation, James suggests, but the problem of conversion makes him adjust the concept so that there cannot be one transformation for all people, nor even one impulse toward transformation for all people. Obligation is many, not one, he now claims. But this fragments the very aspect of moral inquiry and universality James expects to build on.

Something vital is lost here. What I miss most in *Varieties* is challenge—any sort of intellectual, moral, or philosophical challenge. The religious landscape unfolds before James, and it seems there is no place he cannot travel and remain stably secure in his thinking. But this means religious inquiry is not like an intellectual inquiry on the edge of discovery—there is no absence or conflict James must struggle against. Religious thinking is no longer a source from which we can expect new ideas and new developments of thought and philosophy. There is no resistance *in* religion; there is only the resistance *of* religion. There are problems to overcome in religious expectations, but not something that might overcome us and the resistance we embody. For James, religion is ultimately about a willful expansion into "an objectively existing higher level of consciousness, in which we all participate," as Ellen Suckiel puts it.[21] Religion cannot get us anywhere intellectually that we cannot get in some other way. That is what I miss most in James's account of religious experience.

And yet, this attitude toward religion is apparently neither here nor there to James. He must not miss what I miss, or he would have approached things differently. But I do see a problem in James's theory about obligation as a result of this condition of idiosyncratic religion. It moves him back from his expectation of a metaphysical overcoming through the moral life to the casuistic mode he desires to leave. The casuistic mode is the state in which every act of will involves keeping our highest goods topmost, as he says. This continual mindfulness is opposed to the overcoming to which James calls attention in the beginning of *Varieties*. Religion is the state in which the power of higher goods becomes the "center of energy," and from this state no backsliding will ever remove us. But James resists this once-and-for-all change, or the change that opens the person to another world of metaphysical substantiality. He resists these conversionistic images and remains with the casuistic.

This return to the casuistic is a philosophical retreat. That James does so return is evident in his fear of the diabolical. Describing instantaneous conversion, he says, "But in any case the *value* of these forces would have to be determined by their effects, and the mere fact of their transcendency would of itself establish no presumption that they were more divine than diabolical" (VRE 243). Evaluating the forces behind a sudden transformation requires examining their "fruits," their results in our action. To speak broadly, therefore, we cannot know whether the forceful emotional impulse in conversion is a good unless we have it stretched out into practices, and these practices can be evaluated in terms of good or ill. Only by virtue of this casuistic evaluation can we determine the divine or demonic character of the force working on us.

James puts this worry forward as another reason to turn away from the expectation of sudden conversion. But the problem is a bit deeper than James realizes. If we must evaluate the force in instantaneous conversion, must we not also evaluate the force at work in what James calls "natural transformation"? Using the term *natural* seems to qualify this force as less troublesome—it is natural, not manufactured. But its form has little to do with its quality of effect. I am sure that a natural transformation could produce the same demonic outcome as a sudden transformation. The form of the transformation gives James no way to distinguish between forces natural, sudden or otherwise. They all must be measured by the standard of "fruitful for life." And this means that the moral soul can never attain a place of stability based on the significance, power, or form of religious transformation. To put it a slightly different way, there is never a platform individuals can attain, from which they can suppose that all they do or endure has meaning. Meaning—moral meaning—is only retail, never wholesale. This is significant because this is not where James wants to end up, and if this description is correct, his philosophical account of the obligation that attends the claim "God is there" in the "Moral Philosopher" goes begging in *Varieties*.

The moral life, obligation itself, arises for James as the result of an encounter with despair and freedom. His worry about the shape that he might become—that inhuman shape of the asylum patient—casts James into despair. If that should come to him, he knows not whether he could overcome it. His despair is not overcome by the conviction that he is able to attain freedom by the force of will. His freedom is like the weight resting on one end of a cantilever bridge. This weight must increase as the bridge extends, or at some point the progression will tumble into the abyss. James avoids tumbling into despair so long as he is assured of his freedom, and his freedom is dependent on achieving further exercises of his freedom. Despair is the limit to his freedom; it is what awaits his first faltering step. And freedom is the limit of his despair—it keeps despair at bay but cannot overcome it. It does not surprise me that worry over a diabolical force sneaks into James's account of conversion. Like the evil deceiver in Descartes' meditations, it reveals more than it intends, and once invoked it cannot be dismissed. James needs obligation to overcome both the potential abyss of despair and the infinite stretching out that freedom requires. Obligation, that reality of a claim upon us that puts our action into relation with the universe as well into relation with all of our past and future actions, draws James forward in the hope that despair may have an answer in a striking conviction of certainty, or at least in a method of outliving despair. Obligation answers freedom by proposing a content to guide the exercise of faculties and desires. It proposes a limit that does not restrain freedom, but makes freedom meaningful.

The transformation of obligation is incomplete in William James's writing. Obligation remains the feature of his moral and philosophical thought that eludes him. The problem of conversion reveals where James most clearly sees his desire leading, but he hesitates to yield his freedom to the discovery required in conversion, where the content stands beyond him and critiques his efforts. For James, conversion is a repetition of the state of the asylum patient—sitting and waiting, a life of exhaustion, unable to have control over what holds him.

William James marks a significant step toward the understanding of religious and moral obligation in American religious thought. James illuminates the conversion anxiety that lurks within our collective soul, and which still evinces the lingering influence of Edwards. James also illuminates the philosophical problematic of adapting language to address, and perhaps overcome, this anxiety. But I do not think that James overcame this anxiety, and to the extent that he did not, his philosophical transformation of obligation remains incomplete.

NOTES

1. Ellen Kappy Suckiel, *William James's Philosophy of Religion* (University of Notre Dame Press, 1996), 3.

2. Stanley Hauerwas, *With the Grain of the Universe* (Brazos Press, 2001), 85.

3. Suckiel, *James's Philosophy of Religion,* 20ff.

4. Charlene Haddock Siegfried, *William James's Radical Reconstruction of Philosophy* (SUNY Press, 1990), 47.

5. See Robert J. O'Connell, S.J., *William James on the Courage to Believe* (Fordham University Press, 1984), 99–102. O'Connell emphasizes the martial and heroic images of James's moral language, which carry the deontological freight of "doing the universe the deepest service we can."

6. William James, *Pragmatism: A New Name for Some Old Ways of Thinking* (Longmans, Green and Co., 1914), 289.

7. Ibid., 286–287.

8. John Stuhr, ed., *Classical American Philosophy* (Oxford University Press, 1987), 95.

9. Ibid., 94–96.

10. Ralph Barton Perry, *The Thought and Character of William James* (Vanderbilt University Press, 1996), 41.

11. Suckiel, *James's Philosophy of Religion,* 110.

12. Richard Rorty, "Religious Faith, Intellectual Responsibility, and Romance," in *Pragmatism, Neo-Pragmatism, and Religion,* ed. Charles Hardwick and Donald Crosby (Peter Lang, 1997). This essay receives an extended response in chapter 8.

13. Patrick Dooley, *Pragmatism as Humanism* (Nelson Hall, 1974), 99.

14. H. Richard Niebuhr, *Christ and Culture* (Harper & Row, 1951), 251. Niebuhr formulates his "ultimate question in this existential situation" as one that divides between "reasoning faithlessness" and "reasoning faith."

15. A. D. Nock, *Conversion* (Oxford University Press, 1933), 14. Nock traces the development of conversion from Oriental and Hellenistic religions prior to the advent of Christianity. In this way, Nock shows that Christian conversion is deeply rooted in human religious identity and practice.

16. Karen Armstrong, *Islam: A Short History* (Modern Library, 2002), 30.

17. This is why I disagree with the way Hauerwas responds to James. Getting after James on the question of God is a losing battle, because it just turns out that God, though real, is impossible to make into an explicit foundation for religious life. If James draws us into this rocky ground he may not beat us, but he will keep us pinned down forever, whereas the reality of transformation can be like the same ground only inverted—so that any argument for transformation, and James has plenty, are difficult if not impossible to *limit* to purely natural conclusions.

18. Joseph A. Conforti, *Jonathan Edwards, Religious Tradition, and American Culture* (University of North Carolina Press, 1995), 69.

19. *Edwards on the Affections and Alleine* (American Tract Society, n.d.). Subsequent references in the text are noted EFL and page number.

20. Dooley, *Pragmatism as Humanism,* 102. Dooley describes conversion in VRE in its positive light, and handles the natural-supernatural question of origin as one based on the fruits of the converted person. "However, if surrender to God issues in a commitment to fellow men, it promotes a better society. In this society, charity and love of fellow man encourage human excellence—respect for the sacredness of all persons and tolerance of individual differences."

21. Suckiel, *James's Philosophy of Religion,* 121.

5

Dwelling in Absence: The Reflective Origin of Conversion

IN THE LAST CHAPTER, I argued that William James stumbles when he deals with religious conversion. James studies religious experience for its contribution to human transformation, but he does not accept the ultimate character of conversion experience and the content of beliefs associated with dramatic and universal personal transformation. This rejection of conversion marks a shift in James's purpose in the *Varieties* from trying to understand religion to advocating a critical deletion in religious understanding. James, who finds good in almost every idea, finds conversion quite troubling.

James is still one of the authorities on religious experience in America, so invoking conversion as a way of rekindling the fires within philosophical pragmatism must run into conflict with James at some point. And so I have. In previous chapters I have argued that conversion, using Jonathan Edwards's work as a model, enables us to peer into the philosophical souls of C. S. Peirce and John Dewey, both to understand their compulsion to describe a philosophy of transformation, and to point out where their philosophies can be critically advanced. Conversion offers a way of suggesting a possible completion of the transformation the pragmatists seek that does not close down inquiry or limit the community. Conversion may be the confirmation that their desire for change is fulfilled.

Taken in this way, conversion in American philosophy leads to a striking disjunction. A great divide appears between James, who raises the issue of conversion directly with the intention of exposing its limits, and Peirce and Dewey, who do not raise conversion but are amenable in many ways to an ultimate moment of reorientation for the person or the community. The aim of this chapter is to explore this philosophical disjunction in pragmatism. In a nutshell, the difference between James and Peirce and Dewey is that the latter two orient their thought toward problems that represent the greatest threat to their reflective control.

They engage philosophical problems that have roots in their personal failings and fears. Dwelling with these problems requires both philosophical sophistication and nerve, and I think that the possibility for genuine conversion emerges within this ability to embrace the moments of absence within our reflection and our tradition.

Conversion reveals William James's deepest fears as well as his most profound hope. His hope is that his life will develop a power and meaning that somehow exceeds the narrowness of what he consciously creates or controls, but without dependence on some alien good or God. What he fears is that the significance of his life, and human life in general, may depend on some reality he does not create or control. James is compelled to explain conversion in *Varieties of Religious Experience* because of the power of the occasions where individuals confront a truth about themselves that remains absent from their control, and yet they are drawn into this absence rather than remain in the world that they do have control over. At this point James's fears outweigh his hope, and he backtracks from conversion as an ultimate and telling kind of experience that puts the person in clear relationship with the powers of the universe. Rather, he proclaims that religious experience has no ultimate figure of change. Only continuing effort toward personal transformation is religious, and any image of finality or the invocation of an external power necessary for such a personal change is inhuman and antireligious. Conversion limits James's philosophy because he cannot understand its attraction or abide its reality.

Let me step back a moment from James's rejection of conversion and place his thought in context with the argument of this book. I have argued that the pragmatists pursue a philosophical transformation that develops toward a dramatic and holistic change of a person or a community. This desire for an effective and comprehensive transformation is the root of the curious relation between American pragmatism and religious conversion, and this desire leads us to the hand of Augustine.

Saint Augustine's narrative in the *Confessions* exposes the problem of understanding the kind of conversion central to Christian testimony. For Augustine, however, the limit of his philosophical understanding is the absence of his control of his own will. The fragmentation he sees in his inability to will one thing is more than an unattained good; it is a sign of his woundedness. Augustine knows what he is not able to do, and that inability becomes the orienting focus of his inquiry leading to his conversion.

Jonathan Edwards reflects Augustine's willingness to face what is most threatening or troubling on his reflective horizon. For Edwards, the trouble comes through the tradition of Puritanism that was showing internal fault lines, especially concerning conversion. The failure of the Puritan community to live up to its own standards plagues Edwards. His adult reflection and influence move squarely against this resistance, resulting in his philosophical and theological positions that are bathed in conflict and disputation. This character of moving toward the most challenging reflective and communal problems, though, also collects the work of C. S. Peirce and John Dewey. They move into their traditions by seeking out the currents of resistance, where their thought is challenged by what it most clearly is not, or where reflective control is most painfully absent. Edwards, Peirce, and Dewey are examples of a philosophical transformation, the accomplishment of a character remarkable for its affection for moving through personal and reflective resistance into the questions that smell most like the abyss of death.

The development of this character is the heart of my project to understand conversion. Conversion means adopting a truth that we are not at present able to articulate or create, and so moving into the absence of this meaning is essential for understanding this experience. I am particularly interested in how this orientation becomes a moving principle in pragmatic thought, how an affection toward absence develops in our tradition. William James drives pragmatism into the neighborhood of religion, where this affection toward what we are not has its original power, even though I find that he eventually resists this affection. James is pivotal in the developmental course of pragmatism, and I think his resistance to this orientation toward absence marks out clear lines of philosophical struggle that continue into our present reflection.

The plan of this chapter falls along three lines of argument. First, I describe the ways Peirce and Dewey discover the limits of their efforts toward philosophical transformation. They represent distinct methods of locating and handling this limit, and they both face the failure of reflection that is part and parcel with discovering truth. Second, I show Edwards's orientation toward the failure of transformation in his inquiry into the religious affections. This orientation toward failure, his failure, humanizes Edwards's otherwise monstrous image. The last step is to bring these three thinkers together in terms of an American response to the limit of transformation in order to understand why conversion remains such a powerful and complicated feature of our religious and philosophical lives.

DWELLING IN ABSENCE: PEIRCE AND DEWEY

William James eclipsed his teacher, C. S. Peirce, in almost every way. James had the position at Harvard, the admiration of scholars, wealth, and international fame. But it was Peirce who started James on his philosophical quest of divining a new name for some old ways of thinking, and James acknowledges that debt. From Peirce James took the lesson that philosophy can produce a transformation of human life if it overcomes itself and its tendency to lose focus. As a mode of critique, Peirce's pragmatism takes modern philosophy to task for not generating the kind of transformation hoped for. The need for a wholesale replacement of the status quo philosophical vision stands behind James's persistence in exorcising dyads such as free will and determinism that have a hold on our thought, but James fails both to make the wholesale replacement he desires and to realize that Peirce is closer to the mark.

Transformation of Inquiry

For Peirce transformation requires a complete habit change, an ultimate encounter with the character of the universe. Discovering an ultimate habit change to the character Peirce calls "the law of mind" is the positive side of transformation that I connect with conversion. This habit change is possible, however, only if there is also a change in the habit of inquiry. The desire for the holistic change of inquiry emerges in a peculiar way.

The transformation of inquiry is actually one of Peirce's primary philosophical goals. It links his logic, semiotic, and metaphysical speculation. If a difference is not accessible through inquiry, if inquiry does not work from a very different platform from current science and philosophy, then the conclusions of inquiry will not be any different.

What sponsors such a need to have a completely different platform of inquiry? For Peirce this is doubt. Doubt appears as the sign of our incomplete control of action and thought. When I wish to recall Kant's argument for the transcendental deduction, but cannot recall the immediate context enough to locate it in my copy of *The Critique of Pure Reason,* I realize one form of doubt. This personal form of doubt leads me to the correction I need. What I do not know is clear enough that my inquiry builds on this absence. The same may be true of an idea that I am trying to write down: my expression does not capture what I intend, and doubt arises so that I can realize the deficiency and correct it, although I may never bring my idea to exact expression. A third sense of doubt is much more catastrophic.

In his essay "How to Make Our Ideas Clear," Peirce drops a little autobiographical hint on his reader, but it is couched in an expression of extraordinary doubt:

> Many a man has cherished for years as his hobby some vague shadow of an idea, too meaningless to be positively false; he has, nevertheless, passionately loved it, has made it his companion by day and by night, and has given to it his strength and his life, leaving all other occupations for its sake, and in short has lived with it and for it, until it has become, as it were, flesh of his flesh and bone of his bone; and then he has waked up some bright morning to find it gone, clean vanished away like the beautiful Melusina of the fable, and the essence of his life gone with it. (CP 5:393)

Most commentators skip over this hyperbole except to note that Peirce's first wife, Melusina, had left him by the time he wrote this. But there is more philosophical significance here than meets the eye. While Peirce treats ideas and cognition with the cool hand of a logician, there is more at stake in it for him than making clear distinctions. Doubt is more than an insufficient belief; it is a kind of suffering related to the absence of a vague but powerful idea. Nevertheless, this overwhelming loss puts a stamp of veracity on our inquiry. What we bump into is *not* what we would produce ourselves—we could not manufacture this loss in a thousand tries—but it is what our inquiry must overcome in order to function as a working organ of thought. Occasions of doubt like this one are the beginning of Peirce's discovery of realism.

How Peirce handles this absence is critical for his philosophy of transformation. Only an encounter with a real that is not us could become the genesis of a completely new habit of inquiry. If we lose this connection with the real and give in to the temptation simply to replace the vague and powerful idea, to take up with another woman, so to speak, Peirce thinks we will find our inquiry turning in a solipsistic circle, answering only the questions we pose to ourselves. Doubt is the key to a transformed inquiry necessary for the refinement of habits that will make real change possible.

Peirce makes one of his most important philosophical discoveries at this point in handling doubt. Doubt is a limit to thought because it marks the boundaries of ideas and practice. Doubt is also the sign of what stands beyond our reason and may destroy it, reducing our efforts to smash. But doubt is also, as I pointed out above, the indication that our thought is moving beyond the well-worn paths of meaning and transgressing the limits of what we know into the strange territory of what we do not know. In this way doubt becomes a key to surpassing the philosophical production of the moderns—for them doubt was simply error to be avoided and not a potentially directive encounter.

Architectonic of Doubt

In his two essays "Four Incapacities Claimed for Man" and "Some Consequences of Four Incapacities Claimed for Man," Peirce describes a form of inquiry that handles doubt as an integral aspect of thought instead of shoving it away. The first of these two essays demonstrates the failure of Cartesian doubt, what Peirce calls "paper doubt" because it appears under the philosopher's pen and does not arise out of the existential conflict of habit. Descartes poses doubt and then creates a system based on overcoming this "error" by introspection and intuition. Peirce discovers Descartes' error, but infers that this is more than a misguided application of philosophy. It is a sign that inquiry must be based on "a very different kind of platform than this." But how to replace it? Can Descartes' failure and that of modern philosophy be a beginning of a more genuine inquiry?

Peirce knows it is necessary not to simply reject the error of modern philosophy and move on, because he would still be seeking an answer only to that rejection, not to his doubt. The challenge is to incorporate this error of modern philosophy into a construction of a more stable platform, so that in this way philosophy overcomes and incorporates its own error within inquiry. The first blush of Peirce's tendency to think in architectonic fashion appears in his suggestion that such a platform for inquiry is framed by four denials drawn from his rejection of Descartes: "1. We have no power of Introspection, but all knowledge of the internal world is derived by hypothetical reasoning from our knowledge of external facts. 2. We have no power of Intuition, but every cognition is determined logically by previous cognition. 3. We have no power of thinking without signs. 4. We have no conception of the absolutely incognizable" (CP 5:265). These four denials are not directives or principles Peirce states as unequivocal foundations for inquiry. Rather, they are leading suggestions that force the inquirer to seek the consequences of these "denials"—if they are true, what would this mean for inquiry? This hypothetical structure opens out into Peirce's development of the main terms of his lifelong philosophical discovery of the continuity of thought, the logical necessity of a community for fixing belief, the theory of semiotic development, and the real "object" that grounds inquiry.

The success of Peirce's new platform finally rests on the nature of the object that he finds is essential for inquiry to have the nature of the real about it, so that what is discovered "is what it is no matter if any person thinks it." If this object is only apparent in inquiry, like a Kantian "thing-in-itself," then Peirce's project collapses before it starts because thought will never connect to "what is" as he puts it. On the other hand, if his platform reproduces the Cartesian error of making a cognition out of what is incognizable, Peirce has also failed. The object of inquiry must ground the process of inquiry, yet it must remain absent from it in order to preserve the reality of error, of missing the mark, in order to confirm that inquiry is oriented toward something beyond itself. But the only possible confirmation that this object is orienting inquiry is a hypothetical relation. If inquiry exhibits an orientation and direction while still bearing the mark of doubt and error, then it is pursuing something like this object. The only sign that inquiry is grounded by a real object is the character of the inquirer that emerges with the inquiry. Peirce says it this way:

> But it is plain that the knowledge that one thought is similar to or in any way truly representative of another, cannot be derived from immediate perception, but must be an hypothesis (unquestionably fully justifiable by facts), and that therefore the formation of such a representing thought must be dependent upon a real and effective force behind consciousness, and not merely upon a mental comparison. (CP 5:288)

Peirce points out that continuity among ideas is not from a representational comparison, but by an inference. And the inference that connects ideas has to do with discerning a resistant character in consciousness that establishes the idea as connected to a "real and effective force." For Peirce this means that a community must exemplify this direction by a "real and effective force" to substantiate the success of its inquiry.

Let me quickly summarize this argument about how Peirce handles absence through inquiry. Doubt is a sign that thought is striking against something that resists it. The question is what the presence of this doubt means. Is doubt an indication that inquiry is failing or an indication that it is succeeding? Peirce claims that inquiry must move into the realm of doubt to face what it is not in order for transformation of thought to occur. Thought seeks its own transformation because it is capable of overcoming its own errors of taking provisional answers for final ones.

Only inquiry from this new platform pushes thought to its limit of finding the limit of the real by error instead of stopping for what works in
the immediate occasion. A transformation of thought that is complete
will emerge only as a result of inquiry that dwells in this absence which
is doubt as the limit of thought.

The fact that all thought must be tested in action commits Peirce to
the claim that an energetic expression of inquiry is required to fulfill this
hypothetical platform. But Peirce also claims that just having a series of
actions or moments of inquiry will not satisfy the claim that inquiry has
in fact reached this new platform. Inquiry must be discovered in its generality for this character to appear. He says,

> The deliberately formed, self-analyzing habit—self-analyzing because
> formed by the aid of analysis of the exercises that nourished it—is the liv-
> ing definition, the veritable and final logical interpretant. Consequently,
> the most perfect account of a concept that words can convey will consist
> in a description of the habit which that concept is calculated to produce.
> But how otherwise can a habit be described than by a description of the
> kind of action to which it gives rise, with the specification of the condi-
> tions and of the motive? (CP 5:491)

The description Peirce seeks requires both an active representation and
reflection on the motive—the guiding principle of that inquiry. In this
way Peirce thinks science must focus on performing critical inquiry and
reaching a self-critical awareness of that inquiry to be truly scientific.

Doubt and the Inquiry of the Community

From this position it appears that the community, especially the community
of scientists, may provide the consequential proof of Peirce's conditional
idea of inquiry. He says that a community is necessary because it "overcomes the vagaries of you and me" by examining more general action.
Inquiry in a community does not have the constraint of individual persons
and their histories or their limitations. Communal inquiry strives against
the limit of time, and may, it seems, hold the prospect for at least containing
the instances of doubt that mark the functional limits of its reach. Is the
community a way out of the absence which begins Peirce's inquiry?

The quick answer is, no, it cannot without squelching inquiry. But how
does doubt become the focus for a development of meaning and ideas in
a community? Especially since Peirce now has invoked the infinite long
run of inquiry in which time is no longer an eater, as it is for Augustine.

Doubt and absence turn up in the community in the 1903 lectures on pragmatism. Peirce proposes a way "the real" is discovered in three types of men (CP 5:210–212). The first type are aesthetes, for whom "action is taken as utterly free and expressive" and who reflect the quality of the real, but push the articulation no further. They do not aim to make practical or self-critical distinctions. Men of the second type are concerned with the immediate challenge of getting things done. Peirce is quite negative here, since these practical types have no care for the meaning of their actions, only the brute efficiency. He pronounces against this focus on the immediate as the gospel of greed in "Evolutionary Love." "Here, then, is the issue," he says. "The gospel of Christ says that progress comes from every individual merging his individuality in sympathy with his neighbors. On the other side, the conviction of the nineteenth century is that progress takes place by virtue of every individual's striving for himself with all his might and trampling his neighbor under foot whenever he gets a chance to do so. This may accurately be called the Gospel of Greed" (CP 6:294). Dewey, we will see, finds immediate goods and acts occasions for attaining a different kind of transformation, but Peirce does not think this is possible. Rather, there is a third type of men, the scientists, who escape the limits of the temporal order and qualitative characteristics to the elements contained in thirdness, the realm of argument, inference, and the expansion of meaning:

> The man who takes the third position and accepts the cotary propositions will hold, with firmest of grasps, to the recognition that logical criticism is limited to what we can control. In the future we may be able to control more but we must consider what we can now control. Some elements we can control in some limited measure. But the content of the perceptual judgment cannot be sensibly controlled now, nor is there any rational hope that it ever can be. Concerning that quite uncontrolled part of the mind, logical maxims have as little to do as with the growth of hair and nails. We may be dimly able to see that, in part, it depends on the accidents of the moment, in part on what is personal or racial, in part is common to all nicely adjusted organisms whose equilibrium has narrow ranges of stability, in part on whatever is composed of vast collections of independently variable elements, in part on whatever reacts, and in part on whatever has any mode of being. But the sum of it all is that our logically controlled thoughts compose a small part of the mind, the mere blossom of a vast complexus, which we may call the instinctive mind, in which this man will not say that he has faith, because that implies the conceivability

of distrust, but upon which he builds as the very fact to which it is the whole business of his logic to be true. . . . That he will have no difficulty with Thirdness is clear enough, because he will hold that the conformity of action to general intentions is as much given in perception as is the element of action itself, which cannot really be mentally torn away from such general purposiveness. (CP 5:212)

The metaphysical condition for action among practical minds is a linear notion of time. In linear time there is no room for an event between two that are separate in time. There is no possible connection between this time and either a past or a future. Linear time is the grounding notion of negative liberty, of absolute freedom from all constraints. Peirce takes the notion of linear time as securing the freedom of action, where that freedom means that it is susceptible to change through criticism. But linear time cannot contain the element of thirdness needed for this criticism. There is no error in absolutely linear time, either considered as a whole, as Hegel does, or in its isolable and fragmented parts, as Rorty makes clear. There is only what is, or what is easiest to think. Anything real is disconnected from the temporal order, or is absent altogether.

Only men of the third type, then, are able to overcome the limit of time while retaining the movement of inquiry, doubt. So the community is not a way of stepping aside from doubt, but a way of uncovering another dimension of it. That is, the community of inquirers of the third type discovers an absence that is not possible in either of the first two types, nor is it possible simply in community *qua* community.

However much Peirce loads his argument toward generality and the community of inquirers in the infinite long run, it remains true that this community is constructed of actual individuals joined in this inquiry. But how does the individual see this community as an enterprise that is actually oriented toward the kind of long-run inquiry without any qualitative recognition that this is so? How does the individual come to participate in the inquiry of the community, or rather, how does the community appear in the thought of the individual? Is the community of scientists sufficient to warrant this identification with the law of mind, as the living sign of thirdness?

Peirce needs a fourth category of inquirer, that is, an individual that stands apart from the dialectic of the first and second type of men and, through standing in his or her own doubt, finds community in the third type of inquiry and the doubt that orients the character of that process.[1]

This type of community of inquiry cannot be continued by an internal reproduction but must continue to draw inquirers from the other types into its reality of dwelling in absence.

In one of his more striking phrases, Peirce says, "Ignorance and error are all that distinguish our private selves from the absolute ego of pure apperception"[2] (CP 5:235). He means that we perceive our individual character as inquirers, separate from the ideal ego of apperception, by noting when our judgments are wrong, when we do not control our action, or when our thought turns out to fail in practice. To join this personal negation with the movement to the community of inquirers mentioned above means that at some point the "personal" source of doubt must coincide with the doubt of the scientifically inquiring community. In this way personal negation remains a feature of absence for Peirce's objective idealism and becomes the limit of his transformation of inquiry. There is no change in human inquiry if this transformation of a person into the third type is not possible. And this requires that the individual somehow is able to stand in the community through dwelling in the absence of their own ignorance and error. Otherwise there is not a working from negation but canceling and rejecting negation.

Peirce's own absence is the absence of transformation, and I think he realizes this most fully in the "Neglected Argument for the Reality of God." In that essay the individual appears to become a sign for the community, not vice versa, and the absence of the individual is the absence of philosophy. The community of scientists is a kind of verification of the emergence of the "muser" into agapism, but despite the instinctive power of the idea of God in its "beauty, for its supplying an ideal of life, and for its thoroughly satisfactory explanation of his whole threefold environment" (CP 6:465), the individual stands as an absence, as that which cannot be overcome by generality of thought or inferential form.

DEWEY: NATURE, ABSENCE, AND COMMUNICATION

Peirce's lonely condition of confronting the absence of the universe in himself perplexes a philosopher like John Dewey. Dewey is not lonely because he sees himself already in relation to a content of the universe from which there is no possibility of escaping into solitude or private reflection. The problem for Dewey is not overcoming personal limitations so much as it is bringing the ground of interaction that stands behind all thought into plain view. This ground of interaction is the source of expanding meaning in the universe and in thought. In this world transformation is not precariously balanced on the development of meaning by an inference from the vague origin of inquiry, as it is for Peirce. Rather, transformation is a worklike process of bringing ideas and habits more and more directly into contact with the ground of interaction in order to soak up the principle of expansion already present there. Transformation, though, must exceed this soaking up or reflexive response with the development of new meaning. How this is possible in Dewey's estimation is the focus of this section.

Dewey uses the term *nature* to refer to the ground of interaction and experience that provides the material for our efforts to transcend habits and meanings. Nature is mostly inert, that is, it is not a superconsciousness or a personality, but it is that to which practice and thought are modified. Nature occasionally appears to have semiconscious effects, especially when Dewey describes its forcefulness in becoming manifest in human practice. Nature almost appears to be a guiding intention behind the development of meaning. But Dewey is careful to return to the position that this intention emerges only in the enlivening interaction of experience with nature.

Dewey builds his understanding of nature from the ground up, so to speak. He begins with the changes in thought and culture that are either an interaction with a stable and directive content or an interaction with a contingent and unordered continuum of non-meaning matter. Dewey is optimistic that every transformation that comes in experience is an opening to inquire into the "ordered richness" of nature. Nature has an effect on human community that can be discovered, and its authority for altering practice can be witnessed and critically appraised. At the same time Dewey absolutely rejects anything that smacks of an onto-theologically authoritative Word. There is no "the greater than which none can be conceived" for Dewey. Nature is all we have and all we need.

But given the fact that nature resists any objectification in knowledge, the only way to bring the ordering authority behind practice into clear view is to develop new habits. Otherwise the authority behind the development of our practice is "beyond" us and is outside our range of intelligent control. Dewey's most fundamental critique of traditional religion is that it removes a large part of the meaning of our practice from critical control by giving it over to blind obedience. This kind of obedience is an abdication of our most human characteristic of bringing reflective control to our action.

The community, as a denotable thing in experience, is an instance of intelligent control of material conditions for some prospective end, and so the community is the assurance of the incarnation of authority without Being. This is why Dewey eulogizes "democracy." But the community is also an instance of resistance to that control, and this is why Dewey describes democracy as "the task before us" (LW 14:224). This complex relation of confirmation and resistance of intelligent control indicates that the community is a rich object for inquiry, especially as Dewey explores its phenomenal aspects in *Experience and Nature*.

Dewey's premise throughout *Experience and Nature* is that the community does not yet have a clear conception of its enlivening authority. As a result of this absence the community remains an open question, both reflectively and existentially. But to bring the nature of community to fuller view Dewey has only to "understand better what is already the common experience of mankind" (LW 1:40). Dewey seeks to transform our "common experience" into a self-conscious community through a reflection on experience and nature. The most telling feature of this transformation arises from bringing to view what is absent in our "common experience." The reflective control of developing meaning in our experience eludes us, despite the fact that this meaning is part and parcel of a response to nature. Exploring this absence requires Dewey to become more explicit about the relation of meaning and nature.

Nature

Nature is the broadest possible consideration of meaning in the universe. But nature is present only as the condition of experience, and the meaning of nature is just the content of experience that develops in this interaction. Experience is not governed by an ideal progress, nor is it representative of a Platonic form. The transformation of the human community that occurs in the interaction with nature is the only material basis for a meaningful understanding of experience.

Since experience arises in response to nature, fully knowing experience means being able to adopt habits self-critically and adapt the direction of that interaction. The universal condition of nature also means that experience cannot be permanently manipulated or held in a false abeyance by cultural accretions no matter how ingrained in practice they might be. The reason such accretions cannot stand is that we are a community in relation to nature. Nature is the perennial transformation of the unstable into the more stable and the recognition of the limitations of static conceptions by their eventual failure in directing practice. Meaning in experience is a result of developing habits that can stand in a productive relation to nature, which for the human community is like drinking from a common cup. Dewey boldly states, "This community of partaking is meaning" (LW 1:146).

In this way Dewey stacks his notion of transformation around the pole of nature. Nature is at once the idea that draws human community forward as the order of interactions that produce a character are collected in an expanding meaning of practice. And nature is also the instance of expanding meaning—since this is a material reality and not an ideal. This interactive materiality is not locked into one form but evolves in an unlimited expansion of value; that is, differences appear in practice that guide development into specific habits but not into terminal habits.

The unlimited expansion of value is reflected in Dewey's understanding of the role of impulse in human nature and conduct. Habits are formed by interactions with conditions that are connected to ends of action, but habits are flexible, changing when an impulse interrupts their continuity. This interruption appears within the action related to a habit, so all of human meaning is not a making from nothing but a reforming of what is already present. Dewey thinks that many of our reflective problems stem from the notion that we make Reality, as he points out here in respect to idealism,

> [Idealism] took re-constitution to be constitution; re-construction to be construction. Accepting the premise of the equivalence of Reality with the attained object of knowledge, idealism had no way of noting that thought is intermediary between some empirical objects and others. Hence an office of transformation was converted into an act of original and final creation. A conversion of actual immediate objects into *better,* into more secure and significant objects was treated as a movement from merely apparent and phenomenal Being to the truly Real. In short, idealism is guilty of neglect that thought and knowledge are histories. . . . Only action, interaction, can change or remake objects. . . . Intelligence is a factor in forming new objects which mark a fulfillment. But this is because intelligence is incarnate in overt action, using things as means to affect other things. (LW 1.126)

What makes interaction with nature the realm for transformation is the disjunction between the present and the *better* that is absent from our habit.

I find Dewey's shifting use of nature problematic. As both the continuum and the interruption that makes transforming change possible nature becomes a gratuitous term—it means both things and does not have an internal complexity necessary for separating these two different functions. This slippery character of the term *nature* flows from the way Dewey uses the term as a sign of absence when speaking in terms of impulse and a continuum of meaning when speaking in terms of habit. Overcoming this aspect of nature is the challenge Dewey faces in developing his account of transformation through communication.

Absence and Communication

Immediate experience is challenged when a different value appears that is beyond the control of the present habit. For instance, when a swimmer sees a shark fin, her ability to swim in relation to the danger shifts her habit toward another value like being out of danger, and this is beyond her present swimming ability. And so she shouts for help. The appearing value is not a threat of non-meaning, but it comes from a realization of incomplete meaning. This absence is a kind of incompleteness apparent in human habit.

Communication emerges from interactions with this recognition of incompleteness in habit. Communication is not a direct interaction with nature, because nature always remains beyond our habits as the founding condition. Thought is distinct from nature in that thought does not aim to represent nature but to respond to it. Here Rorty is exactly right about the metaphysical ground of Dewey's pragmatism. Practice reveals all the meaning nature has for us. Our action is all that nature can mean. But how this action expands *like* nature is the question.

What puzzles Dewey is the expansive property of human habit in meaning that cannot be strictly tied to a contingent shift in material conditions. Communication is the movement in meaning that is possible when habits are challenged to become *better* than they are by virtue of criticism rather than material conditions. This *better* and the ground of this criticism of habit brings us to another sense of absence related to nature. The interaction that propels habit past itself toward a *better* for the sake only of this *better* is communication.

The praise of communication cannot be overstated. Dewey says, "communication is a wonder by the side of which transubstantiation pales" (LW 1:132). Communication appears miraculous because natural conditions are reproduced as reflective content, as meaning. He describes a mythical relation of two individuals, A and B, where A proposes the consummatory experience of possession of a flower and B accepts or rejects. The miraculous moment to the interaction is that "the thing pointed out by A to B gains meaning" (LW 1:142). No other sentence in Dewey's corpus carries the freight that this *ex nihilo* appearance of meaning does. Between the individuals blankly denoted by A and B, a community is formed around "significant things [which are] actually implicated in situations of shared or social purpose and execution" (LW 1:142). A word "gains meaning when its use establishes a genuine community of action" (LW 1:145). The transformation of individuals A and B into a community is now a "denoted" object.

Communication is a tool that joins elements of consciousness into a "partaking of meaning" like sharing a common meal. Transformation of experience is possible when communication becomes a conscious aspect of our habit forming and reforming, and this is what Dewey means by "intelligence." Communication reveals the ability of consciousness to anticipate the direction of a habit and redirect it toward another appearing value. Nature is newly discoverable in this function of hosting anticipation, but the character of nature as a condition of experience takes another step into the shadows. Transformation of human value occurs because some aspect of interaction reveals a lapse or an emptiness, and it is not clear that this absence can ever be a proper aspect of nature. Dewey says "without reference to the absent, or 'transcendence,' nothing is a tool" (LW 1:146). He makes the same point at another place; "when we name an event we speak proleptically . . . we invoke a meaning, namely, the potential consequence of the existence" (LW 1:150). When Dewey names the community of partakers, he anticipates such a community of partakers where meaning obtains. But he also anticipates the transformation of meaning that is communication when he says that communication is a tool, in fact "the tool of tools"[3] (LW 1:146). So what is transcendentally absent here, communication, or the community? The ambiguity centers on the question of who or what is refining or using the tool. Is communication the tool the community uses to get clear about itself, or is the community a tool communication uses to continue to dwell in the absence related to expanding meaning?

Dewey's account of communication leads toward this further reach into absence. What intrigues Dewey is that communication fully emerges as a good only when it requires the individual to give up a secure world, though flawed in some aspect of its authority, for a new world that cannot be presented in any descriptive terms. All that can be promised is based on a metaphorical relation of this ultimate move into flux and prior moves into the same kind of space in particular habits. This peculiar undergoing is seen, Dewey says, "when an old essence or meaning is in process of dissolution and a new one has not taken shape . . . the intervening existence is too fluid and formless for publication, even to one's self. . . . This process of flux is intrinsic to any thought which is subjective and private." The subject arises in continuity with the reconstitution of experience from pure flux. Dewey continues, "The point in placing emphasis upon the role of individual desire and thought in social life is that it shows the genuinely intermediate position of subjective mind: it proves it to be a mode of natural existence in which objects undergo directed reconstitution" (LW 1:171). But communication as a conscious moment in our orientation toward nature marks a shift in the direction in experience. In communication the subject is not defined by an effort to get into a better relation to nature, but trying to consciously adopt and adapt the process by which nature molds and influences action. To this end, communication must contain the same kind of absence nature does in order that it can represent another possibility beyond the active habit.

This repetition of absence between nature and communication turns into a threat for Dewey's account of the transformation of experience. Once communication becomes a habit of reconstitution in the community, where it is in full control of its expansion of meaning, it is possible to supplant the authority of nature with some other content. This is possible because the state of flux necessary for communication to obtain means that a disconnection from nature is also necessary. The "new world" that appears before it is realized cannot be discriminated from any other world except by being fully realized. There is no standing outside and evaluating a world of value for Dewey; there is only entering into a world and assessing its ordered richness from within. This becomes a problem, for instance, when philosophy replaces the transformative impulse of nature with the nonnatural good of an ultimate and static being. The change of habit possible in communication can be skewed in this way by an alternative content that can be evaluated holistically only in relation to the expansion of nature. There must be a concrete instance of communication related to nature, therefore, in order for this discrimination to take place at all.

The philosophical challenge for pragmatism is discriminating between content in human action once the range of communication is employed within the community, because this is the condition within which all philosophy emerges. Separating communication that is grounded in nature from communication that is not is Dewey's focus in books such as *The Quest for Certainty* and *The Public and Its Problems*. Nature is absent in a more powerful way in these reflective pursuits because the mode of habit change that reflects our natural condition itself becomes a problem. Reflection that follows the authority of an alien content is doubly dangerous because communication is changed into a negative product. It is impossible to describe this problem by formal criteria because it reflects the pattern of responsive change to conditions. This ambiguity is the reason Dewey is positive toward religious impulse but expressly negative toward traditional religion.

Dewey ultimately arrives at a crucial philosophical problem in *Experience and Nature*. Content that is less than completely reflective of nature cannot be revealed as incomplete except by projecting the characteristic direction of these habits. And since the material form of the community or its habits never amounts to an exhaustive image of nature, the only distinguishing difference is that the authority that nature properly has over habits (in Dewey's model of community) is an authority that other content cannot duplicate. The authority of nature cannot be reproduced by anything other than nature itself.

The authority of nature, then, is what is most powerfully absent in reflection that is less than it can be. Dewey works to reveal this absence of authority in other modes of reflective reconstruction. Communication becomes the feature that manifests the dialectic of authority because it collects all habits in their elemental "being-for-reconstruction." Dewey says, "If a man has experienced a world which is good, why should he not act to remake a bad world till it agrees with the good world," or, "at least so act so as to get the renewed *sense* of a good world?" (LW 1:259–260). Who gives up an old world unless a new one is found or remembered? And can this remembering or giving up be described apart from the "sense" of a good world? Dewey does not explain what that sense is.

The force behind remembering a sense of a good world is what Dewey means by authority. He puts it this way in *A Common Faith*: "The authority of an ideal over choice and conduct is the authority of an ideal, not of a fact, of a truth guaranteed to intellect, not of the status of the one who propounds the truth" (LW 9:15). The absence Dewey finds in communication is that authority of an ideal that refuses objectification.

Dewey is confident that the failure of reconstructive efforts in individual and social practice is not because of a failure in the content of experience. It is not a failure of nature, but a failure in the appearing authority of the content of nature. This is the deeper absence Dewey's philosophical transformation struggles with. This authority transcends both knowledge and conditions, and catches the human consciousness up in that search for a content that could reproduce the effect of that on the whole community.

Authority

The absence of nature that finally propels the expansion of meaning in the community is its authority over transformation and communication. Trying to bring this absence to clearer expression is one reason Dewey takes a tentative step toward religious language in *A Common Faith*. He seeks to open up the transformative value of authority for all people, not just those who have had religious experience. But this authority evades his attempt to isolate it from its traditional garb and to use it for expanding the meaning of the democratic community. Instead, Dewey's *A Common Faith* provoked a firestorm over his use of "God" and the notion that there is a transcendent value that he is surreptitiously beholden to.

One problem Dewey creates for himself comes from the way he opposes nature to all things nature cannot contain. This opposition carries him into a deep ravine because the authority he seeks to multiply and express must be beyond nature; it must be authority in experience, and so it is in one sense already supernature. Authority in experience that cannot be created or controlled by manipulating conditions becomes a compounded problem because of Dewey's dogma of naturalism. Dewey is able to display this authority only if he can construct a content that can be holistically tested in practice, and so he turns to education. But even if he succeeds in this construction, he has no assurance that he has not made another false step since the Truth of nature is always one more remove away from practice. He must fail to develop the authority he seeks, and he must deny that it can come from anywhere else but his construction. Dewey can finally only point to and remain within the absence of authority.

To Dewey's credit, he realizes the deficiency of his own content and resists claiming the authority that appears in most philosophical productions. Dewey retains the character of a servant of the universe, an apostle of the possible value of community and experience, and the great goodness of the enterprise in making this value manifest. He knows the good is not his own creation, and neither is the product of the community dependent on his content, but the authority nature bears on its own. Dewey is a priest of sorts, realizing that his skill in metaphorically revealing this authority is the key for communal transformation. He tried but failed to make God a utility term for the authority of nature by coining his phrase "natural piety." Beyond natural piety, however, Dewey is clearly captured heart and soul in this enterprise. We read this statement toward the end of *Experience and Nature:* "Fidelity to the nature to which we belong, as parts however weak, demands that we cherish our desires and ideals till we have converted them into intelligence, revised them in terms of the ways and means in which nature makes possible. When we have used our thought to its utmost and have thrown into the moving unbalanced balance of things our puny strength, we know that though the universe slay us still we may trust, for our lot is one with whatever is good in existence" (LW 1:314).

Pragmatic Paths in Absence

Edwards prefigures both Peirce's and Dewey's means of dwelling in absence. Like Peirce, Edwards is struck that his ability to discern fully his own presence in the community depends on his own transformation. Discovering what remains absent for him and the community is the same thing. His transformation, then, is like the transformation of the community, and on the basis of this continuity he can speak to his community and to himself in one voice.

Like Dewey, Edwards realizes that his failure to articulate the pressing authority behind the good of the universe limits the prospects for his temporal community. Transformation is limited by the rhetorical power revealing the authority of the content of nature and God. But also like Dewey, Edwards knows that the content he serves does not wait for his creative act and neither will its final success be reduced by his failure.

Beyond Peirce or Dewey, however, Edwards finds the compelling source of absence for his reflection in the affections of human hearts. The affections, our most powerful desires and lively ideas, reveal a character that cannot understand its own ordering. There is an absence in the principle that makes our desires into a character. Unless we are able to bring this absent order to view we will not fully understand all that we are or what, in fact, we most deeply desire. Edwards does not have to convince people that they are affectively dissatisfied. If this dissatisfaction is not apparent to the person there is nothing anyone can do or say that would work a transformation in that person. To do so would be to force an adoption of some linguistic formula without genuine connection to the person's habits—it would mean nothing. But people do desire to know themselves, and to know themselves through the transformation of their desires.

Dwelling in absence leads Edwards to the question of how the structure of inquiry and the appearing content in experience become the platform for an alteration of the affections—not a change in desire, but a discovery of the principle of desire that attests to the soul's transformation from what it is in its present incompleteness to the holism it can attain with an orientation toward God. Philosophical absence, for Edwards, becomes the absence of conversion.

EDWARDS DWELLING IN ABSENCE

Edwards's emergence as one of the most significant American philosophers of religion followed a protracted period of corporate neglect. For some reason after his death Edwards became a sign of what his culture could not face, and so it excluded him from its identity. At least it tried to. Edwards is the kind of thinker, however, who trusts the truth of what he has discovered. Neither he nor any person can subvert the force of transformation that works within human life, inquiry, and religious practice. This conviction gives Edwards's thought a resilience that we are currently rediscovering in the midst of our postmodern and post-Christian wanderings.

But Edwards's confidence is not built on the power of reason, rhetoric, or intellectual creation. Edwards's confidence is built on his awareness of the human condition that precedes transformation, the lack of order, coherence, or satisfaction that becomes an overwhelming absence within a person. This order can be recognized only in its absence before it is approached as the proper object of our understanding or an orienting moment of our desire. Edwards's task in the *Affections* is describing how this absence appears and the connection it makes to transformation.

H. R. Niebuhr, in *The Kingdom of God in America,* explores the character of America's founding religious thought that sought to translate the pressing reality of God into a constructive Protestantism. Niebuhr identifies Edwards as the leading theologian whose "faith in regeneration was solidly founded upon a supreme conviction of the reality of divine sovereignty."[4] The pressing reality of God's purpose necessitated the transformation and conversion of man, not just a better moral state, but also a new nature. Given this acknowledgment of Edwards's power it is surprising that Niebuhr uses F. D. Maurice rather than Edwards as the example of an advocate of "Christ the Transformer of Culture" in *Christ and Culture.*[5] In this way I think Niebuhr confirms the American resistance to mixing the topics of philosophical progression and religious conversion. But this is exactly where Edwards dwells. If conversion is human, it will show up in the philosophical discovery of our world and ourselves.

Edwards's philosophical range has been the topic of a variety of interpretations and expansions. John Smith argues that Edwards's response to Locke describes his focus on the development of a "spiritual taste" in the *Religious Affections,* although he thinks that Perry Miller and others drive this dependence on Locke's empiricism too far.[6] Michael Raposa, on the other hand, develops Edwards's emphasis on perfect moral obedience in the twelfth sign in the *Religious Affections* using terms of Peirce's theosemiotic philosophy, supported in spirit by the work of Sang Lee.[7] These are just two examples of the philosophical completions Edwards's *Religious Affections* invites. But something more than these kinds of completions is necessary to probe the power of the *Affections.*

Despite the ways Edwards appears in continuity with aspects of our philosophical tradition, the transformation of thought he proposes does not cohere with a linear or ascending character of intellectual discovery. The transformation Edwards philosophically describes comes only by standing in the radical discontinuity of absence he identifies as "evangelical humiliation." While philosophers dismiss this reference to sin as a holdover from Edwards's reformed tradition, I do not think this adequately addresses the issue. Evangelical humiliation, as we will see in a moment, completely undermines the potential success of every form of continuous human thought, and this includes aspects of Edwards's Puritan tradition as well. Edwards does not repeat the formulas of his tradition, like original sin, without establishing the ground of these ideas in reflection. The progressive discovery of conversion from the blindness of our natural state into a new nature is not one feature among many in his thought—it is the whole story. This puts Edwards at odds with all forms of philosophical continuity narrowly conceived.

On the other hand, conversion is discovered only within human reflection. As such it is within the realm of human responsibility to seek reflective control over thoughts and action in relation to conversion. Edwards does not pose God as the ineffable ground of experience that cannot be explained, as James does in "The Will to Believe." For James, the ineffability of the object behind religious questions or commitments puts discovering it beyond control and thus beyond our responsibility. Edwards disagrees. While God's character is absent from us, discovering this absence is possible in reflection and is thus the most determinative aspect of our character.

Edwards begins where Dewey and Peirce end by driving the questions of structure and content toward the Christian tradition and the soul. Finding the place of absence in our reflective ordering becomes a sign of grace and an opening for reflection. Edwards does not begin with revelation of supernatural content, but what is discovered to the soul is the supernatural depth of the absence of the affections.

Progressive Discovery in the Signs of Affection

In the twelve signs of gracious affection in *Religious Affections* (RA) there is a clear sense of movement and progression in religious understanding. Unlike the twelve signs of what *are not* gracious affections in Part II, the last part of the *Affections* moves to a positive statement of what kinds of affections signify the effect of God's active grace. This moving discovery of what is present in the affections of the saint gives Edwards's account its character of building toward a conclusion of God, rather than simply proclaiming faith or knowledge based on intuition or revelation. In this way Edwards not only contravenes Locke's claim of supremacy for ideas immediately held in the mind; he also shifts the focus of his tradition from its expectation for an undeniable perception of God's revealed truth to the way that truth does emerge with power in the affective lives of people. The affections progress from the recognition of a spiritual sense of love to God, to an attraction for God's moral perfection, to the awareness of a sense of the heart. The progression moves in depth from conclusions that can be intellectually held to those that can only be sensed. Edwards says, "The one is mere speculative knowledge; the other sensible knowledge, in which more than the mere intellect is concerned; the heart is the proper subject of it, or the soul as a being that not only beholds, but has inclination, and is pleased or displeased" (RA 272). God becomes a feature of sensible intuition only by virtue of the character inclinations make possible in the heart.

But progression toward a sensible knowledge in the affections runs on another track than positive discovery. The love the saint has for God is a love that arises without human control. Edwards says "that God loved us, when we had not loved him. God's love to the elect, is the ground of their love to him" (RA 249). Love toward spiritual things, for Edwards, is coupled with the recognition of what the saints perceive in their affections but that does not arise because of their power. Also, God's moral perfection appears as a beautiful thing, but it shows an order that is not our own but a further sign of God's holiness. This absence of the order that appears in the "great manifestation of God's moral perfection" (RA 272) provides the ground for what the sense of the heart might be that it is not. Without the opposing order of God's moral perfection, the order of the saint's inclination and will would not ever be recognized as an absent condition that might be satisfied. This absence of the heart appears only in light of God's moral holiness.

Edwards's discovery in these first six signs of affection is that the soul can progressively move toward God only by a continued attraction to what is most absent in the soul. The sense of the heart that follows the conviction of the truth of the gospel concerning Jesus is not the culmination of this progressive discovery. It sets the ground for the discovery of the sensible knowledge that is most painfully absent in the affections. The progressive discovery in the *Affections* resolves toward an absence that the soul knows cannot be overcome by any reason, intellectual production, or willful act.

EVANGELICAL HUMILIATION

Evangelical humiliation interrupts the apparent ascent of the affections. This humiliation, in which the true depth of our separation from God is discovered, is not an intellectual grasp but sensible knowledge of the heart. This sense confronts the saint; it is not what would ever be aimed at intentionally, and this sense cannot be produced by any active work of the intellect or will. In evangelical humiliation the holiness of God reveals what is absent from the soul, but this is revealed in the affections of the saint. Edwards distinguishes between two forms of the recognition of error:

> There is a distinction to be made between a *legal* and an *evangelical* humiliation. The former is what men may be the subjects of, while they are yet in a state of nature, and have no gracious affection; the latter is peculiar to true saints: the former is from the common influence of the Spirit of God, assisting natural principles, and especially natural conscience; the latter is from the special influences of the Spirit of God, implanting and exercising supernatural and divine principles: the former is from the mind's being assisted to a greater sense of things of religion, as to their natural properties and qualities, and particularly of the natural perfections of God, such as his greatness, terrible majesty etc. which were manifested to the congregation of Israel, in giving the law at Mount Sinai; the latter is from a sense of the transcendent beauty of divine things in their moral qualities . . . ; a sense of this is given in evangelical humiliation, by a discovery of God's holiness and moral perfection. . . . In legal humiliation, the conscience is convinced, as the consciences of all will be most perfectly at the Day of Judgment: but because there is no spiritual understanding the will is not bowed, nor the inclination altered: this is done only in evangelical humiliation. (RA 311–312)

Evangelical humiliation is the awareness that the content that is absent in the affections is the order of God's moral perfection and holiness. Time or reflection is not sufficient to develop this quality or order in the affections because no continuum of progress can overcome this absence. The heart is not determined in its character by the long run of inquiry. The inability to construct an entity out of linearly compiled acts or thoughts is *the* human absence Edwards strikes upon.

In light of evangelical humiliation the unordered soul leaps to the inference that the absence within the person is the absence of God in the world. The prior signs of the epistemic and moral incompleteness of the soul are confirmed in this humiliation as the demonstration of the blindness of human consciousness. In opposition to his philosophical tradition Edwards finds that intellectual power and reflection are finally means of a clearer discovery of human limitations that can be revealed only in light of the unity of God's moral holiness.

Gracious affections flow out of this brokenness in self-abasement. Self-abasement is not an exercise of decrying valuable efforts as not valuable because the scripture says so. Rather, genuine self-abasement follows the realization that we are not the order of "the divinity of Divinity." God's character, as the origin of excellence, becomes clear in the discovery of this absence in ourselves, and nothing else can produce this disjunction. Just as Dewey finds nature emergent in human habit, Edwards finds the character of God emergent in relation to the soul only through the discovery of this absence.

God, for Edwards, is discovered to us only in conversion. The mystery of Christ appears as the order of the tradition that holds human time together, both the time of the power of human reflection as it constructs the ground for our identities through the compiling of actions and reexamining those for an order, and the breaking apart of that time by the discovery of the impossibility of overcoming error. Christ is for conversion, where this continuity and discontinuity of the soul becomes one thing—the work of God. This close connection between human conversion and a description of God's character is one of the reasons Perry Miller sees Edwards as a closet naturalist. Edwards does not herald a peculiar divine conviction that shoots into the soul or mind *ad extra* to confirm or create the positive character of God. God is only known through the Christological absence in the affections.

TRADITION AND CONVERSION

In this analysis of the *Religious Affections* I have paid attention to the negative or absent aspect of the progression of the soul's awareness of gracious affections. I have tried to show at each level of self-awareness, from the love of the saint for God, the recognition of God's moral perfection in the revelation that there is a unity of will and intellect in the sense of the heart and in the experience of evangelical humiliation, that Edwards's discovery is what the soul most deeply lacks. Absence in the affections, however, leads to the content that answers the Christ of the gospels. Christ is not just a focus of faith or a claim that must be accepted; Christ is the linchpin between the soul's search for content in light of its failure and the tradition of Christianity that also finds its unity in this one that cannot be a construction by human mind.

The truth of Christ emerges in the tradition of scripture by which the soul is now able "to behold the amiable and bright manifestations of the divine perfections, and of the excellency and sufficiency of Christ, and the excellency and suitableness of the way of salvation by Christ. . . . Which things are, and always were in the Bible, and would have been seen before, if it had not been for blindness, without having any new sense added by words being sent by God to a particular person, and spoken anew to him, with a new meaning" (RA 281). Without this absence of meaning in the scriptures, that there are things "not seen" that become the ground for a new meaning, there is no transformation of the affections. The gospel tradition is an external confirmation of the sign that Christ is the essential content for the soul only if the Christ is the essential content for that tradition. This locates the Christ between the soul and tradition built upon scripture.

Without this content that links the tradition and the soul every adjustment will only be to another incomplete form of ordered affections or another incomplete tradition. And if a complete ordering of affections is possible without Christ, then scripture is not true in regard to Christ. But more, if ordering the affections is possible without Christ, then all humanity is awash in a destructive absence that it should be able to rescue itself from, but so far it has not or will not. If it is possible to order our affections and our tradition in some other way, and yet this remains undone, what hope remains? Human life and affections will continue to show the absence of solidity, resistance, and entity, unless some transforming content appears. In sign 7 Edwards confirms the divine purpose of the discovery of Christ as this transformation:

> "But we all, with open face, beholding as in a glass, the glory of the Lord, are changed into the same image, from glory to glory, even as by the Spirit of the Lord" (II Cor. 3:18). Such power as this is properly divine power, and is peculiar to the Spirit of the Lord: other power may make a great alteration in men's present frames and feelings; but 'tis the power of a Creator only that can change the nature, or give a new nature. And no discoveries or illuminations, but those that are divine and supernatural, will have this supernatural effect. But this effect all those discoveries have, that are truly divine. The soul is deeply affected by these discoveries and so affected as to be transformed. (RA 340)

Discovering transformation is the proof of evangelical humiliation, just as stabilizing opinion certifies Peirce's self-correcting inquiry. We discover the beauty and power of the scripture tradition in light of our deepest awareness of failure. Edwards raises the case another metaphysical level. Not only are our errors an essential aspect of the discovery of God, the explicit rejection of Christ, in the heart of the individual and in the tradition, makes transformation a local healing, a return to the place of error where error must be corrected. The individual returns to the tradition, and the tradition returns to the individual. This mutual dependence is possible only on the condition that we cannot give ourselves the same order as the tradition, and that the tradition cannot create us in our true individuality. The truth of this discovery is played out in the continuing search for the unity of inquiry and community that forms the backdrop for the American philosophical tradition. Conversion becomes a reflective origin of American philosophy, standing for the possible unity of sense and reflection, and experiential truth that can be known only in the living of it.

FROM EDWARDS TO PRAGMATISM

Speaking philosophically of Christ, and speaking religiously of Dewey's notion of habits and Peirce's notion of inquiry, brings this study to its most difficult point. How is it possible to connect the tradition of philosophical discovery with the tradition of Edwards and his Christ? Is absence a ground that enables us to move between these traditions? Can we claim that pragmatism moves into *all* the reflective problems of men and women, including religious absence? Can we also claim that Edwards's understanding of the affections retains any effective application to the human community today?

One way to examine the possibility of such a connection is to see how the deepest problems of Edwards correspond to the problems of the pragmatists. Edwards does collect Peirce's confusion about the structure of the self and the community. For Peirce, the truth that is present as an object of inquiry establishes the continuity of the community. The object that recedes in our inquiry resembles Edwards's co-emergence of Christ in the individual and the community. But even more compelling is the significance of inquiry for the individual. Peirce and Edwards deal in the same discovery of absence that defines the individual. For Edwards and Peirce the individual is poised at the limit of the community. It is also true for Edwards and Peirce that conversion (or manifesting the law of mind) is not possible unless the individual realizes that she is the sign of the community's continuation. Peirce's difficulty in describing the way the centering of the community occurs through inquiry and how it becomes a content that might inform the individual's habit, is shared by Edwards. Exploring the structure of the individual and the community brings Peirce to the limit of the will, and this becomes a question of facts about particular habits that are adopted and overcome. The possibility of transformation is held within Peirce's category of secondness, the brute fact of actions. Conversion is not a matter of the intellect so much as the will.

Dewey's sense of nature as the content that draws the community forward has its origin in the kind of discovery that Edwards describes. The authority of that content stands apart from the content itself. Authority is what cannot be produced from the side of experience. We cannot *make* something authoritative for us and for our community. We discover ourselves only within that authority, or not. What makes community is the recognition of an authority in experience. Dewey explores the absence that Edwards finds, looking for a content that would satisfy every transformation of human habit. This means that Dewey's pragmatism seeks a Christological completion, or at least it reflects a Christological absence. The community of transformation has this content that exceeds nature as its limit.

Conversion is yet to be fully explored, but dwelling in absence is a necessary feature of this exploration. Without a discovery of absence all creations and expansions of habit are disconnected from the core realization that we must exceed the aspects of our thought and practice from within that practice to attain real transformation. All of our habits must emerge in relation to the nature of our experience, as Dewey says, but this is not the most determining limit. How these habits reflect an order beyond that nature is the question. What Dewey desires is a loft to practice, where practice attains an ideal production that transcends what is now appearing with what might express a value not yet conceived. Peirce, on the other hand, longs for confirmation that the individual inquirer, namely himself, becomes not only a part of the community but that his inquiry becomes a sign of the agapistic expansion of meaning in the universe.

For Edwards, the opening for meaning for individuals and for the community of saints far exceeds all the expectations of our discovery. The soul becomes expansively unlimited as the answer to the Christological absence in the universe. Seeing what it is *not,* the soul sees what it is yet to be. Edwards says this material for growth of the meaning of the soul is vast: "Spiritual good is satisfying, as there is enough in it, to satisfy the soul, as to degree, if obstacles were but removed, and the enjoying faculty duly applied. There is room enough here for the soul to extend itself; here is an infinite ocean of it" (RA 379). This is true freedom, where our discovery is never limited by the content we inquire into but only by our efforts toward it.

But the only way to prove out this absence is precisely what William James says it is—it must become a part of action taken at the risk of losing everything on the hope of gaining a place in the universe. But instead of taking for true that which we think we can live, as James does, the witness of Edwards, Peirce, and Dewey is that real freedom is living beyond what we are exactly sure we can. This means that freedom must explode beyond our expectations and our thought into the kind of life that exceeds what we can imagine or control. God, or whatever is real, must be like a flood coursing through valleys that can never hold its fullness. There is always a spilling over and backing up into other valleys. To use a different metaphor, our inquiry must always be getting away from us, bringing us to ever new discoveries in places that we thought were plumbed for all the good there. Transformed inquiry must also be breaking into places that before were reserved or cut off from our view as possible areas for exploration. The conversion that emerges out of absence means that we do not know the areas in which our discovery will expand, but our inquiry there will be a discovery just the same, and that we are not yet as free as we are intended to be.

NOTES

1. This point of a fourth kind of inquirer follows on the analysis of Carl Vaught's criticism of Peirce's categories from the basis of analogy. Vaught analyzes a difference that is accessible only by being given an autonomous place within a judgment of analogy. He says, "We often make judgments of this kind, and they are cognizable just to the extent that we are willing to grant that analogy is an intelligible conception that cannot be reduced to identity and difference. . . . this phenomenon can be understood only in terms of the Fourthness of analogy, and that Peirce made a disastrous blunder when he insisted that feeling, will and law; quality, existence and generality; possibility,

fact and mediation are the only universal dimensions of human experience." Carl G. Vaught, "Semiotics and the Problem of Analogy: A Critique of Peirce's Theory of Categories," *Transactions of the Charles S. Peirce Society* 22, no. 3 (summer 1986): 325.

2. See also Henry W. Johnstone Jr., *The Problem of the Self* (Pennsylvania State University Press, 1970).

3. Dewey, *Experience and Nature,* 186. See also 247, where Dewey calls the self the "tool of tools," as *the* means implied in every means. This presents another topic of concern than the one here, but the question is profound. Dewey cites the self as a tool because of the necessity of its having a prior order, an opaque essence. This opaque presence of order accords the self a quality that can sustain deep inquiry, almost precisely the same sort of inquiry that communication sustains. Dewey is close here to the psychologism that Husserl suffers in *Cartesian Meditations,* which Derrida makes critical use of in *Speech and Phenomena,* 13.

4. H. Richard Niebuhr, *The Kingdom of God in America* (Wesleyan University Press, 1988), 101.

5. Niebuhr, *Christ and Culture* (Harper & Row, 1975), 220. Niebuhr explains his choice by referring to the way Edwards's thought has been diverted by "shabby revivalism," as a sociological science of mass-producing the knowledge of grace. Maybe moving beyond Edwards is necessary, but even this acknowledgment by Niebuhr suggests that Edwards opened up this potential in his preaching and writing. I wonder how Edwards's reintroduction into American academic view would have been altered had Niebuhr resurrected him instead of moving beyond him.

6. John Smith, "Jonathan Edwards as Philosophical Theologian," *The Review of Metaphysics* 30, no. 2 (December 1976): 311.

7. Michael Raposa, "Jonathan Edwards's Twelfth Sign," *International Philosophical Quarterly* 33, no. 2 (1993): 153–162.

6

Creative Transformation: The Work of Conversion

AMERICAN PRAGMATISM represents a rich collection of arguments and issues that circulate around the transformation of life. This interest in transformation can make pragmatism appear less rigorous or less analytically powerful than competing philosophical models. My suggestion in this book, however, is that pragmatism aims to dwell within the power of philosophy that focuses on the systemic alteration of practice and the discovery of philosophical character. The rigor and analytic power the Americans seek can be measured only in the creative transformation of life, and developing the philosophical tools needed for this transformation is their primary concern.

In previous chapters I have dealt with the structures of transformation of which these philosophers are most aware. Peirce is most aware of the continuity of inquiry and practice and the realization of character within this continuum. Dewey is most aware of the emergent authority that makes criticism of practice both possible and productive in terms of growth. James is most aware of the psychological and personal dimensions of adjustment. Through these individual treatments, I have been trying to construct a broader argument that holds these philosophers together.

The cohesion of Peirce, James, and Dewey into a tradition depends on the strength of their philosophical approaches to incorporate conceptions of habit, inquiry, character, and authority around the pole of transformation. I do not think that these philosophers take it upon themselves to promote transformation in others or measure their success in this way. Rather, they perceive a transformation that is already present in their philosophical tradition and their culture. In this light, they devote their efforts to describing, illustrating, and expanding transformation in order to develop more access to its power and unveil its potential for being discovered through creative inquiry. The creative work of these pragmatists is bounded by transformation. This boundedness to the hope of a holistic transformation is the basis for their connection to Edwards that warrants my intuition that the problem of conversion is deeply embedded in the American philosophical enterprise.

In this chapter I want to extend the critique of transformation in American philosophy and begin to look at conversion thematically. Again, this is not an effort to incite transformation or conversion. Genuine transformation cannot be produced by argument but only by experience and discovery. While describing one's expectations may incline auditors toward the power of transformation, the pragmatists are confident that no person can manipulate this truth. Transformation is a reality that can be discovered with the help of another person or an intellectual guide, but unless transformation resists all efforts to become a function of utility or a domesticated form of thought it will only generate another semiotic iteration of ourselves. My claim is that the American philosophers are convinced that a genuine transformation of the form, content, and character of habits and inquiry is possible in experience. The origin of this transformation transcends experience and complete conscious control, but this transcendence can be discovered only by approaching the limit of self-consciously controlled change. The remainder of this chapter contains, first, some considerations concerning the shared methods of approach to transformation, especially in light of the religious character of this discussion in the pragmatists, and second, a thematic account of the transformation that becomes conversion.

HISTORICAL AND THEOLOGICAL ARGUMENTS FOR TRANSFORMATION

Using transformation as an incorporative theme in the development in American thought, as I am doing here, has similarities to H. Richard Niebuhr's *The Kingdom of God in America,* in which Niebuhr argues that transformation is a fact of our culture through the presence of institutional Christianity. In some ways Niebuhr celebrates precisely what Dewey laments, the authoritative hold of Christianity on the expectations of common faith. Dewey could not displace this character, although he tried. But Niebuhr does not fear external critics such as Dewey as much as the internal loss of the church's identity and integrity. Niebuhr states, "I felt strongly that the times called for a rejection of 'Culture Protestantism' and for the return of the church to the confession of its own particular faith and ethos."[1] The particular ethos Niebuhr is looking to is the sustained effort of the American church to transform itself and society under the power of the kingdom of God. The loss of this power in the church is evident in its inability to speak to the present conditions of social and religious life. In response to this loss, Niebuhr hopes to awaken this ethos by showing the development of constructive and formative resources of that faith.[2] His method is most striking. Niebuhr simply describes the habit of historical American Christianity, doing "theology in the guise of history." He recalls the formative impulses in the figures central to American Christianity: "For the king-dom of God to which these men and the movements they initiated were loyal was not simply American culture or political and economic interest exalted and idealized; it was rather a kingdom which was prior to America and to which this nation, in its politics and economics, was required to conform."[3] In this way, Niebuhr offers an understanding of American culture in relation to American Christianity by using this lat-ter as the starting point. But Niebuhr also explores the transformation at the core of American Christianity as a historical resource for the present reconfiguring of the church and its faith. He has confidence that the pat-tern of transformation evident in the development of constructive Protestantism will provide the grounds for a recovery of this power. He struggles against the possibility that the content that inspired transforma-tive work in our past will do so again. Transformation requires an ever new response, albeit a response that maintains the integrity of the com-munity from which it extends.

Finding such an element of integrity and reformation is also evident in Ellen Charry's work on historical theology, *By the Renewing of Your Minds*. Like Niebuhr, Charry discovers a peculiar character within Christian doctrine. Although she sets out simply to read historical theol-ogy, Charry finds that a pattern emerges in those sources that connect them in a striking way. She says, "When Christian doctrines assert the truth about God, the world, and ourselves, it is a truth that seeks to influ-ence us. As I worked through the texts, the divisions of the modern the-ological curriculum began making less and less sense to me. I realized I was uncovering a norm of theological integrity that had become unin-telligible to the modern disciplines."[4] Charry identifies this norm as an *aretological* intention, that is, these texts aim to produce excellence in the readers. But accessing this theme means resisting the epistemological assertions of modern philosophy and their theological criticisms. "The modern understanding of reason, and truth constructed by Locke,

Hume, and Kant is too narrow to be adequate for theological claims."[5] The theological claims she is principally interested in relate not to how one arrives at a better propositional basis for belief, but how one is to change, "to experience the nobility and truth of God whenever we use our minds rightly."[6] She likens theological "knowledge" to the practice of medicine as a knowledge that also requires skilled judgment. "The proper practice of Christianity, like the proper practice of medicine, requires compassion and care and a watchful eye. In neither case can good treatment be limited to mechanical application of rules or practices."[7] Recovering the category of skilled judgment enables Charry to reinvest biblical material with theological reflection. In relation to the Pauline school she writes, "Christian excellence is spiritual maturation effected by both a rehabilitation of mind and practiced behaviors that renew the self in the likeness of God (Eph. 4:17, 23–24). The imperatives of verses 17–24, urging readers not to return to the darkness of pagan futility, suggest that Christian behavior cannot be coerced. Although the author realizes the important role sociality and communal leadership play in Christian formation (4:11–13), the decision to luxuriate under the lordship of Christ and be guided by the Christian community, rather than wallow in impurity, must be undertaken intentionally. Humans are socially influenced but not socially determined."[8] Charry sees this pattern in theology that makes it a platform for discovering "fresh means of atonement," much as St. Paul suggests is the result of the response of the Gentiles to Christ in the letter to the Romans. The premise of theology is that this change offers new vantages for reading historical texts and making skilled judgments concerning immediate experience.

The consideration of whether transformation is a historical oddity or doctrinal characteristic peculiar to the Christian community finds its complement in the theology of David Ford. He appropriates transformation as a vehicle for expanding doctrinal questions into contemporary thought. Actually, Ford's question in *Self and Salvation: Being Transformed* is whether a theology of salvation can go to the heart of Christian identity. "How can an approach to salvation act as a focus for the gospel story in its biblical setting while also having universal implications?"[9] Instead of tracing out the historical power of conversion as Niebuhr does, or developing a synthetic theological vision as Charry does, Ford examines the transformation of salvation to see if it can collect the work of contemporary thinkers. He argues that it does, taking his lead also from Ephesians:

"The message of salvation is that there is a new humanity which is already a reality in Christ and that even in relation to the deepest hostility (religious, racial, cultural, etc.) one starts from a situation in which the dividing wall has been removed, giving free access to God together."[10] He wends his way through the contemporary voices of Ricoeur, Levinas, and Jungel to display a language of transformation and conversion that is richly open to development.

Each of these three writers deserves an extended analysis. My point here, however, is to demonstrate three different directions from which the question of transformation can be fruitfully approached, and to suggest that each of these ways begins a kind of expansion that obliterates the charge of narrowness or cultic opacity often associated with conversion. My own direction into the question of conversion differs from these three. Rather than proposing that there is a truth that is accepted within culture but presently diminished in its power, or that the expectation of transformation has been present throughout the tradition and just needs a fresh unveiling, or that traditional sources of Christian transformation need additional power from an extension into contemporary voices, my argument is that the transformation of conversion emerges in the thought of the American philosophers when they try to do what philosophy does best, in critically evaluating the origin and prospects of thought and action. There is twofold character to this claim. First is discerning the limit of *self-controlled* transformation, and second, perceiving the reality of transformation that breaks beyond that power of self-control. Pragmatists move into this space, flowing back and forth between self-control and transcendent power. I cannot say that Christianity is or is not the most determining influence on the pragmatists' focus on transformation, but that neither strengthens nor diminishes this argument. The pragmatists' criticism of the demand for transformation clearly connects them with their religious culture, and it also becomes a platform for a creative transformation of philosophy. This is the element I find missing in the three theological models described earlier.

The power to mold a tradition on the basis of a critical advance sets the pragmatists apart. This is also what connects them to Edwards, whose tradition changing power is a result of his work on conversion. Edwards's clarification of conversion became the origin of a creative extension and transformation of American Christianity and culture that continues to influence us today. This extension stumbled intellectually under the leadership of his disciples in the New Divinity, but in many ways the pragmatists recovered this ground philosophically. This access from philosophy makes the transformation at the root of American intellectual and religious culture a different kind of discovery. It cannot be separated from the religious tradition; it is not a purely "natural" theology, but it is natural in the sense that any desire for transformation that emerges in experience is a sufficient ground for this philosophical inquiry.

THEMES OF THE CREATIVE TRANSFORMATION OF CONVERSION

The purpose of this account of conversion is to make an advance on the self-critical awareness of the spirit of transformation that invests pragmatism. My goal is not to make something of the pragmatists that they are not. Rather, I am attempting to get a truer measure of the depth of their arguments for transformation by relating them to religious conversion and Jonathan Edwards. I believe that religious conversion is the proper framework within which a critical sense of the pragmatists' philosophical power may be brought to view and therefore also to a critical assessment. Just as Ellen Charry found an aretological impulse while reading historical theology, when I read Edwards, Peirce, Dewey, and James I find them leading to the question of ultimate transformation. In this section, I use a thematic description of conversion to follow these leadings. In the process I will try to demonstrate what keeps transformation present in their thought without it collapsing into a static theory or a dogmatic doctrine. This goes for Edwards as well, who finds flexibility in the meaning of conversion and expansiveness in the discovery of this life that opens into a continual process of creative transformation of the self and the community.

I have chosen to follow the four main themes I identified in Edwards's twelve signs of gracious affections for the structure of this general account of conversion. Using Edwards's themes as a guide makes it possible to integrate elements of transformation in the pragmatists with his expressly Christian fidelity, showing the resonance between Edwards and the pragmatists as well as their deepest points of conflict. Principal among these points of conflict is Edwards's Christological character of conversion that brings the evaluation of pragmatic transformation to a critical juncture. The four themes that bring us to this juncture are (1) aesthetic moral sense, (2) human understanding and the orientation of inquiry, (3) orienting content and the change of nature, and (4) the return to life conversion makes possible. This focus on the return to life as the *telos* of creative transformation is shared by Edwards and the pragmatists as the true good of revelation and reason.

AESTHETIC MORAL SENSE

The first three signs of gracious affections cohere around a sense discovered in the affections that indicates an active and divine influence. Edwards begins his description of gracious affections by saying, "I. That they do arise from those influences and operations on the heart, which are *spiritual, supernatural,* and *divine;* II. The first objective ground of gracious affections, is the transcendentally excellent and amiable nature of divine things, as they are in themselves; and, III. Those affections that are truly holy, are primarily founded on the loveliness of the moral excellency of divine things" (RA 197, 240, 253). The aesthetic sense of divine moral beauty is the unequivocal beginning of an inquiry into the ground necessary for transformation because it reveals the distinction between spiritual and natural excellence and the attraction that draws the heart from the natural to the spiritual.

One of the most difficult aspects of the *Religious Affections* and of any analysis of conversion is distinguishing between transformation as a completed act and transformation as a progressive discovery. Edwards seems to flip back and forth between these two, as is apparent in this first step of his argument. This ambiguity demonstrates that the transformation of conversion is a genuine moment of human and divine interaction, since otherwise conversion would be either only known as a preordained completion or only experienced as a temporal progression in our ideas. The preordained completed quality is evident in the attraction that would have no ground if not for the initiating influence of God, yet even this initial movement of the divine appears as a kind of invitation.

The divine initiative Edwards has in view is not general grace, but special grace that is saving if it is taken up as the initiation of an inquiry and opening up of the affections toward transformation. Thus, aesthetically motivated transformation can be followed into the realm of conversion. But the attraction to divine beauty is not a product of a temporal progression of ideas. While all beauty reveals a discovery of an order beyond the elements perceived, as the symmetry of a tune becomes apparent apart from the particular notes heard, the order of God's holiness is also perceived by a discovery of symmetry and harmony of acts that human thought can discover but not generate. And this realization of a spiritual discovery is, for Edwards, the opening or beginning of every experience of divine influence that begins an inquiry into transformation.

It is essential for Edwards that the discovery of transformation moves on attraction. Transformation is a response to gracious influence and love, because the method of revelation is continuous with the object revealed. The scripture speaks of the changed heart that loves God, and so this change must be brought about by love, not imposed against one's will or desire. Edwards does not claim that God is somehow ontologically prior within the understanding and then uncovered by some experience or rational principle. Revelation is part and parcel of the divine character of moral holiness, and the revelation of this character cannot be otherwise than an expression of this holiness. God's holy character is a human transforming holiness and so it can be known only in the reality of transformation. The creative transformation that Edwards discovers in himself is attended with the experience of his power to affect his own character through a response to an invitation to find something lovely. This love is not a mysterious element in transformation that eliminates or cancels human power of directed inquiry. The love of God's moral beauty provides a "first beginning and spring" of gracious affections for inquiring into the nature of aesthetic attraction that otherwise remains opaque in the affective lives of men and women.

The pragmatists reflect an aesthetic awareness of a moral quality that stands beyond them, although there is a reluctance to call it *supernatural* the way Edwards does. Dewey's sense of "what holds" him and his community in *A Common Faith* comes to mind as an example of this attraction that begins inquiry. In Dewey's thought, the sense of attraction to an order beyond the present order of practice comes in a powerful way, as does his trust that a "spiritual" order supervening on present practice is a great good and a satisfaction of human desire. James's sense of attraction to an ultimate moral claimant in "The Moral Philosopher and the Moral Life" also describes a kind of spiritual order that bears resemblance to God's holiness. In fact, James's identification with this moral sense of obligation and God's character is a pivotal moment in the development of his understanding of human will. James moves back and forth between the sense of attraction and obligation in connection to the divine, resolving finally on the side of attraction that must therefore dispel obligation. I think this original point of symmetry between obligation and attraction invests James's religious philosophy with a living tension.

Peirce is most clearly enrapt in the sense of aesthetic attraction to divine things when he speaks of "earnestly loving and adoring his strictly hypothetical God" (CP 6:467). God's moral beauty emerges in his account of the harmony within the universes of experience, a harmony that is not a static repetition of an ideal principle, but the discovery of an order that itself is growing and expanding in meaning. This living character of ideal is central to Peirce's notion of God, as he writes to William James in a letter of July 26, 1905:

> Forgive me for harping on the subject of theism, it is impossible for a person who puts metaphysical definitions aside to think that the object of one's love is not living. The idea is a vague one but it is only the more irresistible for that. . . . It is really impossible, except by sophisticating the plain truth, to think otherwise than that there is a living being. . . . So then what I mean by a living being is something approaching the nature of an ideal. I am far from ideal, it is true: but the shortcomings that make me so are out of harmony with something within me which would make me a thoroughly living being if it were not for those defects.

Peirce's awareness of the defects that prevent his being a "thoroughly living being" arise from the objective character of his love, but this love is also an opening for inquiry into the living character of an ideal of God. While Peirce does not associate this object of love with the holiness of God described in the scripture as directly as Edwards does, it is clear that the idea he is attracted to emerges with great consistency from his Christian religious experience. Just as James struggles to integrate obligation and attraction, Peirce struggles to integrate the universal attraction to God and his peculiar experience in the Christian tradition.

Where we may extend an analysis of Peirce, James, and Dewey *via* Edwards's spiritual sense is in relation to the claim that such an attraction constitutes a new principle of nature, and that this new nature and attraction are a kind of invitation to follow this inquiry into a fuller account of transformation. On one hand, the pragmatists work out of this confidence that a new kind of spirit is present in their thought and for people who desire this difference in reflective living. On the other hand, the pragmatists seem also to have this hope without ground. At this point Edwards draws confidence from his tradition: "The only certain foundation which any person has to believe that he is invited to partake of the blessings of the gospel, is that the Word of God declares that a person so qualified as he is, are invited, and God who declares it is true and cannot lie . . . for the Scriptures are full of invitations to sinners, to the chief of sinners, to come and partake of the benefits of the gospel" (RA 223). If Edwards means anything in a global sense for American philosophy, it is confidence in the invitation to follow the attractive leading of mind and spirit into a progressive transformation that may yet become a conversion. Detracting from this desire to inquire into transformation or limiting the potential range or significance of transformation to me is an unpardonable philosophical sin.

Edwards's philosophical character is the best proof of the creative result of following this invitation to follow the aesthetic moral sense with productive inquiry. The challenge Edwards represents for the pragmatists is not to bend the knee to his tradition, but to match his inquiry into the springs of human thought and action. Edwards follows this aesthetic invitation with the articulation of the distinction between spiritual versus natural excellence, and in many ways this becomes the central issue of human transformation. Contrary to Dewey's assertion that classical philosophical and theological models privilege security and permanence of ideas, Edwards argues that the issue relating to the understanding is its transformation to a quality of character that is beyond what is presently available or even potentially available in action. Without a similar demand that our practice must exceed its own limits, the pragmatists have no ground for the reconstruction of habit they work for. Dewey's reconstructive urge turns precisely on the distinction between what has been the historical progress of reason and culture and what it should be in light of the fact that we have substituted the god of security and perfection for the God of democratic interactionism. This fructified interactionism is a kind of divine beauty for Dewey.

William James, as much as I think he substitutes himself for God, follows the attraction to the "more" in experience with powerful philosophical analysis. This analysis generates a unique vision of religious experience, in which transformation is a key component. I will not rehearse previous arguments about his views on conversion, except to make the point that Edwards and the pragmatists are very close in the ways they handle this attraction through cultivating and discerning the power of human understanding. But it is the differences here that show the richness and conflicts within the American reflective tradition.

UNDERSTANDING AND THE ORIENTATION OF INQUIRY

The distinction between the natural and spiritual senses of excellence leads to the second theme of transformation. Apart from this distinction, Edwards claims, there is no possibility of difference in human understanding that would amount to a real difference. The spiritual order in the understanding that incorporates the whole self becomes apparent only in relation to a divine ordering that is open for understanding through the truth discerned in the scripture. Also, like the initiating spiritual sense above, this order must be discoverable in experience and provide a platform for intentional direction and willed change. The signs that collect this theme of the effect on the understanding are "IV. Gracious affections do arise from the mind's being enlightened, rightly and spiritually to understand or apprehend divine things; V. Truly gracious affections are attended with a reasonable and spiritual conviction of the judgment, of the reality and certainty of divine things; and VI. with evangelical humiliation. Evangelical humiliation is a sense that a Christian has of his own utter insufficiency, despicableness, and odiousness, with an answerable frame of heart" (RA 266, 291, 311).

The internal dialectic central to Edwards's account of transformation appears very clearly in this section of the *Religious Affections*. From his philosophical reading Edwards knows the power the mind has to understand its own order. But this power can take possession and overrun the understanding that is of divine origin. Indeed, the mind begins with the discovery if its natural order and ordering power before it finds the spiritual order it was meant to exhibit. How this ordering potential of the mind follows out the discovery of the supernatural principle and discerns the disjunction between spiritual and natural excellence is the intimate version of the larger story of God's redeeming work in human history.

Edwards connects the potential ordering of the mind to the apprehension of an order within the habits that comprise one's character. Sang Lee juxtaposes Edwards's understanding of habits as constituting character to the Scholastic understanding of essential nature. The relation between actions and the relation of different relations emerge into a "dispositional ontology." Lee says, "To say that the abiding nature of entities consists in habits and laws is to maintain that entities are abidingly active tendencies. Things are essentially dispositional and thus inherently and unceasingly tending to actual existences through the exercise of habits and laws and through the immediate exercise of God's own power."[11] The advance in human understanding that is possible only through divine transformation has to do with habits of understanding that reflect an emerging influence of divine power by becoming reordered in likeness to divine habits. Reordering habits by a spiritual influence requires that the natural understanding of habit is an analogical other to the divine, where the divine habit is distinguished as resolving to a single principle within the understanding and the will, eliminating any discontinuity internal to the habits of practice. The person becomes an instance of discovering the dispositional character of the divine character emerging in his or her own understanding. Indeed, persons cannot fully understand the sense of their heart without holding together their will and understanding as the source of habit formation emerging from their prior self-understanding. Transformation of the order of the understanding is central to Edwards's approach to conversion. He declares that such a discovery is the content basis of our ability to know our own transformation. The mind, Edwards says, is the proper seat of the affections.

Given the emphasis on changed habits of understanding, the conviction of the truth of the gospel concerning Jesus in sign V is less a matter of producing correct propositional truths than it is a feature of recognizing that the habit and tendency in recorded revelation is the same principle of order that discriminates the natural faculty of understanding from the spiritual. At this point in the *Affections* the conviction of the truth about Jesus is the sign of the discovery of the sense of the heart—this sense of the heart must have the divine order within scripture as its object in order to be awakened. Illumination can come no other way than by perceiving the order of divine habits in the narrative revelation of Jesus in the scripture taken as a whole. But the space of divine revelation is not limited by the particularity of the finite Christian tradition. Revelation is limited only by the human discovery that follows the opening that appears in the reflective understanding aware of its need for a sense of the heart. Edwards is sensitive to the deist charge that a peculiar divine revelation that is compatible with human understanding is challenged by the presence of non-Christian religions. Edwards responds to this charge by affirming a version of Origen's *prisca theologia*. This ancient doctrine holds that a divine and saving revelation stands at the root of all religions, not as a perfect original that degenerates in specificity or truth, but a permanent if obscured impulse toward reflecting the habit of divine tendency universally distributed in the power of human habit seeking order.[12] There is light to follow in all traditions through which all people may discover the demand for a sense of the heart.

The pragmatic focus on the ultimate character of a transformation of the understanding follows the conviction that the mind is the seat of the affections. Pragmatic inquiry begins by challenging the bifurcation of willing and knowing in modern philosophy. Peirce's most common phrase defining his pragmatism is "you shall know them by their fruits." Further, the pragmatic argument that the division between thought and act is false couples with the drive toward discovering an order in thought and practice as the only method of productive inquiry into truth. The pragmatists clearly reflect Edwards's principle that the reflective life is not determined by the need for satisfactory responses to problems of reason but by the desire to develop a holistic response of the understanding and will to what is real. For this reason there are analogues to Edwards's sense of the heart in the pragmatists, principally apparent in the rejection of the modern philosophical platform of inquiry. The pragmatists demand a different heart of philosophical inquiry.

The analogue of the sense of the heart in Dewey is his projection of progressive intelligence developing new meaning in experience. Such progression implicates both the community and individuals in the same project, collecting the understanding of the communally driven impulse toward growth with the individual will to break beyond confining habits. Dewey recurs to the devotion of men and women for whom natural piety is the order of their action in discovering the task of democracy. The ultimate character of this coordination of understanding and will in a spirit of devotion appears in Dewey's pedagogic creed:

> I believe that every teacher should realize the dignity of his calling; that he is a social servant set apart for the maintenance of proper social order and the securing of the right social growth. I believe that in this way the teacher always is the prophet of the true God and the usherer in of the true kingdom of God. (EW 5:595)

The relation of this prophetic individual to the growth of the community is also apparent in Dewey's emphasis on the individual's settled act of will in *A Common Faith*. But beyond these platitudinous references, Dewey's appreciation of the discriminating force of this "sense of heart" comes out most apparently in his frequent rejection of the "supernatural" order of understanding. For Dewey there is no possible discovery of a coordinating sense between the community and the individual in relation to the traditional character of supernaturalism.[13] Although I disagree with this analysis and have shown Edwards's rich sense of discovery in relation to the supernatural, I think Dewey is exactly right about forms of knowing that occur without due consideration of the relation of the heart and devotion. Where I think Dewey errs is his assumption that the supernatural always turns into a selfish desire for a private salvation. If Dewey had kept his focus on the inability to construct an order of the understanding simply by reference to private ends, and had avoided taking the "supernatural" as the generic failure of that attitude, I think his story of philosophical reconstruction would be much richer.

James reflects on the desire for a sense of the heart as a psychological function of the structure of religion. His suggestion that religious experience coincides with the development of the widest possible self reflects the same expectation that the understanding and will resolve into a single principle. The sense of the heart is not so much an individual achievement for James as it is a possibility determined by the framework within which religion and reflection are combined. In *Varieties of Religious Experience* he aims to alter the conceptual framework of religion in order to secure the ground for an accurate estimation of the prospects available for individuals. James does not worry about encouraging people to faith or witnessing to the power of the content he discovers, but he does intend to say where such content may or may not properly arise and what the effects of such content may or may not be within a properly refined understanding of both psychology and religion. James relies on the expression of the self in its deepest and most profoundly affective dimensions as the linchpin between the creation and the discovery of order in the reflective life. His preference for mysticism in the *Varieties* raises the content of the self to a religiously powerful discovery, primarily because of the limited criticism that can be brought to bear on it. This dependence on mysticism makes James's antithesis to Edwards's position clear, since for Edwards there is no motivating principle that can be cordoned off from critical evaluation. Even though James's focus on the personal dimension of religious experience is often associated with Edwards, their arguments about the difference in the capacity of human understanding in light of religious experience deeply conflict. James claims that one is justified in believing what one hopes to be true, or in our terms here, the sense of the heart is a product of intense appreciation of the content of one's anticipation of a more expansive personality. Edwards, as we have seen, resists any content as the order of the sense of the heart that would have to translate the Christ event into a private accommodation of one's prospective personality.

This conflict between James and Edwards over the order of understanding discovered in conversion brings to light a vitally important criticism of pragmatism. Apart from this conflict, the full dimension of James's alteration of the expectation of human understanding cannot be fully accounted. James argues that the understanding can attain the same affective order in terms of its effects as Edwards claims can occur only in light of the sense of the heart revealed in relation to Jesus. James's resistance to Edwards is the only way into this particular ground of criticism of the ordering of the understanding. The opposition centers on whether the order of the understanding is a personal creation, as in James, or that which is the result of a discovery in relation to a tradition, as in Edwards. American philosophy has pretty thoroughly handed over its religious concern to the spiritualism of human self that informs James's philosophy. This explains some of the tension that has developed between pragmatism and religion despite the clear religious characters of these three classical pragmatists, and despite William James's effort to isolate the peculiar good of religion. Pragmatists have repeated his criticisms while rejecting most of his positive attitudes toward religious activity, a response that has done more to isolate pragmatism from its full potential to reform American practice than any other philosophical habit.

Peirce, in nearly diametrical opposition to James, develops an account of understanding that depends on overcoming the "vagaries" of the self in order to approach real character. Peirce's emphasis on the Law of Mind discovered through the logical analysis of the continuity of thought, corresponds to Edwards's claim that human understanding seeks a completion of an ordering principle it cannot provide on its own. Peirce's notion of a developing character in human inquiry and Edwards's notion of conversion as a complete reordering of the understanding both avoid the problem of an ontological priority of a divine essence, at least in the phenomenological sense with which these claims become available and effective for ordering practice. Edwards and Peirce agree that claims, even ultimate ones like the final character of the individual and the universe, must be testable in practice. While Edwards does not propose a logical test of the "sense of the heart," I think a Peircean analysis of this aspect of transformation is appropriate. For if the sense of the heart cannot be described in relation to practice *and* doubt, I would agree with Peirce that it has no meaning.

The sense of the heart proposed by Edwards could be tested only by comparing it to an alternate ordering of the understanding that is shown to fail in comprehensiveness of self-understanding or self-control. This pragmatic evaluation would amount to showing what the "sense of the heart" makes possible in practice that another principle of understanding could not. The test for comprehensiveness requires an act that completely changes the order of understanding by virtue of a self-critically willed appropriation. I think this ground of a complete change in the structure of habit and habit formation appears in Peirce's "Neglected Argument for the Reality of God," although I think his effort comes up short in the end. Peirce realizes that the limitation of his synechism is that it cannot contain a terminus in action but only the infinitely distant *telos* of a continuous series. Conversion challenges Peirce's logic, and in fact, challenges it on its own terms in a way unavailable from any other position. Only the expectation of a complete change of the order of the understanding by virtue of an ideal that completely orients the will can bring Peirce's semiotic theory to its ultimate test.

Peirce more clearly diverges from Edwards over the principle of evangelical humiliation. The character of Peirce's agapism is really beyond the product of self-controlled inquiry, but when he comes at the issue from the side of logic, he claims that the character of agapism is immanent in the practice of pragmaticism. For if it is not a character that can be potentially realized it is a useless abstraction. If agapism means something we cannot perform, even in principle, even given the hypothetical distance of a temporal long run, then agapism is an idea that is discontinuous with our thought. We have reached the opacity of nominalism. Edwards might provide an interesting response to Peirce at this point concerning the negation that emerges in relation to the character aimed at in self-critical inquiry. Although there is no apparent limit to realizing such a character in practice, this completion cannot be attained in the same active production of the understanding that occurs in inquiry. Edwards's notion of evangelical humiliation might provide a further dimension of Peircean inquiry rather than a metaphysical meltdown. If pragmaticism would discover its own lapse by identifying the character it seeks to emulate, and, with this character, discover its inability to reproduce this in terms of a living content, then it would be closer to the truth concerning us. Even when we know the good, we do not do the good. Peirce does not have an appropriate category for the rejection he perceives at the end of his essay "The Law of Mind."

> A difficulty which confronts the synechistic philosophy is this. In considering personality, that philosophy is forced to accept the doctrine of a personal God; but in considering communication, it cannot but admit that if there is a personal God, we must have a direct perception of that person and indeed be in personal communication with him. Now, if that be the case, the question arises how it is possible that the existence of this being should ever have been doubted by anybody. The only answer that I can at present make is that facts that stand before our face and eyes and stare us in the face are far from being, in all cases, the ones most easily discerned. That has been remarked from time immemorial. (CP 6:162)

Peirce's admission of puzzlement here pushes this analysis of the orientation of the understanding to another level. It is one thing to realize that the order the understanding gives itself is insufficient, as Peirce does. It is another thing to claim that the order that appears sufficient is still a deeper remove into absence. The question is how this principle of absence becomes the "foundational" term of the person, guiding the inquiry and habit development that generates truly self-critical expansion of the soul. In his description of evangelical humiliation in the *Affections* Edwards holds out a prospect of personal freedom that is different from Locke's notion that freedom is the ability to resist the last determination of the understanding. Locke's negative account of freedom builds from the notion that only an appearing good can become the focus of the will, although his account just pushes the question back one step. What does the will focus on if not the good appearing to the understanding? Without some space between the choice of the will and that appearing good, there is no ground for human freedom. Here the role of Edwards's sense of the heart is most clear. The sense of the heart follows from an evaluation of the great good of the affections, and yet it is not the same thing as cleaving to a principle that corresponds to that sense of the heart. The great good desired by the soul is not a disguised love of self but the genuine reflection of the desire for God's holiness as the order in the understanding, recognized as an order beyond the creative power of the will. The distinction between the transformation of under-standing and conversion proper is the difference between desiring an order for the understanding and desiring the content that makes such an order possible. It is the love of the object that makes the will susceptible to the change of character that becomes a complete change of character. The choice for the object itself, not for the "object that orders the sense of the heart," is the basis of Edwards's argument in the *Freedom of the Will*. Free choice of the will cannot be seen in any particular choice, not even the choice of a holy order of the understanding, but only a choice to will as God wills for the soul, that is, that the soul has the will of Christ. Only in this way does the soul reflect the holiness of God in the true human freedom that "comprehends all the true moral excellency of intelligent beings: there is no other true virtue, but real holiness" (RA 255). The excellence that is truly the excellence of the human capacity for trans-formation is realized only in this complete alteration of the foundation of the person in willing to be as God wills.

ORIENTING CONTENT AND THE CHANGE OF NATURE

The most explicitly Christological aspect of the *Religious Affections* begins in this third theme of transformation that introduces the "com-plete change of character" that is Edwards's language for conversion. Edwards presents Christ as the central content of God's transforming work with humanity. This theme brings pragmatic conversion to a criti-cal test. The signs comprising this theme are "VII. Gracious affections are attended with a change of nature; VIII. Gracious affections differ from those affections that are false and delusive, in that they tend to, and are attended with the lamblike, dovelike spirit and temper of Jesus Christ, or in other words, they naturally beget and promote such a spirit of love, meekness, forgiveness, and mercy, as appeared in Christ; and, IX. Gracious affections soften the heart and are attended and followed with a Christian tenderness of spirit" (RA 340, 345, 357).

For Edwards, the mystery of transformation appears most clearly in the discovery of content that changes the nature of the person. The interaction with the content of Christ becomes the orienting fact of the affections, not by dint of power, as in a compulsion of truth that cannot be denied, but by changing the desire of the soul to exercise its excellence. The mystery further appears in the manner that the soul knows this orientation because it has been changed. Otherwise the orientation of the affections remains opaque.

But why is Christ the content for such a change? We have seen that for Edwards the revelation of Christ is a principle that inhabits all scripture. But Christ also manifests a spirit of perfect submission to God's will for an order beyond himself. The self-effacing life of Christ, laying aside the power of a deity to become incarnate in order to redeem human life, is also the character every human can appropriate in discovering an order to the affections. God trusts Christ's sufficiency as the content by which all people may discover this orienting change. In pragmatic terms, the test of Christ's sufficiency is only the continuing and complete transformation of human life writ large.

This is firm ground for the pragmatists. The content they seek is that which will transform and change the nature of themselves and their community. James seeks the orientation to the self that reorients all activities toward this expansion. Such a change requires him, in a negative way, to set aside the orientation and change of Christian conversion. His opposition shows that his transformation is in the same neighborhood as Edwards, but they trust a different content.

For Dewey the change of character results from content developed exclusively in experience. Thick experience becomes the orienting ground of Dewey's transformation, and individual or communal change is oriented by an emergent or growing content of experience. This focus on the content of experience approaches Edwards's Christological ground in the sense that conversion must have individual and communal dimensions. The content of experience must provide orientation for both. Dewey is aware of the power of Christian conversion in terms of producing a different kind of life that manifests openness to change and a lamblike spirit of service to the community. Dewey's vision of the democratic community is a naturalized replacement for the content of Christ that serves as both the content needed for a change of personal character and as the ideal all people seek. Although Dewey claims that his democratic vision is a broadly held ideal, this claim goes begging in terms of its effectiveness to produce a change in human character. There is no tradition of personal transformation built around the realization of the democratic community like there is concerning Christ. Democracy is a powerful idea that orients practice toward more fruitful and humane ways of interacting, but proposing that democracy is *the* content of orientation for all human transformation exceeds propriety. Still, Dewey seems faithful to the mystery of an orienting content that produces human change to the bottom of the heart. I think that Dewey's democratic faith is a kind of orchidism of the universal aspect of Christological content; it is the flower without roots or stalk. Dewey carefully tends the attraction of the democratic ideal in the hope that its universal appeal will determine the character of transforming content.

Peirce models the continuing inquiry that an orienting object such as Christ sustains. The complexity of the self, locked in the semiotic folds and expansion of meaning, matches the complexity of the continually receding object of inquiry. This content keeps slipping away from Peirce, both in terms of a change in himself and in terms of the content his inquiry seeks. Pragmaticism is an orientation in inquiry toward that which always draws it forward. This drawing forward implicates the normative progression of the control of behavior with the normative progression of conclusions of inquiry. The mystery of Christ for Peirce, if I may use such an allusion here, is the harmonization of human thought and action by one content—although that content always remains beyond cognitive realization. This model of transformation coincides with Edwards's suggestion that conversion is a continuous project, and that gracious affections reflect a tenderness of spirit that increasingly takes on the character of Jesus. Peirce interprets this as the fundamental urge toward the gospel of Christ where every man casts in his lot with his neighbor. But Peirce cannot formulate the realization of this character in a way that would not end inquiry. Continuous inquiry becomes not only the means but also the object for Peirce. Even though Christ for Peirce is the continuum of action and thought, and not a "miracle monger," he still hears the call of the savior and is granted permission by the Master to take communion. The focus on content that I am raising here challenges Peirce's inquiry to find an object that is consistent with his notion of continuity and yet provides a platform for practical or moral orientation. A practical conversion like this would strengthen Peirce's concept of the self as both oriented inquiry and distinct expression of normative realization. To repeat my point in the last section in a slightly different way, this addition of conversion requires Peircean thought to account for a different aspect of negation as a holistic error of orientation. Again, it is possible to discover this error only in light of a positive orientation that becomes the root of comprehensive change in a person. Such a change of character eluded Peirce in his lifetime, as Joseph Brent documents. His dissatisfaction with his own character and his feeling that he had squandered his gifts is a sad ending to a life of service to inquiry and philosophy. We may try to redeem Peirce by our appreciation, but our redemption has its limits. Real redemption follows only if Peirce's example enables us to seek, as he did, and to find, as he did not, a truly redeeming content.

CHRISTOLOGICAL GROUND IN CONVERSION

In this portrayal of the intersection of pragmatic transformation and Edwards's conversion, I have indicated at several places how Christ emerges as a point of conflict or challenge to philosophy. I have done so at the risk of producing an abrupt disjunction between transformation and conversion, so I think it is appropriate to pause in this account of transformation to dwell on this issue of Christ. The first point to make, however, is that Edwards, as a sign of fidelity to his tradition, adjusts the meaning of Christ in relation to the transformation of human life. The test of creative transformation for Edwards is the manner in which his theological tradition reflects openness to appropriate modification. In this sense, conversion is continuous with philosophical transformation. Both aim to appropriate the content necessary for full human life. The pragmatists resist the claim that Christ is the limit of creative transformation. This raises the bar on Edwards, so to speak, to find in Christ the ground for a creative transformation of his tradition that corresponds to the American philosophical desire for a transformed tradition. If no aspect of creative transformation emerges from a positive relation to Christ, then this study comes to a quick conclusion. In this case, conversion in American philosophy is not possible.

One way that Edwards negotiates the issue of Christ in his tradition is by pointing out what appears to ground a theology of conversion, that is, that such a transformation must coincide with a natural human quality. Only if Christ is the expression of a natural power of human character can there be continuity between conversion and human action. Conrad

Cherry locates this impulse in Edwards's proposal of Christology that mediates between the Calvinist conviction that man has no power to achieve salvation, and the Arminian claim that salvation depends on a human act of faith. He summarizes the point in this passage:

> The crux of this proposal is Edwards's distinction between "natural" and "moral" fitness. Faith is a "naturally" fit, not a "morally" fit relation. A person is morally fit or suitable for something when his own moral goodness, holiness, or excellence commends him to it. So, if one were morally fit for salvation or justification, the holiness or excellence of his act of faith would commend him to salvation. Then God would reward man with salvation because God respected the "moral excellency, or value or amiableness of any of his qualifications or acts." On the other hand, one is naturally fit for something by virtue of the "natural concord or agreeableness" that exists between the human qualification or act and the reality that is attached to that act. Here man is naturally fit for *salvation by faith* because the two things belong together. God does not reward man with salvation because of the holiness of man's own act; rather, He looks on it as fitting that two things that belong inseparably together, are together; and out of His love for order He sees to it that Christ's righteousness flows to man through the union that man has with Christ through faith.[14]

On one hand, the proposal that faith in Christ is a natural fit or order of human consciousness seems to beg the question. But in light of his tradition and experience Edwards discovers a need to inquire further into the tradition of conversion without dismantling it. The fitness of human nature for Christological transformation restores a sense of humanity to his tradition that is sometimes absent in Calvinism. The transformation Edwards describes extends beyond the limits of Reformed theology and into the nature of man and the products of reason. It also extends beyond the Arminian demand that persons choose their own value apart from any prior ground of grace. Edwards's argument for "natural fitness" confirms the character of human inquiry as an adequate approach to the original nature. Within this approach the revelation of Christ is fully manifested, and thus Edwards alters his tradition on the ground of securing the possibility of creative transformation.

Transformation, however consistent with our nature, still rests on the fact that Christ is the principle of revelation. Gerald McDermott notes Kinmach's summary that "Edwards came to the conclusion that while fallen reason can prove religious propositions to be *true,* it cannot make them seem *real.*" McDermott then quotes from Edwards miscellanies to support the point that the reality of divinity depends on revelation. Natural truths, Edwards says, are not taught

> in that manner in which it is necessary for us to know it, for the knowledge of no truth of divinity is of any significance to us any otherwise than it some way or another belongs to the gospel scheme, or has relevance to Christ the Mediator. It signifies nothing for us to know anything of any one of God's perfections unless we know them as manifested in Christ, and so it signifies nothing to us to know any part of our duty unless it will [bear] some relation to Christ. It profits us not to have any knowledge of the law of God, unless it be either to fit us for the glad tidings of the gospel or to be a means of our sanctification in Christ Jesus and to influence us to serve God through Christ by an evangelical obedience and therefore we stand in the greatest necessity of a divine revelation.[15]

In these lines we see that Edwards identifies Christ as the principle that makes intellectual discovery real in terms of its having a role in God's large scheme of revelation. Christ is the criterion of understanding that supports the realization of God's intention to transform humanity through an ultimate realization of fitness. Our great need for revelation is shown by the reality of Christ in our discoveries that become part and parcel of our realization of divine transformation. Without such a mediating content, our efforts to discover transforming truths would fail.

For Edwards, Christ is above all else the assurance that our desire for transformation is not in vain. H. R. Niebuhr says, "Yet faith is not simply loyalty; it is assurance, too. It is confidence in the object toward which the inner passion is directed. It is the trust that the cause will not fail us, will not let us down. Such trust, to be sure is mated with a kind of objective uncertainty; but it is not the uncertainty that makes it faith."[16] Christ is the object that, for Edwards, assures human passion and trust in the possibility of transformation is not an empty hope.

Edwards finds room in the meaning of Christ to transform his understanding of the cosmological force of inquiry and practice toward a prospective integration. Through this integration it is possible to anticipate practice that perfectly reflects the best order of the mind. Christ is the ground of this complete reorientation of practice that reveals a fundamental change in character. This expands the meaning of Edwards's traditional view of Christ as the image of both perfect moral practice and complete self-understanding through the will of God. But Edwards's vision of Christ alters his tradition, and it is this power of tradition altering inquiry that forms the ground of the pragmatic philosophical tradition. Edwards's fidelity to Christ makes it possible to transform his tradition creatively. Through his encounter with Christ, Edwards finds that his tradition becomes a way of discovering not only the ultimate character of divine reality but also the reality of our own practice seen through the lens of its possible transformation. Edwards's transformation of the tradition focuses on confronting the person with the questions "Is Christ good. Is Christ of God?" Edwards has confidence that raising this question with all possible power is the true measure of his subordination of his efforts to the will of God. This confidence appears in his philosophical project that arrives at the same question; "How does Christ become implicated in the reflective transformation of life?"

The question of conversion for the pragmatists is what to do with Christ. In their critical assessment of transformation, pragmatists must offer a rebuttal showing how Edwards's Christological conversion fails in terms of providing an order of the understanding or as the ground for transforming tradition. Pragmatists must respond to Edwards's account of a holistic change in the person that affects a reorientation of the understanding and the tradition, in such a way that apart from this holistic change nothing is good that may appear good. But this challenge also moves from the pragmatists toward Edwards. The Christological dimensions in the pragmatists raise new questions about the sufficiency of a model of conversion, like Edwards's, to interact positively with the philosophical tradition. Pragmatism pushes conversion continually in the direction of creative transformation.

RETURNING TO LIFE THROUGH CONVERSION

There are two purposes behind Edwards's *Religious Affections.* One purpose is to justify the occurrence of the revival and to provide a warrant for that revival as a genuine work of God. The second purpose is more creative, in the sense that Edwards trusts that his examination of conversion will support and extend the lives of the saints through an active inquiry into their transformation. I think that these two purposes fall together for Edwards. The genuine work of God generates the life of the saints, at least that which makes them peculiar and separate from a "natural" human life. The principle of Christ distinguishes the transformation of conversion from natural transformation. Edwards focuses on the product of living in this distinctive way in the last three signs: "X. Another thing wherein those affections that are truly gracious and holy, differ from those that are false, is beautiful symmetry and proportion; XI. Another great and distinguishing feature of gracious affections is that the higher they are raised, the more is a spiritual appetite and longing of soul after spiritual attainments increased. On the contrary, false affections rest satisfied in themselves; and, XII. Gracious and holy affections have their exercise and fruit in Christian practice. I mean, they have that influence and power upon him, who is the subject of 'em, that they cause that a practice, which is universally conformed to, and directed by Christian rules, should be the practice and business of his life" (RA 365, 376, 383).

The goal in these last signs is to describe a form of living that increases the harmony within the active and reflective life of the person. The demonstrable effect of this changed life is a recognized obedience to "Christian rules," according to Edwards. Proof of an altered inclination can have no other "logical interpretant" to use Peirce's language, than a life. This demand for proof of the change wrought in transformation by examination of one's living is in continuity with the pragmatic tradition. Edwards and the pragmatists hold up this ability to return to life as the final criterion by which any transformation, divine or natural, can be judged. Discovered truths are known fully only if they are implicated in the practical stuff of life. This may be reversed to say that only within the practical stuff of life is the platform for discovering the ultimate aspects of transformation and conversion truly possible.

THE WOMAN AT THE WELL

Instead of describing the force of this last aspect of transformation in terms of Edwards and the pragmatists, I am going to reflect on a story that all these thinkers would agree demonstrates an experience of transformation and conversion. I have chosen this story for two reasons. First, I think it provides a fitting conclusion to this positive statement of creative transformation—although there are disagreements in part, I believe that Edwards's notion of conversion and the pragmatists' view of transformation reconnect in a powerful way in terms of a story about returning to life. Second, the account of this woman's interaction with Jesus that occasions a return to her community illuminates the interplay between reflective transformation and conversion within a dialogue based on religious tradition and reflective access to that tradition. This story is not only a fitting image of conversion; it is also a sign of the human desire for such occasions and the discoveries that form the continuity within human life from which transformation grows as a demand and as a hope.

The account of the woman of Sychar and Jesus (John 4:1–43) reads this way in the Revised Standard Version:

> Now when the Lord knew that the Pharisees had heard that Jesus was making and baptizing more disciples than John (although Jesus himself did not baptize, but only his disciples), he left Judea and departed again to Galilee. He had to pass through Samaria.
>
> So he came to a city of Samaria, called Sychar, near the field that Jacob gave to his son Joseph. Jacob's well was there, and so Jesus, wearied as he was with his journey, sat down beside the well. It was about the sixth hour.
>
> There came a woman of Samaria to draw water. Jesus said to her, "Give me a drink." For his disciples had gone away into the city to buy food. The Samaritan woman said to him, "How is it that you, a Jew, ask a drink of me, a woman of Samar'ia?" For Jews have no dealings with Samaritans. Jesus answered her, "If you knew the gift of God, and who it is that is saying to you, 'Give me a drink,' you would have asked him, and he would have given you living water." The woman said to him, "Sir, you have nothing to draw with, and the well is deep; where do you get that living water? Are you greater than our father Jacob, who gave us the well, and drank from it himself, and his sons, and his cattle?" Jesus said to her, "Every one who drinks of this water will thirst again, but whoever drinks of the water that I shall give him will never thirst; the water that I shall give him will become in him a spring of water welling up to eternal life." The woman said to him, "Sir, give me this water, that I may not thirst, nor come here to draw." Jesus said to her, "Go, call your husband, and come here." The woman answered him, "I have no husband." Jesus said to her, "You are right in saying, 'I have no husband'; for you have had five husbands, and he whom you now have is not your husband; this you said truly." The woman said to him, "Sir, I perceive that you are a prophet. Our fathers worshiped on this mountain; and you say that in Jerusalem is the place where men ought to worship." Jesus said to her, "Woman, believe me, the hour is coming when neither on this mountain nor in Jerusalem will you worship the Father. You worship what you do not know; we worship what we know, for salvation is from the Jews. But the hour is coming, and now is, when the true worshipers will worship the Father in spirit and truth, for such the Father seeks to worship him. God is spirit,

and those who worship him must worship in spirit and truth." The woman said to him, "I know that Messiah is coming (he who is called Christ); when he comes, he will show us all things." Jesus said to her, "I who speak to you am he."

Just then his disciples came. They marveled that he was talking with a woman, but none said, "What do you wish?" or, "Why are you talking with her?" So the woman left her water jar, and went away into the city, and said to the people, "Come, see a man who told me all that I ever did. Can this be the Christ?" They went out of the city and were coming to him.

Meanwhile the disciples besought him, saying, "Rabbi, eat." But he said to them, "I have food to eat of which you do not know." So the disciples said to one another, "Has any one brought him food?" Jesus said to them, "My food is to do the will of him who sent me, and to accomplish his work. Do you not say, 'There are yet four months, then comes the harvest'? I tell you, lift up your eyes, and see how the fields are already white for harvest. He who reaps receives wages, and gathers fruit for eternal life, so that sower and reaper may rejoice together. For here the saying holds true, 'One sows and another reaps.' I sent you to reap that for which you did not labor; others have labored, and you have entered into their labor."

Many Samaritans from that city believed in him because of the woman's testimony, "He told me all that I ever did." So when the Samaritans came to him, they asked him to stay with them; and he stayed there two days. And many more believed because of his word. They said to the woman, "It is no longer because of your words that we believe, for we have heard for ourselves, and we know that this is indeed the Savior of the world."

This setting is one of the most fleshed out vignettes in the gospel tradition, and the writer was assiduously aware of geography, local custom, and religious history of the Samaritans. But the setting makes sense only because of the dialogue between these two who met by chance at a well. In a sense, they were both hiding. Jesus was trying to move without raising the attention of the Pharisees, and the woman was hiding from interaction with other water gatherers who would choose either a closer water source or a cooler time of the day. She wanted to be alone, and the choice of Jacob's well was intentional.[17]

The dialogue that emerges between these unlikely partners flows between Jesus' breaking social barriers in initiating the conversation, and the woman's deflective and pithy rejoinders. She knows where she is and she knows what separates him from her. When he reveals her marital excesses, she points him to the Jewish excesses of claiming Jerusalem as God's chosen place of worship without any scriptural backing.[18] In this repartee, Jesus finds the place to reveal himself. The Samaritans expected a prophet like Moses, a Taheb, a prophet who returns, who will sort out the problems of their racially mixed past and their conflict with the Jews.[19] "I, the one speaking to you, I am the one," Jesus says.

Jesus' claim that he is the restorer she seeks is the last word recorded between them. The woman leaves when the disciples, oblivious of the interchange that has taken place, come back. Whatever meaning the words had that passed between them the result was that the woman returns to her village and proclaims, "Come see the man who told me everything I ever did. Could this be the messiah?" It is this return that makes the difference in the narrative. From her isolated venture to the well, the woman receives a word that bubbles out of her, and she shares the prospect of a spiritual return that the people of her village desire as well. There is no time to stop and discern the meaning of the tradition, there is only the word of confession that prompts the people to come and see for themselves the source of this restoration.

The creative transformation in this narrative in John's gospel is typical in many ways of the gospel tradition that inspires Edwards and the pragmatists. The word that strikes into their experience exceeds the form of its first apprehension, and explodes in significance for themselves and their communities. This creative word is often overlooked by the very groups who are identified with it, like the disciples in this story, so there is no sense in trusting an institution to bring about this discovery. The founding figures of American philosophy desire to return to their communities with a saving word, as this woman does. They long to construct an encounter with truth in the ordinary paths of life that would bring new meaning and a new orientation to the activity of life itself. This is the desired return that I find coursing through the tradition of American philosophy. The desire for the creative transformation of life is the goal that connects the philosophical work of the pragmatists and conversion.

Notes

1. James W. Fowler, *To See the Kingdom: The Theological Vision of H. Richard Niebuhr* (Abingdon, 1974), 98.

2. Ibid., 116.

3. H. Richard Niebuhr, *The Kingdom of God in America* (Wesleyan University Press, 1988), 10.

4. Ellen Charry, *By the Renewing of Your Minds* (Oxford University Press, 1997), viii.

5. Ibid., 9.

6. Ibid., 147.

7. Ibid., 15.

8. Ibid., 53.

9. David Ford, *Self and Salvation: Being Transformed* (Cambridge University Press, 1999), 2.

10. Ibid., 115.

11. Sang Hyun Lee, *Philosophical Theology of Jonathan Edwards* (Princeton University Press, 1988), 50.

12. McDermott, *Jonathan Edwards Confronts the Gods* (Oxford, 2000), 96.

13. Douglas R. Anderson, "Smith and Dewey on the Religious Dimension of Experience: Dealing with Dewey's Half-God," *American Journal of Theology and Philosophy* 14, no. 2 (May 1993): 167.

14. Cherry, *The Theology of Jonathan Edwards* (Indiana University Press, 1966), 97.

15. McDermott, *Jonathan Edwards Confronts the Gods,* 65–66.

16. H. Richard Niebuhr, *Christ and Culture* (Harper & Row, 1951), 252.

17. F. F. Bruce, *The Gospel of John* (Eerdmans, 1983). Bruce points out (101ff.) that if the traditional place of Sychar is the modern Askar, the trip to Jacob's well would take her past another fountain and across a stream.

18. Ibid., 109.

19. Raymond Brown, *The Gospel According to John I–XII* (Doubleday, 1966), 172.

7

The Evasion of Conversion in Recent American Philosophy

I COME NOW to the conclusion of this argument for returning a consideration of conversion to American philosophy. I first found this issue emerging with my reading of the classical figures of pragmatism, Peirce, Dewey, and James. The pressure of their thought toward a transformation that carries persons into an active and extendable relation with their community and with reality most broadly conceived held me, and still holds me, in their thought. So strong was this impulse toward transformation in their thought that I expected it to be clearly repeated and extended in the philosophical work that flows in response to them. But I did not find things as I expected. By and large the argument for transformation is sublimated by the philosophical warrant of making a better argument than the previous commentator, or getting to the truth about X within the thought of A, B, or C. I missed the holism, the comprehensive word about what we are up to. What happened to conversion? This remains my question.

The rekindling of interest in American philosophers such as Peirce, James, and Dewey has produced an abundance of critical work on pragmatism and its origins. There are also signs of an extension of pragmatism in contemporary philosophical discourse, but not yet with the power that these "founders" possessed. I think one of the reasons for this lack of power is that the idea of transformation has been left for some other goal such as philosophical currency or historical curiosity. There are many attempts to repeat, codify, classify, and honor the original arguments that developed into pragmatism, but there is little awareness that anything more can or should be done, or what may be required of us as the people who hold ourselves apart as intellectuals and teachers of the next generation. We have produced philosophically exactly what we want—a safe haven, free to explore reason at its limits, secure from any truth that might grip us and toss us into the rough and tumble of life. We have domesticated pragmatism and made it into a cultural artifact, a banner to wave, an allegiance to a set of thinkers who stand opposed to another set of thinkers, a way of reading the history of philosophy that points to the "truth" as all that we can expect, or all that we can justify. We have for all intents evaded the demand for transformation that sponsored the tradition we laud.

We are not alone, however, and there is comfort, if not satisfaction, in numbers. From time to time a person emerges who seeks to disrupt this comfort and challenge our sanctified tradition with a new reading or a new demand on philosophy. Their mistaken understandings are pointed out, the tradition is reaffirmed in its ability to resist yet another level of criticism, and things go on. But we are waiting, waiting for another person like Dewey, who can reorient the philosophical ground on which we are standing. Or a person like James, who can affect a role in our culture that transcends the divisions between philosophy and religion by virtue of an analysis that strikes to the core of our souls. Or a person like Peirce, who, almost unseen, drives an argument about the structure of inquiry into the very heart of our understanding of ourselves and the human enterprise. We wait for someone who does not stand on the periphery of reflective life, snipping at the edges with a new and momentarily fashionable critique, but one who is able to bring an epoch-making reorientation.

In this chapter I focus on three philosophers whose thought moves toward this reorienting change. Richard Rorty has most nearly approached this kind of stature and effect in American philosophy, although I will argue here that he avoids the fundamental issue of personal transformation, which his own argument demands. Cornel West has attained the public notoriety of an intellectual with a program for transformation, drawing on Christian and philosophical resources for his sermonic challenge to culture. West also evades conversion, but differently than Rorty. Conversion is central to West's self-understanding, but it falls out of his programmatic speech. West fails to establish the ground from which others might enter the same converted place as West himself. Robert Corrington approaches philosophy from within the American perspective, but draws its thought up into the ongoing challenge of consciousness with itself. Transformation of human consciousness is the reality Corrington approaches from a platform of ecstatic naturalism. He shows how thought that is held between the demands of coherence and obligation evades conversion in order to sustain inquiry, and at what cost this evasion is made.

These three voices correspond in tone to James, Dewey, and Peirce, respectively. Rorty shares James's rejection of authority, West reflects Dewey's aim for a philosophical speech that obliterates the distinction between fact and value, and Corrington emulates Peirce's pursuit of the origin of inquiry. My argument is that these three voices represent what American philosophy has come to. They are, in a sense, the fruits by which we know who we are. Conversion is only the linking clue that can hold these personalities and reflection together long enough for us to develop a clear idea of what transformation means for us, and what sort of platform we may yet need to construct to further the project of understanding the ways we can change and should change, both ourselves and our communities.

RORTY AND THE TRANSFORMATION OF PHILOSOPHY

Few books have had the epoch-making effect of Richard Rorty's *Philosophy and the Mirror of Nature* and *Consequences of Pragmatism*. Rorty aims for and achieves a kind of transformation of philosophy by following out the problematic dimensions of analytic thought in Quine, Sellars, and Davidson, showing that the path analytic philosophers are traveling is a dead end. The way out is pragmatism. "On my view," Rorty says in the introduction to *Consequences of Pragmatism*, "James and Dewey were not only waiting at the end of the dialectical road which analytic philosophy traveled, but are waiting at the end of the road which, for example, Foucault and Deleuze are currently traveling."[1] Rorty is not concerned to extend philosophy in its current form but to affect a complete transformation to what he calls "pragmatism."

Rorty's entrance into this transformational project comes from his interest in setting to rights philosophy's epistemic expectations and methodological controls. The analysts, Rorty claims, lost the control of knowledge they sought, finding instead a refurbished Platonism. The transformation this failure indicates, though, is not a change of discrete conclusions, or a shift of emphasis on problems from one sort to another. A complete turning over of philosophy is required, for philosophy is its own problem. Only by "extirpating" the ground of epistemic expectations that Philosophy should or could produce a description of the "world" that would be True universally and eternally, will philosophy really get going again on the problems of men and women and science.

Rorty's transformation of philosophy requires a death and resurrection. Robert Brandom summarizes Rorty's impact this way:

> In his classic work, *Philosophy and the Mirror of Nature,* he notoriously prophesized approvingly the "death of philosophy." Although he now regrets this bit of rhetoric—he certainly never meant to deny that we would always need professors to help students read the great books that make up the philosophical tradition, for instance—he has never relinquished his commitment to the dissolution of a certain sort of philosophy: philosophy as a discipline with epistemology at its heart, a sort of super-science, limiting the limits of the knowable, explaining the nature of the relationship between reality and our representations of it.[2]

Despite the "dissolution" of philosophy as a discipline with epistemology at its core, Rorty continues to focus on the problems of epistemology as the main route into his criticism. In his ongoing conversations with Jürgen Habermas and others, Rorty continues to answer the question "What was Epistemology?"[3] His arguments against representationalism focus not so much on the method of analysis and argument, but on the goals and final expectations of all such enterprises. The epistemological failure of analytic philosophy is in supposing that eternal verities in any form, call them science or language, correspond to a discoverable *telos* of inquiry. Rorty's self-imposed task is "to dissolve the modern version of the problem of reason—the notion that there is a problem about the possibility or extent of accurate representation which is the concern of a discipline called 'epistemology.' Insofar as it succeeds, this attempt frees us from the notion of human knowledge as an assemblage of representations in a Mirror of Nature, and thus reinforces the claim of part I that we can do without the notion of our Glassy Essence."[4] Setting aside the reality of these verities is part and parcel of Rorty's transformation of philosophy. This means that philosophy does not have a goal intrinsic to its own practice that it can hope to complete. It also means that human culture, which alone is the content of all reflection, also has no final good or standard to be achieved. Rorty, however, does not collapse into a fashionable nihilism that disestablishes the possibility for a warrantable standard of human life; he simply argues against the advisability of looking for any such warrantable condition or standards. Philosophy must change its own expectations and must change the expectations of the wider community. Contingent narrative is all there is, and suggestions to the contrary are evasions of the necessary and coming transformation.

Rorty takes up pragmatism as the activity of dispelling any authority that challenges the contingency of life.

> So my preferred narrative is a story of human beings as having recently gotten out from under the thought of, the need of, *authority*. I see James's suggestion that we carry utilitarianism over from morals into epistemology as crucial to this anti-authoritarian movement of the spirit. For James shows us how to see Truth not as something we have to respect, but as a pointless nominalization of the useful adjective we apply to beliefs that are getting us what we want.[5]

The conversion Rorty requires in philosophy is taking up this authority for itself, embracing its power that it is not derivative on any good or ideal, but dependent only on human enterprise that knows itself for what it is, simply its own enterprise.

From the philosophy of Dewey and James, Rorty constructs the "pragmatist." The pragmatist is the one disabused of philosophical expectations of authority, fully embracing the thoroughgoing linguistic character of human reality, able to withstand the tendencies that lead back to intuitions of morality or Truth. "He is a pragmatist just because he doesn't have such intuitions (or wants to get rid of whatever intuitions he may have)."[6] Further, Rorty says, "the pragmatist is urging that we do our best to *stop having* such intuitions, that we develop a *new* intellectual tradition."[7] The pragmatist is concerned about not only developing a personal character but also promulgating this character as the ground of a proper vision of small-p philosophy. This is not an easy transition. It requires a platform of objective disengagement from the intuitions that appear organically as the guiding premises of our reflective lives. The "pragmatist" must make a compelling argument that whatever ground is attained by these intuitions, it is a false and dangerous ground.

> So the pragmatists' quarrel with the intuitive realist should be about the *status* of intuitions—about their *right* to be respected—as opposed to how particular intuitions might be "synthesized" or "explained away." To treat his opponent properly, the pragmatist must begin by admitting that the realistic intuitions in question are as deep and compelling as the realist says they are. But he should then try to change the subject by asking, "And what should we *do* about such intuitions—extirpate them, or find a vocabulary which does justice to them?"

Changing the subject from these intuitions does not challenge them on the basis of coherence or consistency, but it enables the pragmatist to say "his *only* argument for thinking that these intuitions and vocabularies should be eradicated is that the intellectual tradition to which they belong has not paid off, is more trouble than it is worth, has become an incubus."[8] And having not "paid off" properly, this tradition must be replaced with another, determined by the character of the pragmatist who alone is able to place himself (for clearly the pragmatist is Rorty) into a framework of reflection that might constitute a new post-Philosophical culture.

> A post-Philosophical culture, then, would be one in which men and women felt themselves alone, merely finite, with no links to something Beyond. On the pragmatist's account, positivism was only a half-way stage in the development of such a culture—the progress toward, as Sartre puts it, doing without God. For positivism preserved a god in its notion of Science (and in its notion of "scientific philosophy"), the notion of a portion of culture where we touched something not ourselves, where we found Truth naked, relative to no description.[9]

This is not just a philosophical conclusion. This is a new way of living in relation to the traditions of philosophy and value. As it is clear from Rorty's reference to Sartre here, this requires a disabused notion of the world of religion too, since this is the great propounder of intuitions that are not paying off. Rorty goes a further step in claiming that the pragmatist must give up the very notion that there is a place to inhabit, a world, constructed in opposition to other worlds, from which a person can move by identification and difference. In "A World Well Lost," Rorty treats what must be eliminated of religious culture. From Wittgenstein's comment that *Philosophical Investigations* ends philosophy, Rorty adds that this

> can only mean that this book might somehow rid us of "the picture which held us captive"—the picture of man which generates the traditional problems. To say that philosophy might end is not to say that holding large views might become unfashionable or that philosophy departments might be plowed under, but rather to say that a certain cultural tradition might die out. If this change occurred, one would no longer think of the standard list of Cartesian problems as a *Fach*: rather, one would think study of the concern that once was felt about these problems as a *Fach*. The best analogy available is the shift from "theology" to "the study of religion." Once grace, salvation, and the Divine Nature were subjects of study; now the fact that they were so is a subject of study. Once theology was a pure autonomous subject; now religion lies at the

mercy of psychology, history, anthropology, and whatever other discipline cares to jump in. Once we had a picture of man as held in the hand of God, and a discipline which discussed alternative ways of describing the fact. . . . We had a discipline which discussed these various alternatives—never questioning that there was *something* of central importance which needed to be said about the relation between man and nature: some bridge to be built, some dualism to be transcended, some gap to be closed. If philosophy comes to an end, it will be because this picture is as remote from us as the picture of man as a child of God. If that day comes it will seem as quaint to treat a man's knowledge as a special relation between his mind and its object as it now does to treat his goodness as a special relation between his soul and God.[10]

The relation between the overcoming of Philosophy and the overcoming of religion in these lines is fascinating. Does the one make the other possible? Are they analogically related, so that the authority of God dispelled in people like Sartre becomes a sign of the same dislocation necessary or possible in Philosophy? The transformation of Philosophy that would bring it to an "end" implicates the rejection of conversion, that there might be transforming grace in the world, that God might hold us as children, seeking our good. Ending Philosophy means, above all evading this object. I do not think Rorty's use of Christian imagery here is coincidental, merely an example he throws up for rhetorical effect. Disestablishing these worlds of Christianity and Philosophy, finding them "quaint," is embedded in Rorty's family past. What he rails against is not just based on a critical evaluation about what is the case about reason. His passion reveals a personal reaction to the fear of being judged or obligated against one's will or in relation to an authority one recognizes and resists. His passion is much like his mother's, recorded here in a response to her father, the eminent theologian and social-gospeler Walter Rauschenbusch. She writes,

> Can't you see, Father dear, that in spite of the fact that you've captured the most wonderful reputation in the Rauschenbusch family, that the greatest good of your children may be secured not by their conservation of your policy, but by having metal enuf [*sic*] to step off by themselves?[11]

Rorty is seeking justification for his having "mettle enough" for this same stepping off that requires him to lose whatever world there once was for him or any other, but that still leaves him bound to have a response that pays off in the social sense of his grandfather's idealism.

Rorty's stepping off is philosophically supported by a synthesis of Heidegger's analysis of the trajectory of Western philosophy and Dewey's move to a historicized development of the democratic community. What Heidegger accomplishes is the articulation of the desire for a humanness not determined by Being, even though this is still a philosopher's problem for him. In "Overcoming the Tradition" Rorty says, "Heidegger's weakness was that he could not escape the notion that the philosophers' difficulties are more than *just* philosophers' difficulties—the notion that if philosophy goes down, so will the West. . . . Heidegger helps preserve all that was worst in the tradition which he hoped to overcome."[12] Although Heidegger does not escape his own critical web, he is able to formulate the threat to which philosophy is most likely to succumb:

> For Kierkegaard, the opposite of Socratism was Christianity—the claim that man is not complete, is not in the truth, but rather can attain truth only by being re-created, by being made into a New Being by Grace, Kierkegaard thought that Socratism was Sin, and Sin was the attempt by Man to assume the role of God, an attempt which found its *reductio* in Hegel's system. A lot of Heidegger can profitably be read as a reflection on the possibility that Kierkegaard was right to reject Socratism but wrong to accept Christianity—or, more generally, on the possibility that humanism and Pauline Christianity are alternative forms of a single temptation.[13]

If much of Heidegger can be profitably read in light of this single temptation, much of Rorty can be profitably read as a reflection on the certainty that we are right to reject Christianity, but wrong to accept anything in its place. How to get to this middle ground of rejecting and not accepting, avoiding this other temptation, is the test of Rorty's philosophical vision. He moves philosophically between hoping this failed hope will die of its own weight of failure, and the philosophical impulse to move beyond such vain hope to what might actually be warrantable. Heidegger can only stand in the current of thought and suffer nostalgically for man before Being.

> Heidegger would like to recapture a sense of what time was like before it fell under the spell of eternity, what we were like before we became obsessed by the need for an overarching context which would subsume and explain us—before we came to think of our relation to Being in terms of power . . . to recapture a sense of contingency of the fragility and riskiness of the human project.[14]

Rorty synthesizes Heidegger's sense of contingency with the "downward escalator ride" to pragmatism, to human will not as will-to-power, but simply as power. This realization of the nexus of power is the proper place for human thought to dwell, where Dewey looks with wonder at the world as the interest of humans in themselves and their environment as all that can be or needs to be understood as Being or Real. Rorty asks, "Can pragmatism let us hear as well as use?" Answering, he says, "Yes, I see Dewey's pragmatism as putting technology in its proper place, as a way of making possible social practices (linguistic and other) which will form the next stanza of Being's poem." Dewey seeks "to combine the vision of a social democratic utopia with the knowledge that only a lot of hard work and blind luck, unaided by any nonhuman power called Reason or History, could bring that utopia into existence."[15] The crux of Rorty's synthesis is that philosophy has brought us to the end of hope, exactly where we need to be. We (pragmatists) just need a push to realize that this place is ours, the only platform from which we can productively work without reifying our hopes into ideals, where technology rules not only our experience but also whatever is left of our souls.

I will not stop to examine Rorty's interpretation of Dewey here, but I will say that Rorty completely covers over Dewey's "sense of a good world" that, though lost, still remains powerful. There is more transcendental meat to Dewey's common faith than Rorty wants to acknowledge. But my question is how Rorty understands the motive for this transformation in philosophy. Why make the push to disestablish what others hold, even if they are wrong? If this activity is not for the good of Philosophy, and not for a more accurate understanding of an ideal for practice, what is the gain?

The gain appears to be philosophy's coinciding with itself. The transformation Rorty engages is not a positive transformation toward some standard or object. Rather, transformation in philosophy follows the failure of human interest to find certain intuitions powerful any longer—when consensus fails and the mask drops away and we confront ourselves without these intuitions. The pragmatic transformation is essential for philosophy to meet its true character as holding fragmented pieces of our power together into a concerted effort toward whatever we can accomplish, while actively resisting any suggestion that our accomplishments mean any thing like the realization of an ideal character or obedience to some remote end. The loss of interest in these ideals and ends makes this true character apparent, and the pragmatist must herewith live in good faith, and in good style. David Hume could not do better.

From this platform of pragmatism, Rorty can evade all reflection that could possibly generate a converting demand on reason. This aggressive evasion comes out clearly in his response to William James's "The Will to Believe." Rorty agrees with James that "[b]oth scientific realism and religious fundamentalism are private projects which have got out of hand. They are attempts to make one's own private way of giving meaning to one's own life—a way which romanticizes one's relation to something starkly and magnificently nonhuman, something ultimately True and Real—obligatory for the general public."[16] Rorty cannot endure the sense of universal obligation apart from one's power any more than James can. Religious faith is not anything like respect:

> The kind of religious faith which seems to me to lie behind the attractions of both utilitarianism and pragmatism is, instead, a faith in the future possibilities of moral humans, a faith which is hard to distinguish from love for, and hope for, the human community. I shall call this fuzzy overlap of faith, hope and love "romance." Romance, in this sense, may crystallize around a trade union as easily as around a congregation, around a novel as easily as around a sacrament, around a God as easily as around a child.[17]

While this vision avoids the problem of universality, this "romantic" vision is not completely compatible with James. Rorty acknowledges James's moods where he needed the assurance that "somewhere, somehow, perfection is eternal." James's interest in religious experience led him to seek an understanding of that ground that would enable him to cut through hard and fast distinctions and get closer to the ideal of perfection. But sometimes working through distinctions is not enough, and James recognizes his need for a confirmation of the effectiveness of this activity. "All of us, I think," Rorty admits, "fluctuate between such moods. We fluctuate between God as a perhaps obsolete name for a possible human future, and God as an external guarantor of some such future. . . . Those who, like me, were raised atheist and now find it merely confusing to talk about God, nevertheless fluctuate between moods in which we are content with utility and moods in which we hanker after validity as well. . . . Sometimes it suffices to trust the human community. . . . Sometimes it does not."[18]

Rorty takes exception to the argument in "The Will to Believe" where James calls upon faith in order to fill up this ground for trust when the community fails. At these moments, James focuses on the cognitive effect of faith. Faith gives us some facts to live on. Rorty reacts: "This attempt to answer questions of justification by discovering new objective truths, to answer the moral agent's request for justification with descriptions of a privileged domain, is the philosopher's special form of bad faith—his special way of substituting pseudo-cognition for moral choice."[19] But he misses James's point, made more clearly in *Varieties of Religious Experience,* that if there is a difference to be made to life at all through religious faith, it must have cognitive dimensions:

> Religion . . . is not a mere illumination of facts already elsewhere given, not a mere passion, like love, which views things in a rosier light. It is indeed that, as we have seen abundantly. But it is something more, namely a postulator of new facts as well. The world interpreted religiously . . . must have . . . a natural constitution different at some point from that which a materialistic world would have.[20]

James is not searching for philosophical justification the same way Rorty is. James is engaging what *happens* in religious experience, presumably his own. Unlike James, Rorty's philosophical categories overdetermine what he can experience. (Once an epistemologist, always an epistemologist?) Rorty struggles to account for the power of James's analysis when the desire for justification takes a backseat to the cognition of the self that is engaged when a person says, "I should never do that again, and by God, I won't." How would such an event not be cognition? Rorty seems to have forgotten Hume's charge, "Be a philosopher, but, amid all your philosophy, be still a man."[21]

I think Dewey's emphasis on the problems of men and women is the heart Rorty knows he needs. Rorty sees the celebration of power in pragmatism, but Dewey sees an obligation to orient that power to the service of growth in others and in the community. Dewey adjusts philosophical power to these ends, not to "extirpate" questionable ones but to fructify common ones. Philosophy asks not what belief it is possible to hold, but what is necessary to explain the movement toward a deeper involvement with the well-being of my community and myself. What makes sense of the obligation that holds me? What ground does my hope seek, and in what ways does this hope translate into a community of shared purpose and desire? If Dewey is out of step with the desire of his community, he knows he has failed. For Rorty, being out of step with the community just means that *it* has failed. He is more like James in this way, where the risk is that he might wind up with a novelist's faith, without a community except as material for criticism. But even this faith can enable hope to crystallize around some feature of experience that develops into objects of action if they have sufficient and compelling power over us. Rorty wants neither Dewey's common faith nor James's mysteriously objective faith, and so Rorty cannot explain his own ground. His replacement of the power of the Christian vision of transformation with pragmatism works until his image of the pragmatist, founded on James and Dewey, dies for lack of sustenance. His desire to evade conversion leads to an incoherence in his philosophical backing and undermines his attempts to find a platform for creative philosophy. To put this criticism in his own words, Rorty's pragmatism does not pay off.

Rorty's service to philosophy is another epistemic iteration of philosophy itself. Epistemic transformation like this fails, however, because there is no awareness of conversion, the kind of demand that enlivens human reason by facing it with what it cannot supply. Rorty tries to supply romance, a personally meaningful attachment to an item, as a replacement for conversion. But romance is possible only from the position of detachment from the prospect of the community. Romantic vision cannot be demanded and any obligation to the community is strictly nominal and voluntary. If the community fails, the romantic is unscathed. Rorty achieves, by religious faith oddly enough, a complete detachment from the expectations of good desired by the community, and the fear of failure.

Robert Neville, listening to Rorty's essay on James several years ago, responded, "The wisdom writer says 'The fear of the Lord is the beginning of Wisdom.' Where is fear in your understanding?" Rorty answered that fear does not have a place in determining right thought or action. But where then, I ask, is risk? Is the Heideggarian riskiness Rorty seeks just the risk of not getting what we want? Is not risk based to some degree on fear, the fear that we might not be who we must be? This fear and respect grounds the reflection of James and Dewey. Working in the fear and respect of the culminating effect of action is, I think, central to the pragmatic spirit of caring for what is produced by our labor. This is the fruit by which we know ourselves. For Rorty transformation is a choice, like a wish for a designer personality, not the satisfaction of a demand we cannot help but serve. Rorty reduces the transformation of the pragmatists to an epistemic problem, and in the process he evades implicating himself in the transformation that might convert us and our community into a truly human community.

CORNEL WEST, TRANSFORMATION OF CULTURE, AND CONVERSION

Shifting the locus of philosophy from the traditional intellectual arena to the pulpit requires a radically different understanding of philosophical inquiry than is usually presupposed; and it is a difference Cornel West is at pains to describe, defend, and proclaim. But at the base of this description and defense is the simple but profound test he claims is the final arbiter of the success of a thinker, of a philosophy, of a preacher: "Is the word spoken *potent*, to common folk?"[22] The transformation West hopes to encourage in American culture and intellectual life would constitute a conversion not only to the gospel of Christ but also to this kind of potency.

Cornel West transforms American philosophy by raising questions of social analysis, communication, and authority. Philosophy is not measured by theoretical power or academic brilliance, but by the usefulness and applicability of the thinker's thoughts and words, about the modeling of an organic intellectual—by persuasion. West may not precisely model the prophetic preacher he describes, but he is insightful and helpful in getting to the philosophical conception of prophetic speech he desires. My interest here is to explore West's radical religious historicism as another permutation of evading conversion. Since his philosophy more than others stands on conversion, I offer a suggestion to enrich West's account of prophetic pragmatism at this point. My suggestion moves along the double axis of confession and prophecy, where doing and being coincide and where structure matches content.

Prophetic Philosophy

Cornel West's work on the American evasion of philosophy was the subject of a symposium issue of *Praxis International*. In this evaluative project, the tension between participatory and egalitarian models of democracy was at the forefront. The tension is this: do we need a democracy where the access to basic human needs is equally free for all—an egalitarian society—or do we need more than that—a society where involvement is encouraged and where political power is spread among all the people? Richard Rorty finds the first sufficient, but West argues that a fully participatory democracy is desirable.[23] West bases this claim to full participation on his understanding of the Christian gospel as the affirmation of every individual's importance.

West's desire to articulate and encourage this sort of democracy stems from two fundamental orientations: the influence of his black Baptist religious heritage and his commitment to Marxist social analysis. His religious heritage reflects a basic connection with American philosophy and with the pragmatism of John Dewey. His descriptions of the black religious environment almost seem to equate the reality of religious dissenters, who gave the African Americans their church polity, with the reality of the pragmatist tradition that works and hopes for change in a fallen world. This religious heritage has built into it the question of the severity of the fallenness of the world. For the "light fall" conception, reconstruction of the tragic circumstances of the world is possible. For the conception of the "hard fall," only destruction and complete re-creation will work. Here is the tension between institutional reconstruction or destruction, between Dewey and Marx, which emanates from the religious predicament of American blacks. The necessary function of individuals and communities in social reconstruction is located along this line of tension, where the question is, which institutions require destruction and which require reconstruction? Individuals engage in the social analysis that identifies these barriers and instantiates the hope for change that sustains the movement toward a more healthful social democracy. West's prophetic call for philosophy blurs the distinction between individual and communal responsibility, relying on individual awareness to identify socially repressive institutions. The prophetic aspect of his philosophy merges with his notion of prophetic Christianity, which he describes this way:

> Prophetic Christianity has a distinctive, though not exclusive, capacity to highlight critical, historical, and universal consciousness that yields a vigilant disposition toward prevailing forms of individual and institutional evil, an unceasing suspicion of ossified and petrified forms of dogmatism, and a strong propensity to resist various types of cynicism and nihilism. Prophetic Christian conceptions of what it is to be human, how we should act, and what we should hope for are neither rationally demonstrable, nor empirically verifiable in a necessary and universal manner. Rather, they are embedded and enacted in a form of life—a dynamic set of communities that constitute a diverse tradition—that mediates how I interpret my experiences, sufferings, joys, and undertakings. There are indeed good reasons to accept prophetic Christian claims, yet they are

good not because they result from logical necessity or conform to transcendental criteria. Rather, these reasons are good because they are
rationally acceptable and existentially enabling for many self-critical finite
and fallible creatures who are condemned to choose traditions under circumstances not of their own choosing. To choose a tradition (a version of
it) is more than to be convinced by a set of arguments; it is also to decide
to live alongside the slippery edge of life's abyss with the support of the
dynamic stories, symbols, interruptions, and insights bequeathed by communities that came before.[24]

West calls his own religious commitment "Kierkegaardian," emphasizing
its fideistic nature that resists philosophical description or defense. This
platform of faith is West's only attempt to place the individual who
engages in the prophetic political struggle for human dignity and operates at a critical level rooting out deep-seated (social) idolatries.[25]

The substance of West's prophetic approach is a formula of critique
that he applies with unfailing rigor to all political and philosophical
positions, including his own. This formula examines three aspects of any
position: its uncriticized presuppositions, its program for (or lack) of
social analysis, and its existential identification with the downtrodden.
These principal tenets are West's formulation of the residual elements of
the strategies African Americans adopted in order to survive their slave
status and develop a center for their communal life. Evaluation and
appropriation of alien narratives can function only because survival
strategies are fallibilistic and open for change. It is this reading of the
gospel that is the unreasoned and indefensible platform of West's philosophy. He claims that this gospel presupposition can be critically accepted
because it is rooted in the historical fact of the black experience and the
historical fact of the crucifixion and resurrection of Jesus. There is no
metaphysical "backup" to this position, only a historical commitment.
What makes West's presupposition critical is its dependence on the black
tradition as a historical context of survival, and West's selective appropriation of this tradition because of its particular existential appeal to him.[26]

The last general thing to say about West's prophetic philosophy
before we examine his historicism is that he rejects metaphysics in the
old style because such systems are idolatrous, raising closed systems up
as the real objects of veneration, and also because they have no commerce with our daily lives. It doesn't make a real difference. West's
Deweyan side overshadows his Peircean side and with a sweeping hand

he displaces universal description with local description. Prophetic philosophy, then, can speak only a local dialect, and the extension of his program must evolve on *ad hoc* terms.

Religious Historicism

For West, context is the crucial feature of all dialogue. The context is the source for all standards of judgment, theories, and conceptions. But context is not primarily a key to critical thought—it is the source and final articulation of the meaning of our philosophical and political activity. West holds the existential appeal of a narrative, like that of the black religious tradition, together with a critical reflection of that narrative that involves evaluating other neighboring narratives. The glue that bonds existential appeal with the critical philosophical reflection of prophetic speech is the fact that historical appropriations have made the black narrative what it is, and present circumstances demand that new strategies be found so the narrative can continue.

This interplay of religious and philosophical discourse is held together by the context defined completely by the institutional apparatus that happens to be present and by the strategies that are being used to survive. So, for instance, the historical adoption of the Christian narrative that comprises the categories of realized triumph over evil in the resurrection of Jesus, as well as the intense longing for relief from present suffering in the category of eschatological hope, is reciprocated by critical reflection that comprises the present overcoming of the vestiges of sexual, gender, and ethnic power structures (Foucault), as well as the hope of social reformation through Marxist social analysis. West holds that Christian faith carries an implicit connection to radical individualism and Marxist analysis which appeals to the felt needs of our present social existence and provides a platform for speaking to other narrative traditions about the central issues of social democratic life. West's critical reflection, mediated through his historicism, is a combination of appraisal, metaphysical reflection (without universal implications), and prophetic speech that calls for a political struggle for human dignity. It is clear that West's analysis is on a different foot than traditional philosophical criticism.

Because of this difference in West's aim and method, his speech is hard to criticize in traditional ways. Let me turn from exposition to a more critical appropriation of prophetic pragmatism that is possible from a platform sensitive to the issues of conversion. Two points of criticism arise here. The first is that there is an imbalance in West's historicist-prophetic project. The existential appeal that draws a person into this narrative is not matched in richness by the speech and historicistic meta-physical reflection West describes. West says that the critically reflective prophet philosopher speaks out of his existential condition, but there is something else involved in the need for existential salvation that does not correspond to prophetic speech. West's prophetic speech does not speak from the existential condition fully; and it is a truncated speech because there is no call for existential conversion implicit in it. Existential conversion is richer than the result of critical reflection and demands richer philosophical categories than West has supplied.

Let me put this point another way. The last chapter of *The American Evasion of Philosophy* is West's most complete description of his prophetic pragmatism.

> Prophetic pragmatism affirms the Niebuhrian strenuous mood, never giv-ing up on new possibilities for human agency—both individual and col-lective—in the present, yet situating them in light of Du Bois' social structural analyses that focus on working-class, black, and female insur-gency. Following the pioneering work of Hans-Georg Gadamer and Edward Shils, prophetic pragmatism acknowledges the inescapable and inexpungible character of tradition, the burden and buoyancy of that which is transmitted from the past to present. . . . [P]rophetic pragmatism denies Sisyphean pessimism and utopian perfectionism. Rather, it pro-motes the possibility of human progress and the human impossibility of paradise. This progress results from principled and protracted Promethean efforts, yet even such efforts are no guarantee. . . . Human struggle sits at the center of prophetic pragmatism, a struggle guided by a democratic and libertarian vision, sustained by moral courage and existential integrity, and tempered by the recognition of human finitude and failure.[27]

West is clear that his turn to Christianity through the black church was the beginning of his turn to prophetic philosophy. Christianity was the existential side of the content he now articulates philosophically. In this same context West makes the claim that prophetic pragmatism need not be tied to the Christian tradition, and that any tradition will do that is rich enough to sponsor this sort of critique.

> Revolutionary Christian perspective and praxis pave this middle pathway [between liberalism and right-wing Marxism]. They are rooted in the

world view found in the bosom of Afro-American culture and in the major institution which provides refuge from the terror in Afro-American life—black churches; they are informed by the social analysis and moral impulse of the best of the socialist movement—progressive Marxism; and they build upon, yet go far beyond, the prevailing viewpoint of the vast majority of Afro-Americans—black liberalism. Revolutionary Christian perspective and praxis incorporate the prophetic dimension of Christianity and eschew the paralyzing liberal outlook.[28]

Although West tries to make this inclusive move away from his tradition, he makes it at the expense of letting the uniqueness of his call disappear. His claim that any tradition will do means that he cannot call others to his specific tradition, which is Christian, but can only call others to recognize the call they might hear from their own tradition. This move to inclusion fails philosophically on two counts. First, it presupposes that West has articulated the essence of a "calling" tradition for prophetic pragmatism, where this tacit move to universality violates his own historicist criterion. Second, his inability to extend the same call he responded to as a speech fully adequate to his philosophical position undermines his claim that the call to the cause of Christ was sufficient to incorporate him into prophetic pragmatism in his own case. There is something in West's own entry into the fold of prophetic pragmatists that is not expressible in the kind of prophetic speech exemplified by his philosophical position.

My second criticism is that surviving, which is the essential activity at the heart of the black narrative, and West's Marxist analysis, do not appear to be held together either by self-reflexive discourse or by metaphysical reflection. West does not persuasively explain why applying Marxist analysis to the world and evaluating competing narratives on these terms is essential to the tradition of surviving.[29] West needs to define "surviving" in a richer way if he is going to claim that something as radical as Marxist analysis is necessary for achieving that goal.

Let me expand this second critique. West claims that individualistic and democratically egalitarian themes of the gospel are appropriated selectively from a tradition that itself is appropriated selectively from a larger tradition. But he argues as if this selective appropriation is grounded on an authoritative principle called "the gospel" that transcends the dialectic of appropriation and makes his reflective assessment of the nature of the gospel a critical rather than an uncritical belief. This gives his Marxist account a more stable warrant for acceptance than it deserves. Individualism and democracy as the foundation of the gospel— at least to the degree that West uses these terms—seems a dubious claim.

For West, critical, selected strategies are fallibilistically held for specific purposes, and descriptions are limited to identifying strategies within a particular context. The general authority of the gospel in his tradition makes it useful for a general approach to the world, where new and different contexts are faced. West's move to combine the gospel and Marxism is embraced because it further expands the scope of a critical approach to problems, and because Marxism adds an intellectual core to the peculiarly contextual belief in Christianity. Christianity that speaks in Marxist idioms is somehow easier to defend than a strictly orthodox version of the gospel. A similar assimilation occurred with the historical introduction of theism as a philosophical-religious term around the middle of the seventeenth century as the "belief in the existence of a Supreme Being as the source of finite existence, with rejection of revelation and the supernatural doctrines of Christianity" to add intellectual clout to belief.[30] Unfortunately, both this move toward theism and, I fear, West's toward Marxism undermine the very contextual peculiarity that vivifies the appeal of Christianity.

What is more troubling about this problem, though, is that West ignores or discards the dialectic between his Marxist tendencies and his understanding of the gospel he appropriates. He claims the two mutually support one another without considering the possibility that both may emerge from the prior ground of a social-political commitment. It is clear, however, why he would downplay this possibility of dialectic. It undermines his prophetic ground. What makes prophetic ground difficult to articulate is that the word spoken in the original context speaks just as well to remote contexts. West wants to replace this double-speaking word with a thoroughly spoken word that incorporates all contexts by virtue of its theoretical extension. This is West's attitude toward Marxist analysis. He thinks it can and must be applied to every social order. By contrast, I suggest that true prophetic ground is recognized by intensionally *descriptive* and extensionally *applicable* speech. A prophetic word, because it emanates from the intensional truths of divine/human intersection, extends to all human occasions. West's prophetic word speaks Marxist analysis as an extensionally *descriptive* analysis. This evasion of the intensional problems of identity and difference, of individual and community, soul and God, favors the expedient and high moral tone of a gospel based on extensional description. The failure of an extensionally descriptive analysis emerges when the need arises for prescriptive work—what should be done here and now? This determination cannot arise simply from description.[31] What should be done in a particular place and time does not follow clearly from the Marxist description West provides. Something else is needed to give the prophetic word its kick into the rough and tumble of immediate action and change.

The distinction between intensionally descriptive and extensionally applicable speech versus extensionally descriptive speech is often difficult to articulate. Peirce gives us an example of this difference and its difficulty when he describes personality. Personality is "a connection between ideas [that] is itself a general idea" (CP 6:155). Vincent Colapietro unpacks the notion that personality is an idea by describing the semiotic system that Peirce constructs around ideas. The move from personality to ideas to the semiotic structure of thought and meaning provides a rich *intensional* description of the self. Yet Peirce struggles to describe the criterion that makes a personality distinct from other ideas, finally claiming that the discriminating nature of a person depends on the same character of reality as general terms.[32] Intensional descriptions like Peirce's theory of personality cannot avoid metaphysics, which is one reason West has an aversion to them.

One of the virtues of Peirce's metaphysical account of personality is its structured vagueness. Peirce can tell us in systematic terms what a personality is, but this "telling" is not exclusionary because it carries such a wide range of possible articulations that inclusion in that descriptive nexus is possible. The abilities of others to see themselves "in" Peirce's intensional description is the test of that description's *extensional* applicability. If it fails to extend to every person Peirce's description has failed.

There is another reason West avoids the dual characteristic of intensional description and extensional applicability for his prophetic speech: it involves opening the content of his speech to indefinite examination with the possibility that *any* failure of that extended word results in its complete rejection as a failed description. But this is just the test that is applied to prophetic speech in the Bible: "I will raise up a prophet from among their countrymen like you, and I will put My words in his mouth, and he shall speak to them all that I command him. . . . But the prophet who shall speak a word presumptuously in My name which I have not commanded him to speak . . . shall die. And you may say in your heart, 'How shall we know the word which the Lord has not spoken?' When a prophet speaks in the name of the Lord, if the thing does not come about or come true, that is the thing which the Lord has not spoken" (Deut. 18:18–22). Prophetic speech in the Bible is more complicated than simple prediction, when one takes into account the self-referential and repeated prophetic themes that link periods of Israel's history together across radical shifts of demographics, politics, cultus, and location. The test of absolute accuracy outlined in Deuteronomy is the demand for completely general extensional applicability of the prophetic word intensionally described as the "word of the Lord." If West wants to speak prophetically he is bringing himself under a severe criterion.

Confessional Historicism

Introducing the need for intensional analysis throws up red flags in a postmodern world. Intensional analysis necessitates a return to metaphysics. It brings up the problem of special knowledge and the power politics of truth. But I want to bracket those questions for the moment and focus instead on what a return to intensional thinking might provide for West's account. And I still want to temper everything with his own fire—if there is no difference to lived experience, there is no truth. In opposition to West, I think this kind of difference is possible only through a return to metaphysics, to the intensional description of human nature, and to the place of confession in the philosophical style of Augustine.

West's philosophical beginning is not a *fully* confessional place. There are two reasons for saying this. First, according to the tenets of historicism, there is no reality to describe that exceeds our historical context. But confession implies the common feature of a human relation to God, where "God" is tenderly offered as an attempt to indicate either the creative source for such a confession, or, more strongly, as the creative source and the presence evoking that confession. Second, confession includes an intelligible account of the content of one's belief. Though this account need not be rational and deductively certain, it must be rational as intelligible, articulate, and well reasoned. The ground of confession is not the non-arguable ground West claims for himself. While giving good reasons for faith does not mean that anyone agreeing with the soundness of the reasoning is thereby forced to admit the conclusion, it must evoke some aspect of belief that differs from, say, the philosophical beliefs or political ideas that one holds. There is the third meaning of confession as the performative act of willing or admitting belief. This is different from faith as an intellectualism. Faith is more than theoretical knowledge because it also involves the heart, as Edwards and Peirce have said in their own unique ways. The problem for West is that his description of religious historicism leaves no room for individual conversion and confession that would be the necessary ground for radical personal change. Such a transformation cannot be completely articulated by the standards of judgment of the context, but rather indicates a radical shift in the orientation of a person's intentions in relation to reality. Dewey shows more religious sensitivity than West in this respect when he claims that the project of a better world is dependent on men and women of personal faith and a "settled act of the will." Dewey may not have understood conversion very well but he sensed the significance of this intensionally charged space for his democratic program.

Like Dewey, West knows that the fragmentation of the community needs to be overcome in order for social melioration to occur. West sees this problem, but his insistence on historicism demands that the ground behind ultimate commitments remains non-arguable. Like West's more generalized account, confessional historicism also speaks to the problem of identity within a community. The imbalance noted before between West's prophetic speech and his commitment to the black Christian community is reflected in another dimension in the appropriation of strategies for survival that constitutes any community. To say it simply, the appropriation of Christian themes and hopes by slaves had to mean more than what West calls "appropriation of strategies." The strategies found within the Christian community make sense only to those individuals who can *identify* themselves at the most fundamental levels with the Christian story. Strategies are not the blossom floating on the surface ready to by plucked by any passersby; strategies are habits like the trunk of a tree that is inseparable from the roots hidden deep in the ground. Appropriation of a strategy that can withstand the vicissitudes of real political life can stand only so long as the supporting reality of that strategy's narrative remains intact. The choice of strategies is not reduced by this view to an acritical "Pascalian wager," but is rather a judgment of the *orientation* of those narratives. Not just any narrative with attached strategies will do, but only those narratives that refract the orientation of *my confessional narrative.* The orientation of the narrative guides the contextual appropriation. West, in his sermonic moments, reflects this aspect of confessional historicism: "Heroic courage to hope [is] grounded in the groundless mystery of the Cross—a prophetic witness to the absurd love of Jesus in a fallen world that views such love as folly and appears to reduce such love to impotence."[33] Christianity is appropriate to this understanding of returning to the difficult circumstances—even to the understanding that this "return" is a proper way of instantiating the word of God. Jesus returned from death to the same social reality that worked to his crucifixion. The disciples were admonished to return to the hostile city of Jerusalem after Jesus ascended. Even the Christian apocalypse points to this return to the concrete and the problematic; for it is Heaven descending to Earth, not Earth escaping its limitations, that inaugurates the physical Kingdom of Heaven in the Revelation of John. The ability of narratives to enable a return to a specific place, to orient myself toward my finite context, lies at the heart of existential survival and life. But it is the orientation that makes the narrative potent, and orientations can be seen only when the narrative is taken as a mode of identification and not just the supporting and dispensable stem of a strategy.

Confessional historicism is my attempt to suggest a strengthening of the non-arguable ground under West's prophecy. I take West's non-arguable position as a limited platform for the ground of mystery in the world, which is the true space of individual change that I call conversion. West shares the loss of the Americans who fail in just this way. The confessional place I propose corresponds to the thematic character in American philosophy following on Jonathan Edwards's religious affections, C. S. Peirce's heart religion, William James's will, and John Dewey's conviction about preserving values. These philosophers, taken as a tradition, speak to the confessional community as the place of mystery and the ground of prophecy and also reveal the moments of absence or evasion of that confession. I think West is correct that the American philosophical tradition is the promising location for a development of prophetic philosophy, and my comments here should be taken as an effort to appraise critically and extend his analysis. West's evasion of conversion is one of the most instructive platforms for the continuing discovery of transformation and its limits.

ROBERT CORRINGTON AND THE
TRANSFORMATION OF CONSCIOUSNESS

Robert Corrington approaches the transformation of American philosophy from the side of cosmogenesis, inquiring into the origin of the emergence of order within nature. Human spirit reflects the impulses of the universe, the openings and resistances, and follows these openings as an invitation to probe into the reality of the order of the universe. There is no foundation, no authoritative guide, and no promise of security in this discovery. Confidence in this path of discovery emerges from the fact that the Christian tradition and all religious traditions are living communities flowing out of this probing activity. Corrington, like Peirce, refuses to make Kant's transcendental deduction, focusing instead on following out philosophical traces of reality as they imprint on religious, philosophical, and psychological practice.

Corrington, although comfortable and familiar with religious notions of transformation, resists conversion language as dangerous because it represents a closing down of possibilities of the interaction with the underconscious of nature and the "selving" activity indicative of human thought. In conversion probes are limited, novelty eliminated by a conception of the soul that is determined prior to its emergence. Corrington latches on to Peirce's notion of a "real" as an invitation to probe without *a priori* determination. The discovery of the real is an exercise of ecstasis for Corrington, a standing apart from the continuum of nature. Such work of ecstasis reflects the best of religion. Not that we must strive to be good without God, like Rorty, for that simply covers over a self-loathing and absence that will reemerge and devastate an individual. Rather, Corrington holds that the reality ingredient in the universe corresponds to human ecstasis, opening toward it but not requiring or demanding human transformation.

From this openness met with activity, ultimate meaning and purpose may emerge. Corrington, in my terms, proposes a transformation of conversion from a response to a defining content to the indeterminate content of ecstasis. His philosophical program, then, revolves around converting religion and philosophy to this expectation of ecstasis—and I think both uses of "conversion" here carry much of the same meaning. In this program Corrington follows Peirce's lead, but realizes he must go beyond this beginning. The final word on ecstatic naturalism is that it is unstable in just the way Corrington resists the stability of Peirce. He must always be beyond himself philosophically, for any repetition becomes a liability to collapse into representation. The question we will resolve toward is whether an argument for ecstasis avoids the same hegemony as "the" correct formulation of human transformation. I break Corrington's work into three main headings: (1) ecstasis and consciousness, which begins with Peirce; (2) semiotic limits and interpretive community, which emerges in relation to Royce; and (3) the underconscious of nature and the Encompassing. These three headings correspond to firstness, secondness, and thirdness, except that Corrington's third, the underconscious of nature, recurs strongly to Peirce's firstness with the additional content of religious "foldings" that provide Corrington the material for differentiation and identity within the indeterminate ground of the Encompassing.

Ecstasis and Consciousness

In some ways Corrington reflects Edwards's path in the *Religious Affections,* discovering the rules for the ways we are transformed. The massive difference between them, though, is that Corrington proceeds apart from the security of a tradition like Edwards, and he includes the discoveries of the depth psychologies of Freud and Jung. The blending of psychology and semiosis has a proper beginning in Peirce, but Corrington has to reorient our understanding of Peirce away from the brilliantly odd logician and Scholastic realist. In Peirce Corrington finds a man dislocated emotionally and intellectually, a melancholy man.

> Peirce was a master of the art of advanced forms of signification. He could enter into several distinctive semiotic systems and codes with great ease and always find pathways for connecting them. Yet in doing so he pulled further and further way from the ground of signification, perhaps originally presented to him by his mother. I am persuaded that Peirce remained haunted throughout his life by a sense of melancholy loss, a loss felt on the fringes of all of his daring analysis of the basic structures of the world.[34]

Peirce struggled to find himself in relation to his founding culture of Harvard elitism and the dimensions of his distracted personality. Peirce, for Corrington, is an example of a person who blazes a novel way into understanding human spirit. This novel and trailblazing character supports further probing development of Peirce's thought. Identifying the tensions internal to Peirce's cosmology and semiotic psychology sets up Corrington's own novel moves. "Peirce," Corrington says, "vacillated between the kind of conversion hysteria that paralyzes all symbolic and linguistic functions, and the abjection or melancholy denial that flies into a hypersymbolic activity as if to fill the universe with signs so that the maternal and its sensed loss is drowned."[35] This struggle with conversion is central to Peirce, and indeed to Corrington as well.

For Peirce the multidimensional character of the self is metaphorically described as a lake. The self is a matter of depth, amorphous like water, a surface that appears above a vastness within which gradients of reality are found by settling down into places that resist peering looks. From this womblike image, Corrington pictures the self emerging by pressing up and out of this indefinite character. Again, he follows Peirce; "Ontologically, self-control is what it is because of the depth structures of cosmic habit within the universe as a whole. . . . The human process derives its energies and vector directionalities from the universe. . . . But this process is a healing one in which the individual welcomes the larger community into its self-constitution."[36] This point seems exactly right. The puzzle for Peirce, Corrington, and me, however, is how the human process derives these universal energies toward reconstitution, and what object or content makes this reconstitution possible and necessary. From this passage we see how the self remains powerful in Corrington's thought; the self is key. For Rorty philosophy remains key, for West the community is key. For Corrington the key is the self and the process of selving, although later we will see why Corrington removes the Augustinian metaphor of healing from his conception of the self.

This aspect of the evolving and emerging self in Peirce's cosmology comes to the fore in an extended rejoinder to Paul Carus, who attacked Peirce as a necessitarian. Carus took Peirce's argument for "real and general" law as a declaration of determinative regularity. Peirce clarifies that his sense of law is *not* that to which "the phenomena of nature *always* conform, or to which they *precisely* conform" (CP 6:588). Peirce locates the openness for this imprecise conformity in a passage that becomes centrally important for Corrington. Peirce first denies that absolute chance is "something ultimate and inexplicable," stating that the chaos to which he recurs is so irregular that existence does not express this merely germinal state of being. "Even this nothingness, though it antecedes the infinitely distant absolute beginning of time, is traced back to a nothingness more rudimentary still, in which there is no variety, but only an indefinite specificability, which is nothing but a tendency to the diversification of the nothing, while leaving it as nothing as it was before" (CP 6:612). Corrington develops this further,

> The true originative power of the universe is a deep nothingness that is more of a tendency than an actual pool of diversified possibilities. We could call this the domain of nature's potencies. . . . The potencies of nothingness are ontologically prior to the possibilities that obtain in what we could call the "lesser" nothingness. Lesser nothingness is the domain of nothingness of cosmic possibility and variety. This is a kind of possible objects and events. . . . Lesser nothingness is the cosmic soup of possibilities that can become actualized whenever emergents take on habits. Deeper down is the greater nothingness that provides the metaphysical goad for cosmogenesis.[37]

This statement is the ground of Corrington's ecstasis, the standing apart possible within the "cosmic soup" that is the primordial origin of meaning and reality. His probe into Peirce's insight of the internally distinguishing fluctuations of greater and lesser nothingness constitutes his trajectory outlined in the next sections of this chapter. Corrington states the object of his inquiry clearly:

> What inner logic determines the movement from greater nothingness (the potencies) to lesser nothingness (the possibilities) to the nascent world of generals (the forms)? Is God the agency within or behind this process, or is God too a product of this process? Peirce downplays the concept of divine majesty which would entail that the purpose of the world and its creatures is to worship its creator. Instead, he makes a case for human autonomy, arguing that God is concerned with establishing independent creatures who do not seek to become part of an all-absorbing divine presence.[38]

Corrington's transformative reading of Peirce begins from this distinction of autonomous selves and the movement of the universe. Corrington is conscious of this transformative reading, and I think we philosophers all read with a similar transformative goal. This is how I have sought to read Edwards, Peirce, James, and Dewey. These readings are the places where disagreements are possible, and thus this is the location of my problem with Corrington's reading. He privileges both the demand for autonomy above any law, which I do not think coheres with Peirce, and the notion that the ground of this autonomy can only be the primordial soup of nothingness. I take the soup of nothingness to mean "that out of which" law emerges, and God, as the mystery of that generation, as having a complement in human autonomy converging on the divine character of agapism, that also emerges out of the relative "nothing" of firstness. In relation to law, the origin is this abyss of indeterminacy. But Peirce is clear that law, not indeterminacy, is the path toward an explanation of how things work. I am not sure what Peirce would think about making firstness the locus of origin for emergent meaning. He might react as Kant did when he denied that anything productive can be said about noumena. In opposition to Corrington, then, I think there is a sense of reverence of the sacred in Peirce. Otherwise we are hard pressed to understand Peirce's desire to subordinate himself to the "Master" and enter communion as anything but a lapse of judgment.

Semiotic Limits and Interpretive Community

In this section I follow Corrington's consideration of a community that emerges from the potentialities described above in the cosmic soup of firstness. Corrington claims that community is not an outgrowth of consciousness, but a mode of responding to a lawlike real emerging from greater to lesser nothing. Hence, community is a feature of the transformation from dependence on consciousness to the recognition of the role of nature. Corrington develops this notion of community in opposition to the philosophical understanding that community is more like a consciousness or more like a text than an emergent character of nature. "Once nature is reduced to a secondary status," Corrington says, "the supremacy of human textuality takes over. The metaphysical ineptness of this devaluation of nature is evident in the pantextualism that sees everything, whether a person or an event, as a text for which there are no stable or reliable interpretations."[39] The fight between textuality and community leads through the prospect of an interpretive community that is not based on a "text" in the way that privileges consciousness. Only if a community emerges within the interpretive act can text-consciousness be overcome in a positive way.

Corrington develops Peirce's rejection of foundationalism and Cartesian introspection connected with first principles. The failure of this introspection leads Peirce to the character of thought as signs. From this platform Peirce arrives at the notion that intuition must be exceeded with communal acts of interpretation. "Signs form living communities,"

Peirce says, and all human thought collects around God as a "living sign" that makes humanity one community through the self-critical advance of scientific inquiry. This is not the living community Corrington claims since he does not accept Peirce's panpsychism—that all that is, is mind. Instead, Corrington proposes that the living sign can only have as its interpretant the human community, for this is all that can be properly claimed from the origin of nature that Peirce turns away from. For community to be possible, according to Corrington, it must emerge within the semiotic flow from nature, and here he follows Royce's development of Peirce's assertion that "all hermeneutic acts are communal."[40]

Royce moves beyond Platonic knowledge about experience, and James's dependence on experience, to a third kind of cognition; interpretation. "It is to this third cognitive process that, following the terminology which Peirce proposed, we here apply the name 'interpretation.'" Interpretation, Royce says, is the main business of philosophy. Its goal is the production of the Beloved Community, which functions to unite diverse hermeneutic acts through the (Holy) Spirit of loyalty. The Beloved community is "the Universal Church, the body of Christ" which is the paradigmatic community of interpretation. Royce completes his thought; "to interpret is to strive to see the world as God sees it and as we would see it in the ideal kingdom."[41] Loyalty in the act of interpretation is Royce's idealized form of the Beloved community that invests the thought of Walter Rauschenbusch and Martin Luther King with practical power.[42]

Royce says in *The Problem of Christianity*, "The World is the Community. The world contains its own interpreter. Its processes are infinite in their temporal varieties. But their interpreter, the spirit of the universal community—never absorbing varieties or permitting them to blend—compares and through a real life, interprets them all."[43] This expression of a world containing its own interpreter is the ground for Corrington's naturalized community. The community of interpretation functions as the horizon and perspective through which all signs "pass on their way to interpretive transparency."[44] Corrington is still after transparency, which entails avoiding consciousness since there is no way for transparency to emerge within such a mediating abstraction. He says, "By shifting the burden of semiotic theory in this direction, Royce made a bold advance beyond Peirce."[45] Corrington thinks Royce also draws toward the same insights as Gadamer while avoiding his language of mysticism. For Royce the goal is not language but community. Setting aside the locus of language, Corrington suggests that he can follow Gadamer, who "links the hermeneutic process to the evolution of human understanding toward a practical evocation of the Good with the life of the community. Understanding is not limited to texts but drives toward interhuman communication. Rhetoric and dialectic receive their grounding in the hermeneutic process of discussion, which allows individuals to enter into horizons not their own."[46] This movement into "horizons not their own" is an essential distinction for Corrington. Science cannot accommodate this movement. Explicit description cannot work the conversion from one horizon to another. Moving between horizons is essential for interpretive cognition, and this movement requires dislocating oneself from any single form or ground of reference.

> The finite interpreter is not somehow added to an already preconstituted community as one more member but derives his or her very meaning only through those intersubjective transactions that enrich the scope and contour of the community. . . . A mind thus becomes an interpreter whenever the traits of self-reflection, temporality, and intersubjectivity function together to secure the ongoing hermeneutic process.[47]

Interpretation is an end in itself since this is the only stable ground of the community. Therefore, loyalty to the interpretive community entails breaking beyond horizons. This keeps the process moving, but still the question remains about what drives the interpretive urge. Corrington's charge against neopragmatism emerges with the following statement: "[I]ndividual liberty does not constitute a sufficient condition for the hermeneutic community. Some form of conscious convergence must also prevail as the locus of future aspiration for the members of the social order."[48] A conscious convergence is an emergent character within interpretive communities, but it cannot be preconstituted or dogmatic, and neither can it be the result of unconstrained liberty.

Corrington acknowledges the power of Christian symbols as aspects of the conscious convergence in "movement toward the Encompassing." The Encompassing is the final dimension of the sign function and it brings the sign relation into the sphere of religion. The Encompassing depends on no ontological ground, yet it "exerts its uncanny lure for human existence."[49]

> The symbol of crucifixion specifically denies that any human or communal value can be attached to this reality. The cross curiously inverts itself whenever we try to fill it with further human content. In its self-negation,

the cross breaks open to that which vastly outstrips human categorial projections . . . whether or not the cross is the most radical symbol of the
Encompassing, it fulfills its role whenever emptiness takes the place of
semiotic density. This emptiness is not a nihilistic absence of meaning but a
radiant evocation of a different kind of meaning not circumscribed by the
signs of the community and its interpreters.[50]

Meaning that is not circumscribed by the community appears to fall
outside of Roycean loyalty. But Corrington's point, I think, is that interpretive acts, like the one related to the cross, are examples of the ecstasis
that escapes the language horizon of Gadamer without becoming dis-
loyal. Such hermeneutic acts tend toward expanding the richness of the
symbols rather than their destruction, and only with this movement
away from "semiotic density" is the ongoing process of interpretation
preserved in the long run. The crux of human transformation is discovering this origin of an interpretation that opens out within the community, unconstrained by the community, but oriented toward the
community. Again, a Christian image is important for Corrington: "For
Royce, Paul was among the first of Western thinkers to probe into the
dynamic structures of community and show how these structures are
animated and deepened by the presence of the Holy Spirit as the agency
of Christ through time. Paul's vision of love, as the divine/human
expression of loyalty became the ethical core for his understanding of
the community as the body of Christ."[51]

The ground of the community is loyalty, and Spirit (or spirit, in
Corrington's view) is the principle of interpretation that is the sign of that
loyalty. Loyalty "brings us to a new knowledge of the self and its community."[52] But what is the end of this knowledge? What is it for? Loyalty to
an interpretation translates into habits of action that still seek teleological
ground in ways that we will explore next. Corrington bridges from this
understanding of the interpretive community to a method of avoiding
both foundationalism and pietistic models of Jesus as the guide for life. The
interpretive community Corrington describes manifests a universal movement toward "transparency" with what is in the world.

Underconscious of Nature: The Encompassing

The last stage of Corrington's reorientation of Peirce's philosophy
appears in *A Semiotic Theory of Theology and Philosophy*. In this book
Corrington resolves many of his theoretical probes toward firstness and

nature, and the community that emerges through this transformation. Corrington blends together semiotic and psychological expectations,

> Instead of trotting out the old grammar of pathology and normalcy, it is far more illuminating to talk of a dialectic involving closure and selving. The former term refers to the perhaps innate need to freeze meaning horizons where they stand so that the functioning self is not brought into thematic awareness. Forms of local control and the tribal assume priority. The concept of "selving," on the other hand, denotes a much more complex process of living in the spaces where awareness encounters the unconscious of the self and the underconscious of nature. Jung's concept of "individuation," while somewhat heroic and narrow, provides an analogue to the selving process. Selving lies at the heart of the human process and, while deeply ambiguous, is a force leading to species enhancement.[53]

The creative aspect of this process is the discovery of this momentum through reflection on the selving process. The platform of selving Corrington describes collects impulses into a process without (as Royce said) blending interpreters, while providing sufficient ground for the resistance of the individual to emerge, like Edwards's notion of entity. The selving process reaches back to the discovery of a primal (if not originary) momentum within nature. Naturalism becomes *ecstatic* when it probes into its own "somber tone" to find an even deeper momentum within nature that also yields its own categorial array. So Corrington's philosophical inquiry retains Peirce's logic but with a different tone. Corrington emphasizes the "world melancholy" (which he says is "far more stoic than a romantic *Weltschmertz*") that forms the necessary foreground for a participation in the ecstatic potencies that are emergent from the underconscious of nature, as mediated through the unconscious of the self. "One of the central tasks of semiotic cosmology is to describe or evoke the traces within the products of the self to gauge how they may, or may not, point to the ever-receding, yet ever-spawning, abyss of *nature-naturing*."[54]

Corrington's discovery of the melancholy of Peirce now makes sense, because in that character he sees the outline of participation in the emergent character of the self. He is careful here to respect Peirce's hesitation to locate a principle of individuation that is positive in terms of the structure of the self or understanding; hence the underconscious of nature is the ground of the unconscious of the self. Both reflect the limit of secondness, which cannot produce or reveal categories. In one sense the real abyss in the semiotic structure is brute experience or second-ness—there is no way out or forward. Corrington says, "The category of secondness, as the name implies, refers to brute dyadic interaction that is prior to signification or fulfilled meaning. . . . Resistance (a form of sec-ondness) in the human order is rarely fully self-conscious, and part of the endless comedy and tragedy of the human process can be seen in our struggles to find clarity out of the sea of projections that emerge from us and return to us."[55]

But secondness is not easily left, and while Peirce moves from sec-ondness to thirdness, and Corrington from secondness back to firstness, I think the resistance of secondness holds much more significance for both their semiotic structures than they admit. Indeed, Corrington depends on an argument from resistance to overcome Peirce. He says that what Peirce failed to grasp was the "sheer otherness of the uncon-scious, even if he had a partial sense of the underconscious of nature with his primal category of 'firstness.' His doctrine of panpsychism made the unconscious too conscious in the sense that mentality is a trait found throughout nature in a vast continuum admitting only of degrees of instantiation."[56] What Peirce fails to consider is the secondness of unconsciousness, and with this evaluation Corrington dismisses his philosophical father. While Peirce charts a trajectory toward a reality that is far different from its origin (nature-to-mind), Corrington answers both sides of this transformation with a single term, nature, that acts as both origin and *telos* in producing the contours of consciousness. Corrington proposes a path of reflective returning that is a rejection of getting beyond the limits of nature. Yet within this return all the com-plexity usually associated with a divine or ontologically separate con-tent remains:

> Ecstatic naturalism clearly sides with the second trajectory, that which speaks of the holy or numinous that represents a fully natural process of sacred semiotic folds impacting on the human unconscious. Further, ecstatic naturalism remains friendly to those feminist theologies that also want to become free from vertical patriarchal language and to probe into the ways in which nature's own pulsations contain religious seeds. The deconstruction of the male language of neo-orthodoxy, where god is envisioned as speaking *von oben* (from above) to sinful humankind, is absolutely essential to a renewed semiotic cosmology in its religious dimension.[57]

Corrington merges the religious dimension of reflection with the turning toward firstness through ecstatic naturalism—the religious seeds give this turn to the abyss of nature-naturing a modicum of warrant via the hope of a satisfying transformation. My interest here is the way this emulates a kind of conversion, albeit one *away* from other forms of conversion. Corrington says the ecstatic naturalist does not respond to a word from above, presumably like Edwards would hold, and not from experience that privileges consciousness, nor from tradition like we see in West that reflects patriarchal patterns. Rather, the turn must be accomplished from a set of infinities discovered in the process of interpretive selving, moving from the actual infinite of things, to a prospective (hermeneutic) infinite, to an open infinite, and finally to a sustaining infinite, like Tillich's "ground of Being":

> [T]he sustaining infinite is neither religious nor anti-religious; it is not creator, nor is it an agent in history or otherwise. It obtains prior to the distinction between good and evil, and prior to any axiological distinctions such as those aesthetic distinctions so prized in process forms of naturalism. . . . Thus the sustaining infinite lives on the cusp of the ontological difference between the two primal dimensions of nature. It does not sustain what lies "below" it, but lives horizontally, as it were, in the world of innumerable signs and sign systems. . . . It sustains, nothing more, and nothing less. . . . The sustaining infinite provides the clearing within which both identities and scopes can unfold or not unfold. But it is directly relevant to neither.[58]

This sustaining infinite is also the generative ground from which both selving and the interpretive community emerge. The intersection of the community and individual, participating in the mutual aspects of selving, extends from religious ground to the work of social reconstruction:

> [F]or a fragile and nascent interpretive community the self will be a precarious foundling that must raise its head and social body above the inertia of the conditions of origin that make it possible. Interpretive communities, whether they emerge from the social elite or the marginalized, are those communities that challenge the inert self-signs that are perpetuated by natural communities. If this process of critique moves into a postmodern horizon, the self actually becomes derailed and loses its emancipatory energies in an ersatz horizon that only *seems* liberating. But if the interpretive self reaches back into its conditions of origin in a creative way, and brings forth emancipatory energies *from* and *through* these prehuman conditions, the prospects of democratic reconstruction are heightened.[59]

While there is care here, the impulse of the sustaining infinite is negative to Royce's Spirit that at least implies a constructive image of the self. Rather, for Corrington, "the spirit simply is its clearing away; it is not a consciousness in its own right that actively goes after persons and their projections," and "[t]here is no centered consciousness in the spirit that could be addressed by human consciousness, even though the spirit can be met in an I-Thou relationship. Lacking consciousness, it must be seen as a gradient that goes where there is a gap or opening in the semiotic world that needs to be transformed."[60] Corrington moves us toward the Encompassing by virtue of its tendency to interpretation; but there is nothing here but a clearing. Conversion from nothingness to nothingness appears to be the only way Corrington can answer a transformation "from above."

With this description Corrington arrives at a significant moment in his struggle to transform Peirce, especially his susceptibility to conversion language:

> Peirce argued that without some form of novelty, habits could not be broken and new laws could not emerge. Hence, for him, novelty is a necessary feature in personal and cosmic evolution. From the standpoint of the self, novelty is necessary for the fulfillment of the selving process as the novel irruption of signs can compel a new self-organization that encompasses past signs and brings them into a new configuration. Yet there is also the tendency to stress the novel traits too much, thus ignoring or abjecting the necessary antecedent conditions for their emergence. This abjection process can be seen most starkly in certain forms of religious conversion which abject the preconverted self as being no longer relevant to the new self that has emerged. Psychologically this is a dangerous move as it utterly ignores the continuing power of unconscious complexes to intrude in the life of the so called "born-again" self. Again, all novelty is novelty in certain respects and not others.[61]

In this passage, we see again the opposition Corrington finds in conversion that has a structure independent of a unique self. Corrington's objection is revealing, because conversion is much closer to what he aims at than he perceives. What he is arguing for is not very far from the ineffable demand for a change to an ineffable character that resists all rational depiction except as that which the self cannot control. The movement toward an "opening" here is not for some articulable good other than matching the selving impulse with the spirit ingredient in the human unconscious. Corrington senses this absence and elides the effect of the transformed sense of religious community with social reconstruction: "The utopian hope that can move our religious community past the stage of compassion into a stage of political and social action is a product of the conjunction of the selving process and the spirit. . . . It is almost as if a gap opens up that has its own vacuum energy, drawing the self toward those centers of distorted energy that must be transformed through democratic transformation."[62] Overcoming socially distorted energy depends on the selving that originates individuals without consciousness. In this way democratic transformation is a demand for continuing openness and interpretation, not for some good intrinsic to social reality itself.

The coordination of the roles of the nutrient religious community and selving impulses leads Corrington to conclude that "if we were to combine the best of the Greek with the best of the Hebrew worlds, we could say that 'sacred folds' of nature are in some sense responsive to our own semiotic and moral probes, and that there are energies that are extra-human that can aid us in the process of moral growth." These powers are not "extra-natural, nor are they in a 'position' to give us a moral blueprint. Yet without their powers, we are truly at the mercy of semiotic inertia and blind habit."[63]

Corrington evades conversion, as his objection to "born-again" language makes clear, in order to describe a different kind of conversion. Like Peirce, Corrington knows the structure of the self is a clue to the transformative potency in the universe, although Corrington rejects the content Peirce finds in God and his choosing to turn away from the abyss of firstness. Corrington seeks to correct Peirce's failure of nerve by displaying how it is precisely this turn toward the abyss of firstness that provides access to truly transformative ground for both individuals and communities. Corrington is more like James in this respect of turning toward mystery without closure, but Corrington is more systematic than James in seeing this turn as a rejection of all connection to consciousness, no matter how much common sense must be overcome. Corrington has Peirce's community without its ground in God, and he has James's mystery without his ground in the self-adjusting self. He is, in a way, mediating an old conflict between friends. Corrington locates an agreement between Peirce and James that transformation must extend from nature and reconnect with it, albeit with a change of content or form. Such a return needs an inbreaking content to overcome the inertia of habits. But Corrington's model does not carry us beyond the transformation that is immanent in nature. I think this is why "born-again" language shows up in this account—he still yearns for this kind of rebirth and reformation. Indeed, to be taken up by the momentum within nature, as Corrington describes, where habits are broken without imposing another content, would be a rebirth to an expectation that there is no separate dimension to be overcome for selving or interpretation to obtain. This absolute immanence contains ecstasis, and therefore conversion is a moment *of* nature that cannot, need not, move beyond itself. Corrington arrives at a dyadic conception of transformation; our conversion is not nature's conversion; nature is the self-same. This is a kind of stoicism, as Corrington admitted earlier, that fully rejects the Neoplatonic lift from fragmentation to the one.

What I appreciate about Corrington is his sensitivity to the fact that conversion is a fundamental aspect of all metaphysics and cosmology, just as metaphysics and cosmology are fundamental to philosophy and theology. Where I have difficulty with his inquiry is the reliance on absence as the category of personal understanding and individuation. He produces an equivocation of spirit as stillness and spirit as the vacuum that draws attention toward the places of semiotic openness and need. Unlike Royce, Corrington cannot abide the Spirit of Christ, only the spirit of Heideggerian absence.

Conversion and Its Evasion

Richard Rorty, Cornel West, and Robert Corrington exemplify the continuing relevance of conversion for American philosophy. In these philosophers we have seen active resistance to conversion, using conversion as a platform from which analysis extends, or recasting the ground of conversion. In response to these "evasions," I have tried to show the difficulties that emerge within these philosophies taken on their own terms. My argument is that the absence of engaging conversion is not a failure of moral will or the rejection of a standard; it is a kind of philosophical failure to face a challenge of the philosopher's peculiar strength. The challenge of conversion is that standing apart from this critical test reason flounders on a beach of its own making.

The evasion of conversion also reveals it as a place of deep resistance to philosophy. Most clearly in James, but even in West, the non-arguable ground of conversion appears to cancel philosophical power or description. Conversion cancels reason, or at least it appears to do so. My larger argument has attempted to show that antipathy toward conversion does not reflect our tradition, but rather just the opposite. Historically, an ultimate transformation like conversion has been a fruitful platform for reflection. This means that philosophical resistance to conversion emerges from another level. The impulse to conversion reflects a willful dissatisfaction with the present self, community, or conception of reality. Philosophy does not handle this resistance well. For all of philosophy's character as critical reflection that embraces difference and change, a change like conversion stands over against philosophy as something it cannot affect except at the extreme limits of its power. In conversion, philosophy sees its dependence on human affections and desire. Philosophy evades this resistance and attempts to replace it with other forms of conflict more easily handled, as Rorty does, or describe the resistance as yet another feature of the continuum, as Corrington does.

Conversion entails an inbreaking content or reality that unsettles practice and overcomes the inertia of habit. Such an inbreaking content shatters categories. Rorty and Corrington provide two examples of resisting this kind of difficulty. Rorty is not interested in any inbreaking content, and Corrington reinterprets the continuum so that it has the signs of an inbreaking content without the categorial difficulties. West makes the inbreaking content the principle of his prophetic speech, but this content is opaque to philosophy. Edwards recognizes the inbreaking content of conversion, but resolves that if there is anything reason should do for us by which its value can be clearly measured, it is getting hold of this inbreaking character and feeling the categorial threat to its limit. Edwards does not want to become this content, but he wants to understand the world in which it breaks in and ourselves as the object and purpose of that inbreaking. Elevated consciousness is not his goal. Rather, the lives of people, transformed into living stabilities by virtue of this inbreaking and shattering word, interpreters of the signs of the divine, are his focus. Such people are living moments of divine transformation that together make the only satisfying argument for real change in the universe, that is, by constituting in their embodied existences the change of the present world into a different one, by the changing of themselves.

Conversion in American philosophy will always be problematic. American philosophy moves around conversion and only occasionally toward it. Philosophical work comes in from the fringes, approaching and receding from this place. The transformation of both knowledge and knower, transformed and transforming communities, and the philosophical origin of transformation, which can also be the subject of transformation, comprise the movement in relation to the vital core of conversion. The philosophical challenge I have undertaken here is holding these aspects of transformation together in order to see these trajectories as a piece of a disposition in relation to conversion. The foundation of personal transformation becomes that of the community, which can follow these trajectories with open eyes, not fearing the discovery that may come, but realizing the continuity of all such transformations with the impulse behind American philosophy to seek and find this place of conversion.

NOTES

1. Richard Rorty, *Consequences of Pragmatism* (University of Minnesota Press, 1982), xvii.

2. Robert B. Brandom, ed., *Rorty and His Critics* (Blackwell, 2000), x.

3. Ibid., 236ff.

4. Richard Rorty, *Philosophy and the Mirror of Nature* (Princeton University Press, 1979), 126.

5. Herman J. Saatkamp Jr., ed., *Rorty and Pragmatism: The Philosopher Responds to His Critics* (Vanderbilt University Press, 1995), 71.

6. Rorty, *Consequences,* xxviii.

7. Ibid., xxx.

8. Ibid., xxxvii.

9. Ibid., xliii.

10. Ibid., 33.

11. John Pettegrew and Casey Nelson Blake, eds., *A Pragmatist's Progress?* (Rowman and Littlefield, 2000), 96.

12. Rorty, *Consequences,* 54.

13. Ibid., 31.

14. Richard Rorty, *Essays on Heidegger and Others: Philosophical Papers* (Cambridge University Press, 1991), 2:31.

15. Ibid., 2:48.

16. Richard Rorty, *Philosophy and Social Hope* (Penguin, 1999), 157.

17. Ibid., 161.

18. Ibid., 163.

19. Rorty, *Philosophy and the Mirror of Nature,* 383.

20. William James, *Varieties of Religious Experience* (Penguin, 1982), 407–408.

21. David Hume, "An Inquiry concerning Human Understanding," in *Modern Philosophy: An Anthology of Primary Sources,* ed. Roger Ariew and Eric Watkins (Hackett, 1998), 493.

22. Cornel West, *Prophetic Fragments* (Eerdmans, 1988), 272.

23. Robert Westbrook, "Democratic Evasions: Cornel West and the Politics of Pragmatism," *Praxis International* (April 1993): 7.

24. Cornel West, *The Ethical Dimensions of Marxist Thought* (Monthly Review Press, 1991), xxviii–xxix.

25. West, *Prophetic Fragments,* 88.

26. Cornel West, *Prophesy Deliverance!: An Afro-American Revolutionary Christianity* (Westminster Press, 1982), 106ff.

27. Cornel West, *The American Evasion of Philosophy* (University of Wisconsin Press, 1989), 228–229.

28. West, *Prophesy Deliverance,* 145.

29. West, *Prophetic Fragments,* 121.

30. Nicholas Lash, *Easter in Ordinary* (London: SCM Press, 1990), 103.

31. Westbrook, "Democratic Evasions," 7.

32. John Smith, *America's Philosophical Vision* (University of Chicago Press, 1992), 44.

33. Hosford Dixie and Cornel West, eds., *The Courage to Hope: From Black Suffering to Human Redemption* (Beacon Press, 1999), 228.

34. Robert Corrington, *An Introduction to C. S. Peirce: Philosopher, Semiotician, and Ecstatic Naturalist* (Rowman and Littlefield, 1993), 22.

35. Ibid., 24.

36. Ibid., 115.

37. Ibid., 179.

38. Ibid., 200–201.

39. Robert Corrington, *The Community of Interpreters* (Mercer University Press, 1987), xii.

40. Corrington, *Community of Interpreters,* 10.

41. Ibid., 24.

42. Anthony Cook, *The Least of These: Race, Religion and Law in American Culture* (Routledge, 1997).

43. Corrington, *Community of Interpreters,* 26.

44. Ibid., 35.

45. Ibid., 35.

46. Ibid., 42.

47. Ibid., 53.

48. Ibid., 58.

49. Ibid., 61–62.

50. Ibid., 63.

51. Ibid., 69.

52. Ibid., 77.

53. Robert Corrington, *A Semiotic Theory of Theology and Philosophy* (Cambridge University Press, 2000), 36.

54. Ibid., 39, 41.

55. Ibid., 46.

56. Ibid., 53.

57. Ibid., 61.

58. Ibid., 112, 113.

59. Ibid., 135.

60. Ibid., 166.

61. Ibid., 201.

62. Ibid., 214, 215.

63. Ibid., 224.

BIBLIOGRAPHY

Anderson, Douglas R. *Creativity and the Philosophy of C. S. Peirce*. Boston: Martinus Nijhoff, 1987.

_____. "Smith and Dewey on the Religious Dimension of Experience: Dealing with Dewey's Half-God." *American Journal of Theology and Philosophy* 14, no. 2 (1993): 161–176.

_____. *Strands of System*. West Lafayette, Ind.: Purdue University Press, 1995.

Armstrong, Karen. *Islam: A Short History*. New York: Modern Library, 2002.

Augustine, Saint. *The City of God*. Trans. John Healy. London: Dent and Sons, 1931.

_____. *Augustine's Confessions and Enchiridion*. Trans. Albert Outler. Philadelphia: Westminster Press, 1955.

_____. *On Free Choice of the Will*. Trans. Thomas Williams. Indianapolis: Hackett, 1993.

_____. *The Confessions of Saint Augustine*. Trans. John K. Ryan. Garden City, N.Y.: Image Books, 1960.

Barron, Robert. *And Now I See: A Theology of Transformation*. New York: Crossroad, 1998.

Barth, Karl. *The Epistle to the Romans*. Trans. Edwyn Hoskyns. London: Oxford University Press, 1963.

Bauerline, Mark. *The Pragmatic Mind: Explorations in the Psychology of Belief*. Durham, N.C.: Duke University Press, 1997.

Benne, Robert. *Quality with Soul*. Grand Rapids, Mich.: Eerdmans, 2001.

Bernstein, Richard J. *John Dewey*. New York: Washington Square Press, 1966.

_____. *Philosophical Profiles*. Philadelphia: University of Pennsylvania Press, 1986.

_____. *Beyond Objectivism and Relativism*. Philadelphia: University of Pennsylvania Press, 1991.

Boisvert, Raymond. *John Dewey: Rethinking Our Time*. Albany: State University of New York Press, 1998.

Bonhoeffer, Dietrich. *Creation and Fall and Temptation*. New York: Macmillan, 1959.

_____. *Christ the Center*. Trans. Edwin Robertson. San Francisco: Harper, 1978.

Brandom, Robert B., ed. *Rorty and His Critics*. Oxford: Blackwell Publishers, 2000.

Brent, Joseph. *Charles Sanders Peirce: A Life*. Bloomington: Indiana University Press, 1993.

Brown, Peter. *Augustine of Hippo*. Berkeley: University of California Press, 1967.

Brown, Raymond. *The Gospel According to John I–XII*. New York: Doubleday, 1966.

Bruce, F. F. *The Gospel of John*. Grand Rapids, Mich.: Eerdmans, 1983.

Buber, Martin. *I and Thou*. Trans. Walter Kaufmann. New York: Scribners, 1970.

Buchler, Justus. *Philosophical Writings of C. S. Peirce*. New York: Dover, 1955.

Buckley, Michael, S.J. *At the Origins of Modern Atheism*. New Haven, Conn.: Yale University Press, 1987.

Calvin, John. *Institutes of the Christian Religion*. 2 vols. Ed. John T. McNeil. Philadelphia: Westminster Press, 1960.

Campbell, James. *Understanding John Dewey*. La Salle, Ill.: Open Court, 1995.

Charry, Ellen. *By the Renewing of Your Minds: The Pastoral Function of Christian Doctrine*. New York: Oxford University Press, 1997.

Cherry, Conrad. *The Theology of Jonathan Edwards*. Bloomington: Indiana University Press, 1966.

Colapietro, Vincent. *Peirce's Approach to the Self*. Albany: State University of New York Press, 1989.

Conforti, Joseph. *Jonathan Edwards, Religious Tradition, and American Culture*. Chapel Hill: University of North Carolina Press, 1995.

Corrington, Robert. *The Community of Interpreters*. Macon, Ga.: Mercer University Press, 1987.

_____. *An Introduction to C. S. Peirce: Philosopher, Semiotician, Ecstatic Naturalist*. Boston: Rowman and Littlefield, 1993.

_____. *A Semiotic Theory of Theology and Philosophy*. Cambridge: Cambridge University Press, 2000.

Daniel, Stephen H. *The Philosophy of Jonathan Edwards*. Bloomington: Indiana University Press, 1994.

Deledalle, Gerard. *Charles S. Peirce's Philosophy of Signs*. Bloomington: Indiana University Press, 2000.

Deuser, Hermann. *Gott, Geist und Natur*. Berlin: W. de Gruyter, 1993.

Dewey, John. "What I Believe." *Forum* 83, no. 3 (1930): 176–182.

_____. "Time and Individuality." In *Time and Its Mysteries, Series II*, 85–109. New York: New York University Press, 1940.

_____. *John Dewey: The Early Works: 1882–1898*. Ed. Jo Ann Boydston. Carbondale: Southern Illinois University Press, 1969–72.

_____. *John Dewey: The Middle Works: 1899–1924*. Ed. Jo Ann Boydston. Carbondale: Southern Illinois University Press, 1976–83.

_____. *John Dewey: The Later Works: 1925–1953*. Ed. Jo Ann Boydston. Carbondale: Southern Illinois University Press, 1981–90.

Dooley, Patrick. *Pragmatism as Humanism: The Philosophy of William James*. Chicago: Nelson Hall, 1974.

Edwards, Jonathan. *Edwards on the Affections and Alleine*. New York: American Tract Society, n.d.

_____. *The Works of President Edwards*. 10 vols. Ed. Timothy Dwight. New York: S. Converse, 1829.

_____. *A Narrative of Some Surprising Conversions*. Worcester, Mass.: Moses W. Grouse, 1832.

_____. *Works of Jonathan Edwards*. 9 vols. Ed. Perry Miller. New Haven, Conn.: Yale University Press, 1957.

_____. *Original Sin: The Works of Jonathan Edwards*. 3 vols. Ed. Clyde Holbrook. New Haven, Conn.: Yale University Press, 1970.

_____. *A Jonathan Edwards Reader*. Eds. John E. Smith, Harry S. Stout, and Kenneth P. Minkema. New Haven, Conn.: Yale University Press, 1995.

Eldridge, Michael. *Transforming Experience*. Nashville, Tenn.: Vanderbilt University Press, 1998.

Fontinell, Eugene. *Toward a Reconstruction of Religion*. New York: Doubleday, 1970.

Ford, David. *Self and Salvation: Being Transformed*. Cambridge: Cambridge University Press, 1999.

Fowler, James W. *To See the Kingdom: The Theological Vision of H. Richard Niebuhr.* Nashville, Tenn.: Abingdon Press, 1974.

Gaustad, Edwin. *The Great Awakening.* Chicago: Quadrangle Books, 1968.

Goudge, Thomas. *The Thought of C. S. Peirce.* New York: Dover, 1950.

Guelzo, Allen. *Edwards on the Will: A Century of Theological Debate.* Middletown, Conn.: Wesleyan University Press, 1989.

Hardwick, Charles D., and Donald Crosby, eds. *Pragmatism, Neo-Pragmatism and Religion.* New York: Peter Lang, 1997.

Haroutanian, Joseph. *Piety Versus Moralism.* Hamden, Conn.: Archon Books, 1964.

Hatch, Edwin. *The Influence of Greek Ideas on Christianity.* New York: Harper and Brothers, 1957.

Hauerwas, Stanley. *With the Grain of the Universe.* Grand Rapids, Mich.: Brazos Press, 2001.

Haughton, Rosemary. *The Transformation of Man: A Study of Conversion and Community.* London: Geoffrey Chapman, 1967.

Hausman, Carl. "Metaphorical Reference and Peirce's Dynamical Object." *Transactions of the Charles S. Peirce Society* 23 (summer 1987): 381–409.

Heidegger, Martin. *Basic Writings.* Ed. David Farrell Krell. New York: HarperCollins, 1993.

Hickman, Larry. *John Dewey's Pragmatic Technology.* Bloomington: Indiana University Press, 1990.

————, ed. *Reading Dewey: Interpretations for a Postmodern Generation.* Bloomington: Indiana University Press, 1998.

Hodge, Charles. *Essays and Reviews.* New York: Robert Carter and Brothers, 1857.

Hoopes, James. *Consciousness in New England: From Puritanism and Ideas to Psychoanalysis and Semiotic.* Baltimore: Johns Hopkins University Press, 1989.

James, William. *Pragmatism: A New Name for Some Old Ways of Thinking.* New York: Longmans, Green and Co., 1914.

————. *Essays in Radical Empiricism.* Cambridge, Mass.: Harvard University Press, 1976.

————. *Some Problems in Philosophy.* Cambridge, Mass.: Harvard University Press, 1979.

_____. *The Will to Believe and Other Essays*. Cambridge, Mass.: Harvard University Press, 1979.

_____. *The Varieties of Religious Experience*. New York: Penguin, 1982.

Jaspers, Karl. *Kant*. Ed. Hannah Arendt. San Diego: Harcourt Brace Jovanovich, 1962.

Jenson, Robert W. *America's Theologian*. New York: Oxford University Press, 1988.

Johnstone, Henry W. *The Problem of the Self*. University Park: Pennsylvania State University Press, 1970.

Ketner, Kenneth Lane. *His Glassy Essence: An Autobiography of Charles Sanders Peirce*. Nashville, Tenn.: Vanderbilt University Press, 1998.

Langsdorf, Lenore, and Andrew Smith, eds. *Recovering Pragmatism's Voice*. Albany: State University of New York Press, 1995.

Lash, Nicholas. *Easter in Ordinary*. London: SCM Press, 1990.

Lee, Sang Hyun. *The Philosophical Theology of Jonathan Edwards*. Princeton, N.J.: Princeton University Press, 1988.

Leibniz, G. W. *Philosophical Essays*. Ed. Roger Ariew and Daniel Garber. Indianapolis: Hackett, 1989.

Liddy, Richard. *Transforming Light: Intellectual Conversion in the Early Lonergan*. Collegeville, Minn.: Liturgical Press, 1993.

Locke, John. *An Essay Concerning Human Understanding*. 2 vols. New York: Dover, 1959.

Lonergan, Bernard. *Insight: A Study in Human Understanding*. Vol. 3 of *Collected Works of Bernard Lonergan,* ed. Frederick Crowe and Robert Doran. Toronto: University of Toronto Press, 1992.

Luther, Martin. *Luther's Works*. 55 vols. Ed. E. Theodore Bachmann. Philadelphia: Muhlenburg Press, 1960.

McDermott, Gerald. *One Holy and Happy Society: The Public Theology of Jonathan Edwards*. University Park: Pennsylvania State University Press, 1992.

_____. *Jonathan Edwards Confronts the Gods*. Oxford: Oxford University Press, 2000.

_____. *Transformations of Mind: Philosophy as Spiritual Practice*. Cambridge: Cambridge University Press, 2000.

McIntyre, John. *The Shape of Sotierology*. Edinburgh: T&T Clark Ltd., 1992.

Menand, Louis. *The Metaphysical Club: A Story of Ideas in America*. New York: Farrar, Straus & Giroux, 2001.

Milbank, John. *Theology and Social Theory: Beyond Secular Reason.* Oxford: Blackwell, 1990.

Milbank, John, Catherine Pickstock, and Graham Ward, eds. *Radical Orthodoxy.* London and New York: Routledge, 1999.

Miller, John William. "Notes on Philosophy 1–2." Unpublished manuscript.

Miller, Perry. *Jonathan Edwards.* Cleveland: World Publishing, 1959.

———. *Errand Into the Wilderness.* Cambridge: Harvard University Press, 1984.

Morgan, Edmund. *Visible Saints.* New York: New York University Press, 1963.

Mormoto, Anri. *Jonathan Edwards and the Catholic Vision of Salvation.* University Park: Pennsylvania State University Press, 1995.

Murray, Ian H. *Jonathan Edwards: A New Biography.* Carlisle, Pa.: The Banner of Truth Trust, 1987.

Neville, Robert Cummings. *The Highroad Around Modernism.* Albany: State University of New York Press, 1992.

Newlin, Claude. *Philosophy and Religion in Colonial America.* New York: Philosophical Library, 1962.

Niebuhr, H. Richard. *Christ and Culture.* New York: Harper & Row, 1975.

———. *The Kingdom of God in America.* Middletown, Conn.: Wesleyan University Press, 1988.

Niebuhr, Reinhold. *Moral Man and Immoral Society.* New York: Scribners, 1960.

Nietzsche, Friedrich. *On the Genealogy of Morals.* Trans. Walter Kaufmann and R. J. Hollingdale. New York: Vintage, 1989.

Nock, A. D. *Conversion.* New York: Oxford University Press, 1933.

Noll, Mark. "The Contested Legacy of Jonathan Edwards in Antebellum Calvinism." In *Reckoning with the Past,* ed. D. G. Hart, 200–217. Grand Rapids, Mich.: Baker Books, 1995.

Ochs, Peter. *Peirce, Pragmatism, and the Logic of Scripture.* Cambridge: Cambridge University Press, 1998.

O'Connell, Robert. *William James on the Courage to Believe.* New York: Fordham University Press, 1984.

———. *Images of Conversion in Saint Augustine's Confessions.* New York: Fordham University Press, 1996.

Orr, J. Edwin. *The Flaming Tongue.* Chicago: Moody Press, 1975.

Paringer, Andrew. *John Dewey and the Paradox of Liberal Reform.* Albany: State University of New York Press, 1990.

Parker, Kelly James. *The Continuity of Peirce's Thought.* Nashville, Tenn.: Vanderbilt University Press, 1998.

Peirce, Charles Sanders. *The Collected Papers of Charles S. Peirce.* 8 vols. Cambridge, Mass.: Harvard University Press, 1934–57.

————. *Writings of Charles S. Peirce: A Chronological Edition.* Ed. Max Fisch. Bloomington: Indiana University Press, 1982–.

————. *Peirce on Signs: Writings on Semiotics by Charles Sanders Peirce.* Ed. James Hoopes. Chapel Hill: University of North Carolina Press, 1991.

————. *Reasoning and the Logic of Things.* Cambridge, Mass.: Harvard University Press, 1992.

Percy, Walker. *Lost in the Cosmos.* New York: Farrar, Straus & Giroux, 1983.

Perry, Ralph Barton. *The Thought and Character of William James.* Nashville, Tenn.: Vanderbilt University Press, 1996.

Pettegrew, John, ed. *A Pragmatist's Progress.* Boston: Rowman and Littlefield, 2000.

Potter, Vincent. *Peirce's Philosophical Perspectives.* Ed. Vincent Colapietro. New York: Fordham University Press, 1996.

Raposa, Michael. *Peirce's Philosophy of Religion.* Bloomington: Indiana University Press, 1989.

————. "Jonathan Edwards' Twelfth Sign." *International Philosophical Quarterly* 33, no. 2 (1993): 153–162.

Rice, Daniel. *Reinhold Niebuhr and John Dewey: An American Odyssey.* Albany: State University of New York Press, 1993.

Ricoeur, Paul. *Fallible Man.* Trans. Charles A. Kelbley. New York: Fordham University Press, 1986.

Rockefeller, Stephen C. *John Dewey: Religious Faith and Democratic Humanism.* New York: Columbia University Press, 1991.

Rorty, Richard. *Philosophy and the Mirror of Nature.* Princeton, N.J.: Princeton University Press, 1979.

————. *Consequences of Pragmatism.* Minneapolis: University of Minneapolis Press, 1982.

————. *Essays on Heidegger and Others: Philosophical Papers.* Cambridge: Cambridge University Press, 1991.

_____. *Objectivity, Relativism, and Truth*. Cambridge: Cambridge University Press, 1991.

_____. *Philosophy and Social Hope*. New York: Penguin Books, 1999.

Rose, Gillian. *Love's Work: A Reckoning with Life*. New York: Schocken Books, 1995.

Rosenthal, Sandra, Carl Hausman, and Douglas Anderson, eds. *Classical American Pragmatism: Its Contemporary Vitality*. Chicago: University of Chicago Press, 1999.

Roth, Robert, S.J. *American Religious Philosophy*. New York: Harcourt, Brace and World, 1967.

_____. *Radical Pragmatism: An Alternative*. New York: Fordham University Press, 1998.

Saatkamp, Herman J., ed. *Rorty and Pragmatism: The Philosopher Responds to His Critics*. Nashville, Tenn.: Vanderbilt University Press, 1995.

Seigfried, Charlene Haddock. *William James's Radical Reconstruction of Philosophy*. Albany: State University of New York Press, 1990.

Shain, Barry Allan. *The Myth of American Individualism*. Princeton, N.J.: Princeton University Press, 1994.

Singer, Irving. *The Nature of Love*. 2 vols. Chicago: University Press of Chicago, 1984.

Smith, John. *Reason and God*. New Haven, Conn.: Yale University Press, 1961.

_____. *The Spirit of American Philosophy*. New York: Oxford University Press, 1963.

_____. "Jonathan Edwards as Philosophical Theologian." *The Review of Metaphysics* 30, no. 2 (December 1976): 306–324.

_____. *America's Philosophical Vision*. Chicago: University of Chicago Press, 1992.

_____. *Jonathan Edwards: Puritan, Preacher, Philosopher*. Notre Dame, Ind.: University of Notre Dame Press, 1992.

Soneson, Jerome P. *Pragmatism and Pluralism*. Minneapolis: Augsburg Fortress Press, 1992.

Stein, Stephen J., ed. *Jonathan Edwards's Writings: Text, Context, Interpretation*. Bloomington: Indiana University Press, 1996.

Stout, Harry S. *The New England Soul*. New York: Oxford University Press, 1986.

Stuhr, John, ed. *Classical American Philosophy*. New York: Oxford University Press, 1987.

Suckiel, Ellen Kappy. *Heaven's Champion*. Notre Dame, Ind.: University of Notre Dame Press, 1996.

Tallon, Andrew. *Head and Heart: Affection, Cognition, Volition as Triune Consciousness*. New York: Fordham University Press, 1997.

Tracy, Patricia. *Jonathan Edwards: Pastor*. New York: Hill and Wang, 1979.

Turnbull, Ralph. *Jonathan Edwards the Preacher*. Grand Rapids, Mich.: Baker Book House, 1958.

Vaught, Carl, G. *The Quest for Wholeness*. Albany: State University of New York Press, 1982.

_____. "Semiotics and the Problem of Analogy." *Transactions of the Charles S. Peirce Society* 22 (summer 1986): 311–326.

Wainwright, William J. *Reason and the Heart*. Ithaca, N.Y.: Cornell University Press, 1995.

Ward, Roger A. "C. S. Peirce and Contemporary Theology: The Return to Conversion." *American Journal of Theology and Philosophy* 16, no. 2 (May 1995): 125–148.

Wedeking, Gary. "Problems in Locke's Agency." *Dialogue* 29, no. 2 (1990): 163–188.

West, Cornel. *Prophetic Fragments*. Grand Rapids, Mich.: Eerdmans, 1988.

_____. *The American Evasion of Philosophy*. Madison: University of Wisconsin Press, 1989.

_____. *The Ethical Dimensions of Marxist Thought*. New York: Monthly Review Press, 1991.

Westbrook, Robert. "Democratic Evasions: Cornell West and the Politics of Pragmatism." *Praxis International* 13, no. 1 (April 1993): 1–13.

_____. *John Dewey and American Democracy*. Ithaca, N.Y.: Cornell University Press, 1991.

Wieman, Harry Nelson. *Religious Experience and Scientific Method*. New York: Macmillan, 1927.

Wilson-Kastner, Patricia. *Coherence in a Fragmented World: Jonathan Edwards's Theology of the Holy Spirit*. Washington, D.C.: University Press of America, 1978.

Witherup, Ronald. *Conversion in the New Testament*. Collegeville, Minn.: Liturgical Press, 1994.

INDEX